The
Living World
of the Sea

THE
LIVING WORLD
OF THE SEA

By William J. Cromie

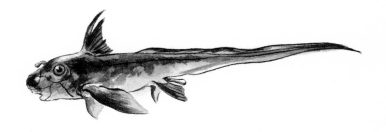

Prentice-Hall, Inc., Englewood Cliffs, New Jersey

Fifth printing. . . . . . July, 1969

This book is dedicated to all those who are fascinated by the creatures of the sea—especially to my wife, Alicia, without whose help it never would have been illustrated and without whose patience and understanding it never could have been written.

Contents

1.
The Origin of Life

"Let the waters bring forth abundantly the moving creatures that hath life."—GENESIS

THE Earth had just formed. Gases poured out of flaws in its heaving, cracking surface and gradually collected into a filmy atmosphere. Held in place by gravity, this seething envelope was extremely poisonous. No living thing that we know of today could have breathed the gas mixture. Intense ultraviolet radiation from the sun burned the barren rocks and would have disintegrated a plant or animal. The new planet had to undergo drastic changes before it could support life.

No one knows how it all started. The universe may have been born 10-15 billion years ago in a tremendous explosion, or it might have always existed. Some five billion years ago the sun, then Earth and the other planets probably condensed from a cold cloud of dust and gas.

In any case, the Earth's atmosphere, oceans and the raw materials of life must have come from its interior. Gases present in and between rocks rose to the surface because of their light weight. Carbon dioxide and water vapor reached the surface through volcanoes, fumaroles and rifts. Water vapor condensed into drops and gradually collected in low spots. The presence of water was vitally important since it absorbs ultraviolet radiation and would shield any creatures that arose in the sea from the deadly rays. At first there would have been just puddles or pools. Then these would have grown and joined into lakes, which in turn would have

1

The LOOKDOWN grows to little over a foot and is found from Cape Cod to Brazil, Baja California to Peru. Its deep, wafer-thin body shines with a pearl-like iridescence and exhibits all the colors of a pale, delicate rainbow.

widened and deepened into seas. Eventually the deep basins
in the Earth's crust would have filled to the brim.

Scientists cannot agree on how long this took. Some say
the oceans filled rapidly at first, almost reaching their present
level during the first one or two billion years. Others believe
they have been growing steadily. Dr. William W. Rubey of
the U.S. Geological Survey estimated how much water is coming out of volcanoes, fumaroles and hot springs at the present time. He says if water has been released at this rate for
the past 4.5 billion years enough would have reached the
surface to account for the two million trillion tons now contained in the oceans.

Either way, a very small amount of water is added to the
oceans each year. This does not produce a noticeable rise
in level because it is masked by other fluctuations, such
as the forming and melting of ice, sinking and rising of land
and subsidence of the ocean bottom under the weight of the
water.

Carbon dioxide, seeping out of the interior of the primeval
Earth, became dispersed through the new ocean and atmosphere. Hydrogen also must have been present for it is
the most abundant element in the universe. Since the carbon
in carbon dioxide combines with an amazing variety of other
elements, it must have reacted with the hydrogen to produce
hydrocarbons. These are the simplest types of organic compounds—compounds not found naturally unless associated
with living things. So here we have the first step on the
ladder of life. Hydrocarbons are the substances out of which
more complex organic compounds can be made—compounds
that form the building blocks of all living things.

How might these more complicated substances have been
produced in the early atmosphere and ocean? Intrigued
with the possibility of finding out, Stanley L. Miller, then
a graduate student at the University of California, performed a famous experiment in 1952. He simulated the
primitive atmosphere with a closed chamber in which he
circulated a heated mixture of water vapor, hydrogen,
ammonia (a compound of nitrogen and hydrogen) and
methane (a hydrocarbon). Some form of energy is required

to make these simple gases combine. For this energy Miller chose an electric spark, which, on the small scale he used, simulated lightning or ultraviolet radiation. The heated gases were passed over the spark, then cooled until they condensed to liquid. The liquid was boiled and Miller recirculated the gases over the spark. He continued this for a week until the liquid became colored. Miller then analyzed the fluid and found it contained many different organic compounds, including *amino acids*. These acids are the building blocks of proteins, one of the basic ingredients of all living things. It is the combination of proteins in an organism that determines whether it is a plant, an insect, a dinosaur or a man.

Russian scientists performed similar experiments using ultraviolet light as an energy source. Billions of years ago much more ultraviolet radiation reached the surface than does today. It could, therefore, have supplied energy needed for the bonding together of organic compounds. Volcanic heat, radioactivity and lightning might have contributed energy also, and biochemists have simulated these in the laboratory with electron beams, gamma rays and heat.

Experimenters at Florida State University produced 14 naturally occurring amino acids by heating a mixture of methane, ammonia and water to temperatures normally found in volcanic regions. One of the researchers, Dr. Sidney W. Fox, linked some of these amino acids together to form more complicated compounds. He did this by simply placing them in a hot lava rock and washing the rock with boiling, sterilized water to simulate rain and tides.

These experiments demonstrate that simple elements in and around the Earth can be turned into molecules * with some of the properties of living materials far more easily than had heretofore been suspected. Some or all of these molecules may have formed in the atmosphere, but eventually they drifted down to the ocean or were washed out of the sky by rain. The early ocean must have provided warm, stable surroundings in which these chemicals could remain unchanged

---

* The smallest unit of any chemical compound. If you break a molecule of water down you no longer have water but two atoms of hydrogen and one of oxygen.

for long periods. There were no microorganisms, such as populate today's oceans from top to bottom, to use them for food. Nor was free oxygen present to break down compounds into their simpler parts. The primitive ocean might be imagined as a dilute broth in which fragile molecules were preserved under the same conditions we associate with efficient canning: sterility and absence of oxygen.

But the molecules must have been very widely dispersed through the oceanic broth. Some means would be needed to bring them together so they could react with each other and form larger, more complex molecules. One way this could have occurred has been suggested by the experiments of Dr. Peter J. Wangersky at Yale University. By bubbling air through a mixture of artificial sea water and dissolved organic compounds, including amino acids, he found that the compounds come out of solution and collect as a film on the bubbles. Continued bubbling results in the buildup of larger and larger clumps of particles. Analyzing the clumps Dr. Wangersky found *polypeptides*, molecules which represent a step from amino acids toward proteins.

Dr. Wangersky believes this may have been an important mechanism in the long process of evolution from inorganic chemicals to life in the sea. Winds and storms would cause bubbling in the primordial ocean as they do today. Simple dissolved material could be converted to blobs of solid particles by sticking to the bubbles. Once they burst, the gobs of goo would presumably continue to pick up more matter as they drifted. Such organic aggregates, says Dr. Wangersky, might be the progenitors of all life, including man.

Even if life does not trace its ancestry back to blobby bubbles, Dr. Gordon Riley believes there would be much less life on Earth today without them. The organic gobs must have been a stable food source from early times. Even today, Riley believes, organic bubbles are the basic food of innumerable tiny plankton creatures in the dark depths and near the surface of the ocean.

Dr. J. D. Bernal of the University of London also believes that "life, like Aphrodite, was born of sea foam." He says that organic material accumulating at the surface would be

concentrated a hundred or a thousand times in the bubbles
produced by breaking waves. "With an onshore wind,"
Bernal writes, "the surface of the sea of hundreds or thousands of miles in extent can be deposited along a few miles
of beach." He likens this to "skimming the scum of the
oceanic cooking pot and depositing it on the beaches." We
know well how effective this process can be when a ship has
an oil leak too close to our favorite shore resort.

According to Bernal's theory, a thin coating of organic
sludge would be left by each receding tide and it would
build up layer by layer to a considerable thickness. The
molecules would adhere to particles of clay in the muds of
estuaries and tidal flats. The deposits would be alternately
wetted and dried, exposed to the sun's ultraviolet energy and
shifted by streams. More and more complex compounds
would be formed as the mixture was worked over and over
again by the forces of nature.

Thus, says Bernal, life could have originated on the
shores of the ocean with the accumulation of large amounts
of material by purely inorganic means. These giant molecules could have separated from the clay somehow and
drifted out to sea where chemical reactions or metabolism
began.* But Bernal does not think things happened this
way. "The story of metabolism runs absolutely parallel with
the story of the concentration of organic matter," he writes,
and, "I believe that metabolism in the wider sense was occurring all the time." Even while the molecules were stuck
to clay particles balanced chemical reactions took place. In
Bernal's words, "The method of living evolved at the same
time as the material of life."

Many scientists agree. Dr. Barry Commoner of Washington University believes metabolism is the only vital function
of life which can occur in the absence of a living cell but
with results closely resembling what happens in the cell itself.
Therefore, he says, "here is the beginning . . . the most
likely starting point for the origin of life."

---

* Metabolism is the sum of chemical reactions that make life possible—
the building of food into living matter and the breaking down of this matter
to obtain energy for breathing, moving, digesting, etc.

In a paper read before the National Academy of Sciences in April 1965, Dr. Commoner outlined the development of life as follows: first, energy-releasing chemical reactions evolved among complex molecules in the oceanic soup. With this energy the molecules were able to add more material and thus grow into larger, yet more complicated compounds. The compounds came together and gradually formed organized structures. These structures then developed the capacity to reproduce themselves and transmit the organization to their descendants.

The "Mother Molecules"

Scientists working under the auspices of the National Aeronautics and Space Administration (NASA) have simulated part of this development in the laboratory. Starting with the same ingredients Stanley Miller used 11 years before, Dr. Cyril A. Ponnamperuma and associates at NASA's Ames Research Laboratory in California managed to make all the

Dr. Cyril A. Ponnamperuma experiments with the master molecules of life in his laboratory at Ames Research Center, Moffett Field, Calif.

National Aeronautics and Space Administration

ingredients of the master molecules of life. The researchers
felt the chemistry they performed was "astonishingly simple"
and could have been duplicated in the early ocean.

Using beams of electrons and ultraviolet light they built
up, in a step-by-step fashion, compounds known as *nucleotides*. These sometimes have two or three units containing phosphorus loosely attached to them. When broken off
the parent molecule such units release a great deal of energy.
Nucleotides present in the primordial soup could have
"frozen" some of the sun's ultraviolet energy into the bonds
that held their phosphate units. By breaking these bonds,
the energy could be released and used to build up large
complicated molecules more efficiently than by using the
raw energy of the sun. This is what Dr. Commoner meant
when he referred to making complicated compounds with the
energy of metabolism.

Another way of putting all this is to say that nucleotides
in the primitive ocean would have enabled chemical reactions to occur which otherwise would not have taken place,
or would have taken place much more slowly. Today all the
vital chemistry in any creature's body depends on *enzymes*—
complicated proteins which make reactions occur much faster
than they would otherwise. Such complex catalysts probably
did not exist at the beginning of life, but Drs. Commoner,
Bernal and others believe the simpler nucleotides could have
done the job. They would have done it at a much slower
rate, but time was not as important then as it is now.

Nucleotides also form the building blocks of the two most
important molecules in any living system—DNA (deoxy-
ribonucleic acid) and RNA (ribonucleic acid). Called the
prime movers of life, these nucleic acids occur only in living things—in all living things—and apparently operate the
same in a single-celled microbe, a seaweed, a lobster or a
man.

DNA is the stuff of which genes are made. It determines
what every living creature is and what its descendants will
be. Nucleotides in the giant DNA molecule are arranged
along its twisted length in sequences which determine how
amino acids are made into proteins. RNA takes this informa-

tion and, in another part of the cell, puts together the proteins which make an organism what it is. DNA also produces
exact copies of itself, making offspring the same as their
parents and enabling species to retain their characteristics
from generation to generation. You yourself started life as a
single cell in whose heart or nucleus was a DNA code speci-
fying exactly how you were to be built. This information is
located in cells throughout your body and is passed on to your
children with slightly different information from your mate.

Scientists have changed the basic character of one-celled
organisms by injecting synthetic, man-made DNA into them.
They have also placed RNA into broth similar to the inside
of a living cell and produced the molecules of which living
tissue is made in the same way that a cell would. Such experiments foreshadow the day when man, modifying and
making genes at will, can fashion plants, animals or human
beings to any desired specifications. Dr. Ponnamperuma is
already trying to join nucleotides into DNA and RNA molecules and believes he has succeeded in linking up two or
three. However, he has a long way to go since it takes perhaps a hundred thousand of these building blocks to make
the DNA of even a very primitive living organism.

Could nucleotides have assembled themselves into a
"mother molecule" in the ocean billions of years ago, and
was this molecule the ancestor of all the multitude of living
things on Earth? Could life have begun when a spiral of
nucleic acid began taking simpler molecules out of the broth
and arranging them around itself in the form of new protein? In 1965 Dr. Sol Spiegelman at the University of Illinois
mixed a strand of non-living RNA in a test tube with an
enzyme and some nucleotides. What he got was a *virus*—RNA
enclosed in a protein jacket and able to grow and reproduce
itself without any further help from Dr. Spiegelman. If such
a virus arose in the primitive ocean, it could have replicated
into billions of like viruses in a comparatively short time.
Then further chemical changes might have caused them to
become more complex and to take on a variety of forms,
and this might have eventually resulted in the development
of different species of living things.

As attractive as it sounds, most scientists do not think this is what happened. Dr. Commoner contends that, under natural conditions, viruses and DNA cannot reproduce alone. He says, "the replication of DNA is highly dependent on the organized structure of the living cell, and therefore could not have appeared in the origin of life until after this organized structure had developed." Bernal seconds this with, "the simple, naked nucleic acid molecule can do nothing by itself."

Here Bernal's ideas on the beginning of life converge with those of A. I. Oparin, a Russian biochemist who has done pioneering work in this field for over 40 years. Both think that early organic material eventually took the form of semi-liquid or jelly-like droplets. With the formation of such droplets potential living matter would be in much less danger of breaking up or going back into solution. Instead of being scattered about molecules would be gathered in separate packages each of which could contain all the essentials for metabolism. Each package could retain its individuality and develop independently of all others.

Some droplets would be better suited for existence in the oceans than others. They would have stable and efficient means of taking smaller bits of organic matter out of the surrounding water. Some of this material would be built into their own structure while some would be broken down to provide energy. As long as these chemical reactions balanced, an organic jelly drop could maintain itself and grow. But any droplet in which the substance was broken down for energy faster than it could be replaced soon disappeared.

Oparin makes the ingenious suggestion that Charles Darwin's principle of natural selection and survival of the fittest began to operate at this level. According to Darwin, those creatures best adapted to their surroundings, by virtue of structure and composition, stand the best chance to survive and reproduce their kind. Creatures not as well adapted become dominated by the others or simply perish. Oparin believes this could have happened at the beginning of life. The best organized droplets added new molecules more rapidly than the others—took "food" out of their "mouths"— and grew more complex at their expense.

Eventually the metabolizing blobs would have to develop some kind of "skin" or membrane to hold themselves together. This would also control smaller molecules that passed in and out as well as right through them. One group of long organic molecules (the lipids) packs together in sheets and these could have supplied the needed partitions. Once in place they would make the highly organized and complex system a self-sustaining box or cell.

Next would follow the partition or separation of internal cell parts, perhaps with different molecules undertaking different tasks. One part might become the core or nucleus—the control center housing DNA and the master plan for the cell. Another part might contain amino acids and other elements for making proteins, and another the enzymes for metabolism. Or maybe all these parts developed separately and somehow came together. Either way, any blob that developed all these characteristics would be a living thing.

This sequence from jelly droplet to living cell is, of course, pure conjecture. The actual evolution of cells is the deepest mystery in biology. But one thing is certain: life arose as a natural and continual process taking place over billions of years. There is no definite point at which we can say, "life began here." No sharp line separates the living and nonliving. The one grades continuously into the other, leaving stages between, like viruses, which cannot as yet be placed in one class or the other.

First Creatures

The first living things may have no counterpart on Earth today. Some very primitive red bacteria harbor virus-size molecules which contain nucleotides and enzymes. These molecules can make their own organic food, too, using the energy of the sun. This fills all the requirements for calling it a living organism, but whether such small bodies ever existed independently remains unknown. Bacteria may have been the first creatures. They are the smallest and simplest of organisms that can definitely be said to be alive, although they are not either animal or vegetable. Often called "germs"

Marineland of Florida

The beginning of life for the SKATE and the CONCH. After developing for about a year, the newborn skate wiggles out of its "mermaid's purse" or egg case. The conch is in the process of producing a "sea necklace"—a helical ribbon consisting of many little parchment-like packets each containing a number of eggs.

Marineland of Florida

or microbes, many thousands could live in a space the size of the period on this page.

Whoever they were, the first creatures had no choice but to live on the oceanic broth in which they arose. All of to-day's one-cell creatures can assimilate or "eat" less organized organic matter. Therefore, this must be a basic ability evolved in the beginning. In the absence of oxygen, the only way creatures can break down this organic food to get energy for their vital functions is by *fermentation*. In this process simple molecules like sugar interact with water and form carbon dioxide and certain acids, like alcohol. The latter have less energy than the former, and the difference repre-sents the energy available to the organism doing the fer-menting.

Certain modern bacteria and yeast cells can live like this when their oxygen is cut off. But fermentation is a wasteful and inefficient process that uses up large amounts of organic material to provide only a small amount of energy. This means the first organisms and their descendants would start out "eating" food much faster than it was being made by inorganic means. They were living on borrowed time.

Before the food ran out, however, some organisms evolved color, or pigment, and with it the ability to utilize directly the energy of sunlight. At first this energy was used only to assimilate organic material more rapidly, thus making the food situation even worse. But since this ability gave them a tremendous advantage over other organisms, the colored group moved ahead of the rest of the ocean popula-tion. In time, they developed a new and wonderful green pig-ment called *chlorophyll* (from Greek words meaning "green leaf"). This chemical enabled them to use the energy of sun-light to make their own organic food from carbon dioxide, water and other inorganic substances. The process is called *photosynthesis*, meaning "putting together by light," and without it life as we know it could not exist.

The first organisms to photosynthesize became the an-cestors of all the grasses, trees and seaweeds. Green plants alone can produce the stuff of life—proteins, carbohydrates and fats—from the elements of water, soil and air. Every animal that ever lived has been dependent on them, directly or indirectly, for its existence.

Not only did photosynthesis free living things from the bondage of ocean-cooked food, it changed the composition of the Earth's air and provided an energy source necessary for the advanced evolution of life. When plants make sugars and starches by combining carbon from carbon dioxide with hydrogen from water, oxygen is released as a waste product. Before plants, there was only a minute amount of free oxygen on Earth, formed high in the atmosphere by ultraviolet rays splitting molecules of water vapor into hydrogen and oxygen. After their evolution, plants gradually used up most of the carbon dioxide in the air and replaced it with oxygen. Today, scientists estimate that all oxygen in our atmosphere is completely renewed every 2,000 years by photosynthesis. Carbon dioxide in the air and ocean, they figure, is changed every 300 years. Thus all the oxygen and carbon dioxide we breathe has been in and out of living things again and again.

As oxygen increased in the early atmosphere it reacted with incoming ultraviolet radiation at high altitudes and formed an energetic variety of oxygen known as *ozone*. Eventually the ozone built up into a thick layer that absorbed ultraviolet energy and prevented it from reaching the surface. Thus this energy was no longer available to participate in the formation of organic material, but since living things had learned to make their own it was not missed. In fact, its disappearance paved the way for the evolution of more complex and delicate forms of life. Ultraviolet rays can break down organic compounds as well as aid in their fabrication. If we did not have an ozone shield about 15 miles above our heads today, the sun's full supply of energy would kill us and most other higher animals. Even the feeble ultraviolet rays that do reach us can cause painful sunburn.

Photosynthesis enabled plants to make their own organic food but in order to get any energy out of it they still had to break it down by inefficient fermentation. A much more efficient way would be to "burn" the food by combining it with oxygen. Such cold burning, or *oxidation*, releases about 30 times more energy than fermentation, or just about all that is in a compound. With oxygen available, it was only a matter of time until organisms evolved the ability to use it. Those that did developed a tremendous advantage over those that did not and the latter soon disappeared into obscurity.

Photosynthesis coupled with fermentation made life self-sustaining. Photosynthesis coupled with oxidation or respiration provided organisms with a surplus of energy that could be used to power new forms of behavior.

One of the new types of behavior was the habit of eating each other. This would have saved some organisms the trouble of making their own food. Animal cells may have evolved separately from plant cells or they may have evolved from such "cannibal" plants. There are one-celled organisms living today that can obtain nourishment either by photosynthesis or by pouncing on the photosynthesizers. Through disuse such creatures may have lost their chlorophyll and turned to living on plants and each other.

How long ago did all this happen? As knowledge and technology have increased, the age of life has been pushed steadily backward from thousands to millions to billions of years. In 1965, a University of California research team startled science by discovering that living things have populated Earth nearly a billion years longer than anyone had realized. They found molecules produced by living organisms inside rocks formed 2.7 billion years ago. Led by Dr. Melvin Calvin, the researchers believe that the molecules came from primitive chlorophyll-bearing plants such as blue-green algae. Familiar as the slimy greenish coating on quiet water, rocks and wharf pilings, these algae are the most primitive plant forms in existence today. They are so ancient the structures inside their cells are jumbled together instead of being separated from each other as they are in higher forms.

The rocks came from northern Minnesota and were dated by their radioactivity. Researchers used a variety of delicate and sophisticated chemical and physical techniques to detect the molecules. The astonishing thing about this finding is that organisms capable of photosynthesis must have been common as long ago as 2.7 billion years. Although blue-green algae are at the bottom of the evolutionary ladder, photosynthesis is a highly complex process that must have taken an enormously long time to evolve—perhaps one or even two billion years. In 1965 a pair of Harvard University scientists discovered evidence of even earlier, simpler life —organisms similar to modern rod-shaped bacteria—in South African rocks 3 billion years old. This may mean that life-making processes began soon after the birth of Earth, some 4.5 billion years ago.

Dr. Calvin and colleagues plan to search for signs of crea-tures in our planet's most ancient rocks—3.3 billion-year-old granite pebbles located in South Africa. Dr. Bernal says the beginnings of life may even antedate the oldest rocks on the Earth's surface. He suggests the possibility of organic mole-cules forming in the primordial dust cloud from which the planets were formed. Writing of these matters in his great book *Origin of Life,* Oparin says: ". . . the modern process of evolution of living organisms is fundamentally nothing more than the addition of some new links to an endless chain of transformations of matter, a chain which extends back to the very dawn of existence of our planet."

Descent of Man

Evolution simply means that plants and animals change slowly over millions of years and as a consequence new varieties of life arise. Mutations or changes in the DNA gene material produce new characteristics within a species. If these characteristics make an organism better suited to live in its surroundings, they will be preserved by natural selec-tion and will persist from generation to generation. Over a long period of time, an organism undergoing a series of such changes acquires new features and functions which distin-guish it from its ancestors and characterize it as a new species or new kind of creature. The whole wonderful concept is neatly stated in the full title of Darwin's famous original work: *The Origin of Species By Means Of Natural Selection Or The Preservation Of Favored Races In The Struggle For Existence.*

There are somewhere between one and two million different species of animals living today. Each started life as a single cell, that is, in the same state as the first animal formed in the primitive ocean broth. This cell grew and divided into smaller cells which in turn grew and divided. Some cells joined to form a single creature just as atoms combined to form molecules and molecules combined to form the first cell. Today animals develop in the egg or womb in much the same way their kind did during the long years of their evolution. The growing embryo roughly repeats the evolutionary history of its species.

Cells group into tissues like muscles, which probably evolved as it became necessary for animals to chase their food or get away from predators. Tissues become organized into organs such as the liver, kidney and heart, and organs are grouped into systems to perform such functions as digestion, reproduction and respiration.

As these levels of organization came into existence for the first time so did new and progressively more complicated creatures. The development was smooth and continuous but today we classify creatures in different major groups or *phyla* based on levels of complexity. The simplest animals, hence the ones that have been around longest, are the single-celled Protozoa like amoeba. Although the lowly amoeba and its relatives are in the evolutionary basement, they are the product of billions of years of chemical evolution and can do most of the things any other animal can do. They breathe, move around, capture food and reproduce.

Some time in the remote past two amoeboid-like cells probably stuck together after division and began a new level of complexity in the animal kingdom: cell colonies. Today such colonies are represented by Porifera, the sponge phylum. Each sponge cell is specialized in performing some particular function in the colony, such as getting food or bringing it to the other cells. But each retains the ability to go off by itself and, by repeated division, form a new colony.

Eventually, cells living in groups became so specialized they could only exist as part of an animal. At this level, each cell or group of cells integrates its actions with the others, and it takes all cell groups working together to keep the animal alive. Certain cells in a jellyfish are organized into nervous tissue which coordinates the action of all its tentacles. Jellyfish, sea anemones and corals belong to the phylum Coelenterata, the most primitive group of multi-cellular and tissue-carrying creatures.

From coelenterates, the tree of life splits into two main branches. One leads through worms to insects and the giant squid; the other leads to man.

Flatworms are the most primitive creatures possessing a head and cells organized into organs. They even show the beginning of organ systems. Their relatives, segmented worms or Annelida, have well developed brains and nervous, digestive, reproductive, excretory and circulatory systems. Segmented worms such as the common earthworm and creatures in the phylum Mollusca (snails, clams and squid) probably evolved from the same ancestor. And lobsters, crabs and shrimps, which are in the same group as insects, are probably direct descendants of segmented worms.

The other main branch of life has at its base an unlikely phylum—Echinodermata (starfish, sea urchins and sea cucumbers). Unlikely because in this position they must have the same ancestors as the higher backboned animals. The reason for suspecting this, despite a primitive and alien appearance, is the character of their embryos. Before birth echinoids have a rudimentary backbone and bear strong resemblance to the unborn of Chordata. Chordata is the phylum which includes all backboned animals or *vertebrates* —some 45,000 different species.

Above echinoids are obscure creatures having only part of a backbone sometime in their lives. Then come the ugly, jawless lampreys and hagfish; followed by gristle-skeletoned sharks, skates and rays, and then bony fish. After fish evolved rigid skeletons of bone, strong enough to hold them upright against the pull of gravity, they could leave the supporting buoyancy of water and venture onto the land. As they solved the problems of supporting themselves, drying up and producing their young in air, fish evolved into amphibians and reptiles. Reptiles then gave rise to both birds and mammals. Mainly because of superior brainpower, mammals have be-

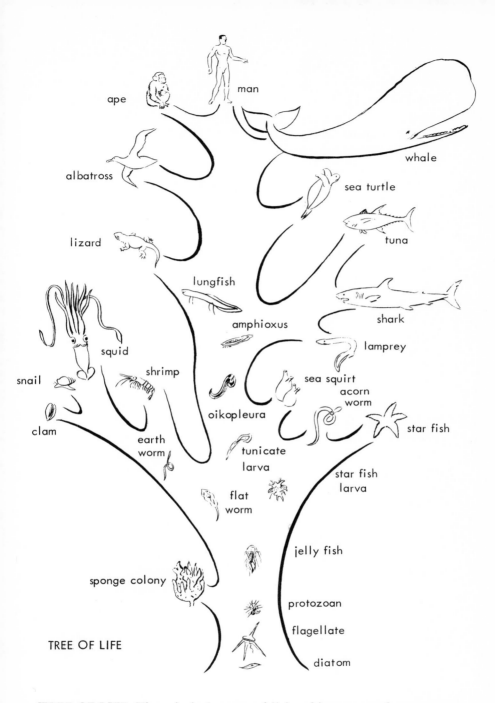

TREE OF LIFE. The principal groups of living things arranged on a growing, branching tree to show their relationships and the supposed order of their evolution.

come the most successful creatures on land and in the sea. Whales are the best divers, among the fastest swimmers and the most intelligent creatures in the ocean. Their cousin, man dominates the land.

Life is the most complex state of organization that matter has achieved, and in man matter has learned to contemplate itself and other living things, to ask questions about life and to obtain answers by reason and experiment. The greatest challenge to this intelligence is the question of whether the origin and evolution of life is "deterministic" or "opportunistic." That is, does it follow some sort of "law" (perhaps established by a higher being), or has life emerged as a result of chance events taken advantage of by natural selection. This question involves life in all parts of the universe. Although other planets in our solar system, with the possible exception of Mars, seem to support no life, telescopes reveal trillions of stars like the sun. Therefore, there may be billions of solar systems and millions of opportunities for life to arise.

Dr. Harlow Shapley, one of our planet's most respected astronomers, makes the conservative and widely accepted estimate that there are 100 million planets suitable for life— possibly 100,000 in the Milky Way galaxy alone. If life is deterministic and arises whenever the proper conditions and molecules are present, then life, even intelligent creatures, probably exists in other parts of the universe. If life arose on Earth as a happy accident, purely as the result of chance combinations, the odds are still such that life—although possibly in entirely different forms—might have arisen somewhere else. There is also the possibility that life originated at one source and has been scattered throughout the universe like seeds on the winds of starlight. In any case, it seems doubtful that life exists or has existed only on Earth.

2.

The Water World

"There is, one knows not what sweet mystery about the sea, whose gently awful stirrings seem to speak of some hidden soul beneath."
                                                    —MELVILLE

HAD the ancients who named our planet known that 71 percent of its surface is covered by water, they probably would have called it "Oceanus" instead of Earth. No other planet in our solar system, as far as is known, has an ocean. For every square mile of dry land on Earth, there are about two and a half square miles of ocean surface. The continents can be thought of as islands rising out of a single *World Ocean* and dividing it into various parts which we arbitrarily name oceans, seas, gulfs, bays, etc. This World Ocean averages 12,500 feet or about two miles deep, and in some places extends to depths exceeding seven miles. If the Earth's surface were smooth, instead of being wrinkled into mountains and basins, the ocean would cover the land to a depth of more than 8,000 feet.

There is about 300 times more living space available in the ocean than on land and in fresh water together. On the continents, life is restricted to the surface and to a shallow zone a few feet deep. (Flights into the air by birds and insects cannot be considered since they are only temporary journeys.) But about two-thirds of the ocean is deeper than 10,000 feet, and all this vast expanse of water—from its sparkling, sunlit surface to its cold, dark, abysmal depths—is inhabited by some form of life.

The deep ocean does not begin where land ends. All continents have underwater extensions in the form of shallow platforms, called *continental shelves.* These relatively flat terraces are anywhere from a few miles to 800 miles wide, with the average around 42 miles. At the outer edge most shelves end abruptly in steep cliffs, called the *continental slopes,* which plunge to depths of 10,000 feet or more. Depths at this "break" or outer edge average about 600 feet.

Five-sixths of the total mass of living matter on Earth dwells in the upper, sunlit part of the ocean. But this living matter is not uniformly distributed. There are deserts and jungles in the ocean just as on land. Coastal areas of the sea correspond to jungles. They are densely populated because of the drainage of "food" materials from the land and the mixing of the water from top to bottom by winds, currents and tides. From an economic point of view these regions are the most important, for here live the majority of animals which man catches for sea food.

Living surrounded by water is very convenient. The best of all solvents, sea water carries in solution and constantly bathes its inhabitants in all the substances necessary for a good life, growth and reproduction.

Water makes up about 80 percent of living things. It accounts for 60 to 70 percent of a backboned animal's weight and as much as 96 percent of some invertebrates like jellyfish. The chief ingredient of blood and the circulating fluids, water comprises 95 percent of human blood plasma. It forms an internal sea, bathing and partly filling every cell. Like the external sea, it carries dissolved food and oxygen to the cells and removes poisonous wastes. It warms, cools, lubricates and nourishes.

Being mostly water, marine creatures have nearly the same weight as their surroundings. In other words, the water supplies them with lift or buoyancy and counteracts the pull of gravity. (Space doctors keep subjects submerged in tanks for days to simulate the effects of weightlessness on astronauts.)

Air offers no such support. Terrestrial animals had to develop strong skeletons, limbs and muscles before coming ashore in order to keep from constantly falling down. The larger a land creature the more of itself must be used for support. This limits their size. Sea-supported animals can grow much larger. The biggest beast in the ocean, the blue whale, weighs as much as 30 times more than an average elephant, the largest animal on land. Whales that beach themselves often die of suffocation because the great unsupported weight of their bodies collapses their lungs.

Marine animals expend less energy than land dwellers to overcome the force of gravity, but they use more in moving through their "thicker" surroundings. Sea water is about a thousand times more dense than air, so it offers much more resistance. The relative thinness of air makes it possible for even poorly streamlined animals to move at considerable speeds. The cheetah can travel up to 70 miles an hour; certain ducks fly as fast as 66 miles an hour. The fastest water animals—tuna, and certain small whales—can maintain speeds of 35 miles an hour or better but only for short intervals. Since all sea creatures must move in the same medium, this reduced speed is no disadvantage to any particular one.

Water absorbs and holds more heat than air, rocks, soil or any substance except ammonia. If all the sun's heat that reaches Earth fell on Antarctica, it would melt the thousands of feet of ice covering that continent in 2½ years. Yet this same amount of heat would raise the ocean's temperature only 2° F. By the same token, the World Ocean can lose large amounts of heat to the atmosphere with little reduction in temperature. Because of this, sea climate is not subject to the wide and sudden fluctuations experienced on land. Temperatures get as low as 127° F. below zero in Antarctica and as high as 136° in the desert country of North Africa. In the open sea, away from the influence of land, the maximum rarely exceeds 86°, the minimum 27°.* In fact, most

---

* Because of the salts dissolved in it, sea water freezes at temperatures below 32°.

near-surface waters never experience a change of more than 10° from season to season and more than one degree between day and night. About 1,000 feet down seasons disappear, and below this the water is uniformly cold, averaging just below 35° F.

Since mild and uniform conditions prevail over vast areas for long periods, sea creatures are not required to make severe and frequent adjustments to their surroundings as many land creatures must do. They therefore become delicately attuned and exceptionally sensitive to prevailing conditions. All marine creatures, except mammals, are *cold-blooded* * so their bodies take on the same temperature as the surrounding water. Even slight variations in this temperature can cause immediate changes in body chemistry, and large and sudden variations may have disastrous results.

Because of this sensitivity, the boundary zone between water masses of different temperatures may be just as effective a barrier as a mountain or desert. Such temperature "fences" occur throughout the World Ocean, particularly where different currents and water masses meet, and keep animals from moving from one area to another.

One fence extends around the bottom of the Earth at 50°-55° South latitude. Here, cold, relatively fresh water flowing north meets warmer, saltier water coming south in what is called the *Antarctic Convergence*. Regions on either side of this convergence have completely dissimilar submarine climates, and the animals and plants that inhabit them are as different as those of forest and tundra.

But all creatures are not equally confined by such barriers. Many whales, some fishes and possibly squid wander over great distances in the water world. But others, particularly animals about to give birth and the resulting eggs and offspring, are highly susceptible to temperature changes. This restricts time of spawning to certain seasons, usually spring when more food is also available. Biologists believe changes in temperature associated with seasons provide the stimulus that induces sexual activity in marine animals.

---

* *Warm-blooded* animals—birds and mammals—have evolved their own "heating plant" which enables them to keep their body temperatures constant despite outside changes.

Commercial and sport fishermen measure water temperature to determine where the fish will be biting. For instance, bluefish move inshore when the mercury drops to 60° F.; they go out again when it gets over 70°. Striped bass come in at about 42°, and mackerel like it between 52° and 48°.

Water temperature also affects metabolism. The rate of living of cold-blooded animals is roughly doubled by a rise of 20° F. Conversely, low temperatures slow down chemical reactions and the organism requires less food and energy to stay alive. This lower metabolism may actually extend a creature's life by inducing a period of suspended animation that permits survival when times are hard and food scarce.

The higher rate of metabolism in warm seas means animals grow faster and reproduce earlier and more frequently. Many generations are born in the tropics in the time it takes one to be produced in the polar regions. This rapid succession presents more opportunity for mutations and results in a greater variety of species. As a result the tropics are inhabited by a bewildering variety of plants and animals, each present in relatively small numbers. The polar regions, on the other hand, are populated by relatively few species, each represented by a large number of individuals.

Cold water animals generally grow larger than similar animals living in warm seas. Polar species are bigger than

American Museum of Natural History

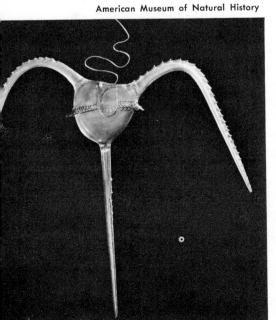

Temperature influences the appearance of this one-celled microscopic creature (*Ceratium*). In warm waters and seasons, its arms or horns lengthen to offer more resistance to sinking in the lighter water. In cold waters, which offer more buoyancy, *Ceratium* gets by with short horns.

their tropical relatives. Deep, cold waters underlying the tropics harbor bigger creatures than those found near the surface. Two species of fish living at 5,000 feet are twice as long as their close "cousins" living at 1,500 feet. This increased size may be due to the fact that cold water creatures take longer to reach sexual maturity. The delay would permit a longer growing period with resultant larger size.

Water temperature, then, exerts a profound influence on sea plants and animals. It affects their reproductive rate, their rate of living and growth, and their size. It also affects water movement, its ability to flow, the amount of gas dissolved in the sea, and the form and thickness of shells and other body coverings.

The Briny Sea

Temperature does not act alone but in concert with currents, light, pressure, food and, particularly, the content of dissolved material. The ocean is a complicated solution of many substances, continually mixed as in a gigantic test tube; billions of chemical reactions are going on at all times. The principal and most obvious ingredient of this solution is sodium chloride, or common salt. Besides sodium and chlorine, the main elements in sea water are magnesium, sulphur, calcium, potassium, bromine, carbon and strontium. These nine ingredients make up 99½ percent of the ocean's salts, combining to form such compounds as magnesium chloride, sulphates of magnesium and potassium, and calcium carbonate (lime). Animals absorb the latter from the sea and build it into bones and shells.

Many other substances exist in smaller amounts. (Probably all the elements known in nature will eventually be found in sea water.) Plants and animals use the ocean's silicon for making shells and body coverings. Plants incorporate phosphorus, iron and manganese into their tissues. From man's point of view, interesting elements include 15 billion tons of copper, 2 billion tons of uranium, 500 million tons of silver and 10 million tons of gold. These treasures, however, are so thinly scattered through 330 million cubic miles * of water that the ocean makes a very lean ore. Plants and animals can detect and concentrate minerals which are present in infinitesimal amounts. Man spends large sums of money to learn how they do it, but except for salt, magnesium and bromine he has been unable to "mine" ocean water profitably.

Most salts are dissolved out of rocks and soil and carried into the ocean by rivers. Each year rivers dump about 400 million tons of dissolved and suspended matter into the World Ocean. The secretions, excretions and decay of organisms; rain washing gases and particles from the sky; winds wafting dust and dirt out to sea, submarine volcanoes belching up chemicals, and meteorites from outer space add additional material. As many as 15 million meteorites, the size of the dot over this *i* and smaller, may plop into the sea every day. If all the salts in the ocean were removed and spread out on dry land, they would blanket it with a thickness of more than 500 feet.

The amount of salt in the sea, its *salinity,* depends on the difference between evaporation and precipitation. Diluted by rain, snow and melting ice, polar seas are freshest. The saltiest part of the ocean lies in the subtropics around 30° North and South—areas of intense evaporation and sparse rainfall. Away from the influences of land, salinity stays quite stable, varying from about 3.4 to 3.7 percent, or 34 to 37 parts of salt to 1000 parts water (abbreviated o/oo). The average salinity of the World Ocean is about 35 o/oo.

In 1884, a British chemist, C. R. Dittmar, made an extremely important discovery as a result of carefully analyzing samples of ocean water from all over the world. He found that although the **total amount** of salts varies from place to place, the kinds of salts and the **relative amounts** of each remain remarkably constant. Sea water may be a bitter brine or almost fresh, but sodium chloride will always account for 78 percent of the salts, magnesium chloride for 11 percent, calcium carbonate for 0.3 percent, etc. This is understandable since all oceans and seas are interconnected and the

---

* One cubic mile of water would fill a lake 26 miles long, 10 miles wide and 20 feet deep.

water flows ceaselessly between them. The water that sloshes against your foot on an East Coast beach may lap the web-foot of an antarctic penguin hundreds of years later, and thousands of years ago it may have splashed a Polynesian fisherman.

Besides mineral (inorganic) salts, the World Ocean contains a considerable amount of organic matter both in solution and particle form. The quantity of this loose, nonliving material is estimated to be at least 50 times greater than that making up living things. One biologist says the dissolved portion in the Atlantic alone equals 20,000 times the weight of the world's wheat harvest for a year. Organic substances come from land via rivers, from animal wastes and secretions and from the decay of deceased organisms.

It was once thought that only bacteria could "eat" this dilute and invisible material. These microscopic specks of life live everywhere in the ocean and on and inside other living things. There may be hundreds of millions of them in a thimbleful of rich bottom mud. In the economy of the sea, bacteria serve as a septic tank, undoing the work of lifetimes of metabolism by decomposing dead creatures. (Sometimes they start digesting a plant or animal before it dies.) As lifeless organic "garbage" sinks toward bottom, they break it down into simpler compounds and inorganic minerals. Bacteria obtain nourishment in this way, and the store of primary food in the ocean's cupboards becomes replenished. This occurs when currents sweep the inorganic leftovers into the lighted portion of the sea. Tiny one-celled plants take in the minerals along with carbon dioxide and water, and incorporate them into living tissue. This plant tissue is eaten by the smallest animals in the sea, which in turn serve as food for larger beasts.

Scientists long believed that the little seagoing plants were the only thing the multitude of tiny weak-swimming animals could eat. However, enough of this vegetable food does not exist at certain seasons and in the dark depths to feed the number of animals known to be present. Then in 1964 Doctors E. R. Baylor and William H. Sutcliffe bubbled air through an artificial seawater mixture at Woods Hole Oceanographic Institution. This is the same experiment Dr. Wangersky performed at Yale, and they obtained the same result—dissolved organic material became reconstituted by sticking to the bubbles. Doctors Baylor and Sutcliffe, together with Dr. Gordon Riley, propose that the organic bubbles form "bite-size" particles of food after they burst. These, they feel, are the "bread"—the basic fare—of the tiniest animals in the sea.

This discovery revealed a vast, unsuspected supply of food in the sea and uncovered a missing link in the chain of life. While debris formed by decaying organisms is small and shows signs of its former life, the bubble aggregates are larger and look like shapeless blobs. After the bubbles break, new matter adheres to the particles as they sink and they grow larger. This is manna from a watery heaven for minute creatures struggling for life in the depths. The quantity decreases with depth for 1,500 feet, then remains steady. Midwinter storms churning the water, and the organic secretions of expanded animal and plant life in spring both increase the amount of bubble food.

Storms and winds also increase the amount of gas in the sea. We do not normally think of the ocean as being full of gas, but this must be so or animals could not breathe and plants could not photosynthesize. Most of the gas enters at the surface as a result of the constant mixing of sea and air. The atmosphere takes up moisture, and gases become absorbed from the air and dissolved in the water. Strong winds, rough seas and breaking waves increase both processes. The sea, then, "breathes" through its surface. When crowded with rushing, tumbling, white-crested waves it is breathing more deeply than when it lies in ripples or quiet rolls.

Salt and Blood

A comparison of ocean water and animal blood reveals a startling similarity. Jellyfish, lobsters, sharks, some fishes, frogs, dogs and humans all have body fluids containing the same salts in much the same proportions as sea water. Certain marine invertebrates such as starfish can substitute ocean water temporarily for their "blood."

In other words, our blood and the body fluids of other animals is nothing more or less than modified sea water. Since all creatures have a common origin in the sea and all are at least distantly related, there should be nothing too surprising about this. Sea water had a salinity of about one percent at the time life arose and this water entered into the composition and metabolism of the first organisms. Despite billions of years of evolution in widely divergent directions, salinity and the proportions of salts have been retained with only minor variations. This suggests that the conditions under which life is possible are very restrictive and have changed little since it first began. The composition of body fluids has remained the same because the conditions under which life is possible have remained the same. The evolution of different creatures has been accompanied by the evolution of mechanisms for maintaining these conditions within the animals.

Life requires that a balance be maintained between this internal sea and its surroundings. If a marine creature such as an octopus is carried into fresh water by currents, it will die in a few minutes. The difference in salinity between the water and the animal's fluids creates an unequal pressure, and water rushes in with such force the creature's cells rupture. This should lay to rest the old story about the octopus that swam up the Columbia River and crawled out into an Idaho hayfield before it was killed by a farmer with a pitchfork.

Water always flows between two regions of different salinity until the salinities become equal and the pressure differential is abolished. Flow of water and salts through the skin of an animal is possible because body coverings and cell membranes are selectively permeable. That is, they allow the passage of water and certain salts but block other salts that come in larger "packages" or molecules.

Strange as it seems, fishes in the sea live in constant danger of "drying up." Their body fluids have a lower salt content than the surrounding ocean, so water tries to pass out of the fishes until the salinity of their internal fluids equals that of the sea. They can counteract this by simply swallowing more water, but then they must get rid of unwanted salt coming in with it. This is done by special cells in the gills which secrete excess salt, keeping the composition of internal fluids constant.

Conversely, fresh water fishes live in constant danger of "drowning." Their blood contains more salt than the surroundings, and water tends to flood inward. To combat this their kidneys discharge excess water and gill cells absorb salt instead of secreting it. The kidneys also take up salt from the outgoing fluid. Since elimination of water and secretion or absorption of salt requires an expenditure of energy, fishes must continually do work to keep from drowning or drying up.

Invertebrates can usually regulate their insides to accommodate the narrow range of salinity in the open ocean. Some are able to make additional adjustments if not forced to do so quickly. If the salinity of water in which California mussels live is slowly reduced to one-half its normal value, the mussels still survive. But if salinity changes rapidly, they may perish. Relatively sudden dilution of water by excessive rain kills young oysters and sometimes prevents oyster females from spawning properly.

There is wide range in the ability of animals to maintain a constant internal salinity in spite of external changes. Some, like the salmon, shad and eel, are equally at home in fresh water rivers or the briny ocean. Others—those living in deep water or the open sea where salinity remains stable over large areas—experience adverse effects from relatively small changes in salt content. Thus, salinity fences exist in addition to temperature fences. Each species in the ocean has a maximum and minimum salinity and temperature that it can endure.

The Restless Waters

Besides influencing the character and range of living things, temperature and salinity play a major role in the movement of water from place to place. These two variables—and to a lesser extent, pressure—determine the *density* or *specific gravity* of water. Large quantities of salts make the water denser, or heavier. The warmer the water the more it will expand and the lighter or less dense it will be. Water always flows from an area of high density to one of lower density until the densities become equal.

Scientists think of the World Ocean as divided into an upper and lower part. The lower part consists of layers of cold water stacked one atop the other in order of decreasing density. The upper part, warmed by the sun, has a markedly lower density. Since it is frequently stirred by winds and mixed by waves, layering in this section is not well defined.

Over much of the ocean a zone in which density increases rapidly separates the upper and lower water. This boundary is known as a *thermocline,* because a pronounced decrease in temperature causes the density increase. The presence or absence of a thermocline depends on latitude and time of year. It is particularly pronounced in tropics and subtropics during summer. Usually a thickness of 50 to 650 feet of warm, mixed water lies atop the colder, heavier masses. Secondary thermoclines may also develop between 1,500 and 3,000 feet. Thermoclines can seal off vertical movement, preventing the mixing of upper and lower waters and even the movements of animals.

The deep layers are formed by cold, heavy water sinking in the northern North Atlantic and Antarctic Oceans. This water spreads out in the depths of the Atlantic, then flows into the Indian and Pacific basins. In the upper part of the oceans, wind and density differences set up a system of horizontally moving currents. Continents and the Earth's rotation deflect this surface circulation into six circular cells or gyres. As shown by the diagram there is one gyre each in the North Atlantic, South Atlantic, North Pacific, South Pacific and Indian Oceans. The sixth gyre consists of water driven eastward around Antarctica by strong westerly winds.

When currents transport water away from land, or two currents flow away from each other (diverge), water rises from below to replace what is carried away. Such *upwelling*

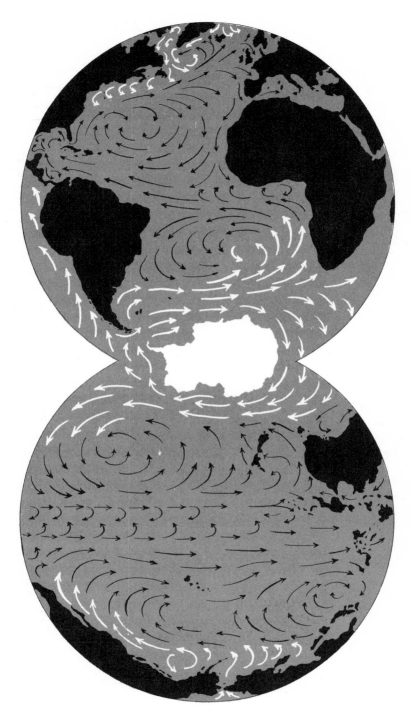

SURFACE CIRCULATION OF THE WORLD
OCEAN. Cold currents are represented by white
arrows. Black arrows indicate warm currents.

also occurs when offshore winds push water away from the coast. Conversely, when winds pile water against a shoreline, or surface currents converge, the extra water builds up at the edges then sinks.

The greatest abundance of life anywhere on Earth is found in areas of upwelling. Cold, rising waters bring up mineral salts that fertilize crops of marine plants. The prolific flora provides food for large populations of vegetarians, which in turn nourish the flesh eaters. Nutrient-rich waters rising from depths of 6,500 to 10,000 feet make the open ocean around Antarctica one of the most fertile regions on Earth. Areas of upwelling in the equatorial regions are two to five times more productive than the central ocean regions to the north and south. Upwelling also occurs along the west coasts of Africa, South America, and to a lesser extent, California. The water off Southwest Africa is probably the most productive local area in the World Ocean, but because of reduced extent it is not as important as the Antarctic Ocean.

Off the west coast of South America, trade winds push the cold, northward-flowing waters of the Peru Current out to sea. A fountain of nutrients upwells to fill the trough that is created, and this produces favorable conditions for life as far as 200 miles off Peru. Enormous schools of small sardine-like *anchovetas* provide food for other fishes, sea lions, birds, and even penguins. As these fish leap and splash in the rich waters, millions of cormorants, gannets, pelicans, terns, and gulls darken the sky and plunge into the sea like rain. Some five or six million birds catch 1,000 tons of anchovetas a day. This teeming marine life has made Peru one of the largest fishing nations in the world and the excreta of sea birds, which makes excellent fertilizer, supports a large Peruvian guano industry.

Upwelling will be discontinuous if offshore winds are intermittent, and a weakening or shifting of the wind may cause it to stop completely. When winds die down off the Peruvian coast and upwelling becomes weaker, a warm current called El Niño moves south from the equatorial regions. The name refers to the Christ-child because it comes during Christmas season, but El Niño brings no joy. It overlies coastal waters like a stagnant blanket, choking off the supply of nourishment on which plants and animals depend. Fish die by the millions. They litter the beaches, and the air reeks with the stench of rotting flesh. The water becomes polluted with poisonous hydrogen sulphide which gives off an odor like rotting eggs and blackens metallic objects. Sailors look over the side to see that *aguaje*—the Callao painter—has been at work on their ships. The fishing and guano industries suffer enormous losses at such times. In addition, the tropical rain belt often shifts, and torrential downpours may occur at places where it sometimes does not rain for a year. The dusty soil is washed away, crops are destroyed and mud houses dissolve and collapse.

Varied and abundant life cannot exist, then, when waters are stagnant. The sea needs movement to support its populations of plants and animals. The restless waters carry food and oxygen to seaweeds, barnacles, oysters and others which spend all or most of their lives fixed in one place. Great and small masses of water flowing and eddying in all directions disperse gases and toxic wastes. Poleward-moving currents bring warmth to higher latitudes, helping to balance the Earth's heat budget and extending the range of warm-water species. Other currents carry cold water equatorward and increase the range of cold-loving creatures.

Currents disperse eggs, larvae and organisms that are weak swimmers or, like plants, cannot swim at all. Many creatures that spend their adult lives creeping, crawling or attached to the sea floor mature from weakly-swimming larvae or floating eggs. During their youth, these beasts may be transported to favorable locations and may settle in areas that would otherwise remain unpopulated. The dispersing action of currents works against the limiting effects of temperature and salinity, so that all places that can support life become inhabited.

But plants and animals can also be carried to locations where adverse temperature and salinity conditions, lack of food, or unsuitable bottom conditions cause their demise. This is the price paid for widest possible distribution.

Hardy organisms that manage to survive in unfavorable

localities may undergo profound changes. As these species struggle for existence, random mutations make some of them more fit for the rigid surroundings. Eventually, these better adapted organisms may become so modified in form and function that new races of animals arise. From new races evolve new species which are totally different from their ancestors, and even unable to survive in regions whence their ancestors came. By persistently pressing creatures into more and more selective environments, currents indirectly play an important role in evolution.

It is generally believed that the species-producing centers are the warm, stable waters of the tropics, with their rich diversity of life. From here organisms spread poleward and into the depths. Through the process of natural selection, new species evolve at the border regions. The more rigorous conditions creatures encounter as they move poleward result in the survival of fewer and fewer species. It is estimated that five species live in warm water for every one living in cold water.

The continuous movement of their surroundings, there-fore, plays a decisive role in the history and fate of all living things in the sea. This movement is part of an all-encompass-ing circulation that is as complete, and as harmonious as that of the blood. It thoroughly mixes and distributes myriad soluble substances. Present in prodigious quantities, these substances form a dilute chowder in which marine creatures live out their lives. It constantly bathes their body surfaces and internal cavities with all the essentials of life. Not only do plants and animals live in the sea, they are part of it and the sea is part of them.

3.
Ocean Pastures

"This is the forest primeval."—LONGFELLOW

IN THE open ocean one sees no green meadows or fertile prairies. Away from the rim of seaweed around the coasts one is aware of only an endless confusion of seemingly barren waves. Yet there are lush pastures in the open sea.

Johannes Muller discovered these invisible grasslands in the 1840's by pouring sea water through a fine gauze net. Examining the contents under a microscope, he found a miniature world crowded with tiny plants and animals of great diversity and beauty. Muller correctly surmised that the one-celled plants of this microscopic cosmos maintain the same balance between the animal and vegetable kingdoms that exists on land. They incorporate the mineral wealth of the water into their bodies and so make it available to the huge and multifarious animal population of the sea.

On land plants have to reach for their food, water and light by branching roots and spreading leaves. In the sea, tiny plant cells can absorb all the essentials of life through their outer surfaces, so have no need for roots, stems or leaves. Each minute cell is a highly organized unit of life capable of carrying out the same basic activities as the tallest tree or the most prolific vine. Untold billions of these cells are scattered over the ocean like a fine dust. They alone can take simple substances like carbon dioxide, water and mineral salts and, with the aid of sunlight and colored pigments, transform them into the complex organic compounds that make up protoplasm.

These motes of plant life feed microscopic grazing animals, present in countless millions. The little vegetarians in turn are devoured by small fishes and other creatures. These creatures provide food for bigger fishes, giant squid, toothed whales and men. All the creatures in the sea can be thought of as parasites living off invisible plants.

No one knows with much certainty how much plant life there is in the World Ocean, but it undoubtedly represents the bulk of all living matter on Earth. Hundreds, thousands, and at times tens of millions, of cells may be present in a single quart of water. Without the microflora the World Ocean would be an immense blue desert with life confined to a narrow strip around the edges of the land.

Immobile plant cells, and those tiny animals that are not powerful enough swimmers to counteract the motion of the waters, must live out their lives drifting passively with the currents. Such organisms are known as *plankton*—the name coming from an expressive Greek term meaning "those who are made to wander." There are some 15,000 different species of wanderers, including the eggs and larvae of creatures that will later become swimmers, or crawlers or be fixed to the sea floor. The animals are called *zooplankton* and the plants *phytoplankton* from the Greek words *zoon* (animal) and *phyton* (plant).

Although the ocean is populated by animals from surface to bottom and shore to shore, plants can live and produce food only in the upper sunlit layers. No sharp line exists between these layers and dark parts of the sea, illumination fading gradually with depth. Sensitive instruments have detected some light as deep as 5,000 feet, but for practical purposes 650 feet is considered the lower limit of light penetration. The lighted zone varies widely, since it depends on the amount of incoming sunlight and the transparency of the water. Sunlight in turn depends on latitude and cloudiness, so it changes from season to season, day to day and even hour to hour. Transparency varies with the amount of material, living and nonliving, in the water.

The largest part of the sun's radiation reaching Earth falls on the ocean. Most of this is reflected off waves and back into the atmosphere, or goes into warming and evaporating water. Only a ridiculously small portion (about .04 of one percent) is used for photosynthesis. Plants, of course, need organic matter to live and grow, so they burn up part of what they produce themselves. Only in the upper part of the lighted region, called the *euphotic zone,* do plants make more organic material by photosynthesis than they burn up by respiration.

This euphotic zone, or zone of food production, varies widely. In the open ocean it extends to about 350 feet. In the plankton-rich, particle-clouded coastal waters, it may be as shallow as 3 feet or as deep as 100 feet or more. In the poorly-lit region between the euphotic zone and darkness, use of organic material approximates production and no effective plant growth takes place. Below this twilight zone eternal darkness rules and photosynthesis cannot occur; nevertheless certain plantlike organisms do live in this region.

Seaweed and Sargassum

Vegetation in the sea exhibits a pronounced lack of variety when compared with the enormous profusion of plant life on land. This dearth of flora forms is in striking contrast to the fabulous assortment of animals. The animal kingdom belongs mainly to the sea, while the plant kingdom is fostered by the land.

With few exceptions, marine flora belong to a group called *algae.* Although responsible for almost all food production in the ocean, algae have many representatives on land—in fresh water, in hot springs, in ice and snow, underground and within the bodies of higher plants and animals. In the sea they range from single-celled plants, visible only through a

microscope, to giant kelps as big as trees. All contain chlorophyll, but this green coloring is often masked by other pigments, so that algae may be red, brown, blue, yellow, green
or even iridescent.

Most seaweeds are algae. Largely confined to a narrow rim
at the edge of land, seaweeds are not very important in the
economy of the ocean. Only about two percent of the sea
floor is shallow enough to provide both a place of attachment and enough light for photosynthesis. This area is further reduced by the presence of loose sand, mud, shingle
and violent surf, which prevent the plants from maintaining
a good grip on the bottom. The majority of seaweeds need
exposed rocks or reefs to anchor to, but some grow attached
to the shells of animals or to other seaweeds.

Algae are classified according to the structure of their
cells and their life histories. Generally, individuals in each
class have the same color pigments. The classes include
green, blue-green, brown, red and yellow-green algae. The
yellow-greens are floating or planktonic plants; the rest, with
the exception of some blue-greens, are attached forms. From
shallow to deep water one finds blue-green and green, brown
then red sea-weeds, with a wide degree of overlapping.

Wandering along shore, you sometimes see a blue scum
or slimy deposit on the water surface and on mud, rocks
and wharves. Along the coasts of the United States you see
mermaid's hair—a dark, fuzzy mat that covers rocks and
pilings. These are blue-green algae, the most primitive and
poorly organized of marine plants. Some of this group are
not blue or green at all, but orange or reddish. The Red Sea,
in fact, gets its name from the blue-green algae *Tricho-
desimum erythraeum*. Much smaller than its name, it periodically blooms in great numbers, coloring the surface of
the sea yellow, orange, and, rarely, red.

Exploring the lower part of the tidal zone down to about
30 feet along temperate and tropical coasts, you encounter
many species of green algae. Most familiar are the large,
showy sea lettuces, *Ulva lactuca* and *Ulva lastissima*. They
reach a length of about 4 feet and grow just below the low
tide mark. You also see grassy, tubular *Enteromorpha;* the

delicate, plumose sea moss *Bryopis;* the spongy, branching *Codium,* and the odd merman's shaving brush *Penicillus.*

To see most brown algae you need diving equipment, or clear water and a glass bottom boat. The scientific name for this class—*Phaeophyceae*—means "dusky or shadowy plants." They grow to depths of 100 feet or more along rocky coasts from the tropics to the arctic. However, they prefer colder water and develop best in higher latitudes.

The more than 1,000 species show great scope in size and structure. Brown algae range from minute, filamentous plants like *Ectocarpus,* through the 15-foot-long mermaid's fishline, *Chorda,* to the giant kelps. The small sea palm, *Postelsia,* grows along the open west coast of the United States where it is exposed to the full force of breaking waves. Masses of the brown rockweed *Fucus,* with its characteristic "berries" or air bladders, color whole sections of the rocky tidal zones north of central California and North Carolina.

GREEN ALGAE

Sea Lettuce to 4 ft.

Merman's Shaving Brush to 5 in.

Sea Moss to 8 in.

Sea Grass to 2 ft.

The giant kelps include the 15- to 20-foot-long devil's apron, *Laminaria,* the 100-foot sea pumpkin, *Pelagophycus* and the 130-foot bladder kelp, *Nereocystis.** Among the largest of all plants and the longest of all algae, the vine kelp *Macrocystis* reaches the surface from depths of 260 feet off the coast of Chile. These trees of the sea form underwater forests among whose dense stipes (stems) and waving fronds myriad animals obtain food and shelter.

The rich kelp beds on the shores of the Pacific are harvested for food, fertilizer and fodder. Since ancient times these plants have been eaten by millions of people in the densely populated areas along the coasts of Asia and the Pacific islands. Today, these people eat some 100 varieties of it.

As rich in minerals as barnyard manure, kelp has been used in fresh or half-rotted condition as fertilizer in Scotland, Ireland and France for many years. On the west coast of the U.S. several factories have been built to make cattle-feed from kelp. Not too long ago, a dairy herd whose food included 10 percent dried seaweed set a world's record in milk production.

Red algae, which grow from a few feet to as much as 425 feet in depth, replace the browns and greens in deeper water. Their love of subdued light makes them important food producers on the continental shelves. Worldwide in distribution, they are most common in temperate and tropical regions. Among the most beautiful and striking objects in the sea, they come in orange, red, purple, olive, violet and iridescent varieties.

The purple laver *Porphyra* looks much like sea lettuce. Its supple structure allows it to yield unharmed to the push and pull of waves. The aboriginal Indians of North America ate *Porphyra tenera,* which still grows abundantly from California to the Gulf of Alaska. In Great Britain, cattle are fond of the dulse, *Rhodymenia,* and sheep wander down to the tidal zone to graze on it in preference to grass. *Rhodymenia palmata* is consumed raw, chewed like gum, eaten with

---

* These lengths are maximums.

fish and butter, boiled with milk and used in ragouts in various parts of the world.

Although not the most desirable dish as far as digestibility and caloric value are concerned, seaweed makes a delicious vitamin/mineral-laden food supplement. About 20 edible varieties are harvested wild and cultivated on sea farms in Japan. Here it is wrapped around meat and rice and eaten like grape leaves, sprinkled on crackers and even transformed into candy. Stipes of brown seaweed are eaten as "sea cabbage" in southern Chile. New Englanders used to prepare puddings from the gelatinous fronds of Irish moss, and lobster or shrimp boiled with seaweed gives it a "taste of the sea."

Algin, a gelatinous compound extracted from brown and other algae, goes into the manufacture of ice cream. It is also used as a stabilizer in sherbets, chocolate milk and

RED ALGAE

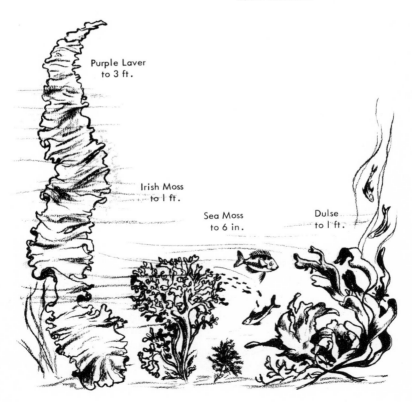

Purple Laver
to 3 ft.

Irish Moss
to 1 ft.

Sea Moss
to 6 in.

Dulse
to 1 ft.

cheese and as a thickener for soups and salad dressings. Agar
from red algae makes a base for jellies and candy. Seaweed
also crops up in some kinds of adhesives, in car polishes and
even in the wax used to take impressions for making false
teeth.

The only seaweed adapted to a nomadic floating existence
is gulf weed or *Sargassum*. Through the south central portion of the North Atlantic there are several species of this
infamous brown algae that float in clumps on the surface. The
abundance of the bushlike plant has given this area the name
Sargasso Sea. The weed itself was named by Christopher
Columbus' crew, who were first to cross this sea. The air-
filled bladders that keep it afloat reminded the sailors of
small grapes which they called "salgazo" back home in Por-
tugal.

For more than 450 years the Sargasso Sea was cloaked in an
aura of mystery and danger. Early explorers described it as
covered with an impenetrable mat of tangled vegetation
which caught hapless ships and imprisoned them forever.
Today on a voyage from New York to Bermuda, which lies
in the western part of the Sea, you can see this is not so.
Crossing the center of the Sea you might spot no more than
a few patches of weed the size of a man's head, or long
stringers of it might be in sight almost every hour. But the
7 million tons of *Sargassum* is so widely scattered throughout
the Sargasso's 1,000-by-2,000 mile area, it would not even stop
a dinghy.

Many books claim *Sargassum* is torn loose during storms
from dense weed beds along the Caribbean and Gulf coasts,
then carried into the Sea by the Gulf Stream. This is where
the popular name "gulf weed" originates. However, no
coastal gardens prolific enough to supply this much plant
material have been discovered. Also most *Sargassum* consists
of two species that are natural floaters never found attached
to rocks. Dr. John H. Ryther of Woods Hole Oceanographic
Institution believes gulf weed lives independently, growing
and reproducing in the open ocean. It reproduces by putting
forth shoots which eventually break off as new plants. Ryther
points out that these floating weeds have a "healthy color

and show new leaves and vigorous young shoots." Some of the weed may be torn loose from the sea bottom and drift in with the currents, but he favors the theory that the great bulk of *Sargassum* is native to the Sea. Its ancestors probably lived attached to the bottom, but Ryther believes present-day plants have evolved the ability to live a floating existence.

Grasses of the Sea

Gulf weed is, of course, not the only plant life in the Sargasso Sea. Like other parts of the World Ocean, this sea contains an incalculable number of microscopic plant cells. If you could strain this vegetation out of the water, you would discover that its total weight is much greater than the 7 million tons of *Sargassum*. Studying the eastern North Atlantic, German biologist Hans Lohmann found between 20 and 240 **million** plant cells beneath each square foot of ocean surface that he sampled. In the Pacific, 500,000 plants have been found in a single quart of water from the Gulf of Panama.

Unfortunately we cannot see these organisms merely by looking over the side of a ship. Suppose, however, we imagine being aboard a special research vessel with microscope lenses for sides and bottom. Everything in the sea around us would then be magnified hundreds of times, and we could leisurely study and observe the marine microcosmos as we sailed along and peered out below the water line.

Diatoms are the plants we would see most and the ones most important in the economy of the sea. Often called the "grasses of the sea," these yellow-green algae range in size from cells that pass through the meshes of the finest silk net to those just visible to the naked eye. Each consists of a blob of living jelly, encased by a cell wall that secretes an external skeleton or shell. The shell is made of silica, which the plant takes out of solution in the ocean and secretes around itself as a hard, insoluble covering. As clear as translucent glass, this cover does not interfere with the passage of light.

These shells consist of two parts, or valves, which fit together like the top and bottom of a pillbox. The pillboxes may be round, rectangular, oval, lens-shaped, club-shaped, starlike or drawn out into any number of odd and fantastic designs. Valve surfaces are ornamented with striations, pits, slits and pores that form intricate and often beautiful patterns. Looking through the side of our microscope ship would be like watching a water ballet performed by a treasure chest of exotic and absurd trinkets endowed with the spark of life.

The living material inside the shell of the diatom contacts the surrounding water through pores and slits in the valves. This facilitates the exchange of carbon dioxide and oxygen, as well as the salts used in metabolism. Some diatoms move in a jerky, zigzag way. These species have a special slit' of *raphe,* and it is thought that the streaming of protoplasm along the raphe is responsible for this movement.

Diatoms reproduce by simply dividing in half. The protoplasm splits into two masses, then the valves separate. Daughters that receive the larger valve can secrete a new half-shell and grow to the same size as the parents. Individuals receiving the other shell get progressively smaller because new half-shells must fit *inside* the smaller valve they inherited. Such reduction in size cannot go on indefinitely, so some diatoms regain their full size by the formation of *auxospores.* Their protoplasm begins to grow, pushing its way out of the old shell. When the bladderlike mass expands to two or three times original size, a new pair of valves is secreted. Other species have shells that stretch during reproduction, so both daughter cells can attain parent size.

Diatoms prefer colder waters. They bloom and flourish best in the Antarctic Ocean, over continental shelves in the temperate and frigid zones, in cool upwelling waters and in the northern Atlantic and Pacific. As our research ship sailed into warmer waters, we would notice the diatoms being replaced by *dinoflagellates.* These curious little creatures, members of a larger group called *flagellates,* are much more interesting to watch. They all have one or more threadlike processes, or *flagella,* with which they propel themselves through the water.

Watching dinos and other flagellates twist and whip through the sea, you might think of them more as animals than plants. Indeed, scientists have not definitely put them in one kingdom or the other. Some zoologists refer to them as *protozoans,* or "first animals," while many botanists class them with the yellow-green algae because many flagellates make their food by photosynthesis. Other flagellates lack chlorophyll and feed by capturing their food as animals do. Some live like plants when there is light and like animals when there is none. In this puzzling primitive group, then, the plant and animal kingdoms have not become fully separated. This suggests that all higher organisms may have descended from an ancient flagellate, or a creature very much like a flagellate.

Photosynthetic dinoflagellates rank second only to the diatoms as basic producers of food in the ocean. They display a magnificent variety of form, and watching them through a microscope ship you would observe some of the most bizarre creatures of the plankton world. Some live naked and others wear a thin, flexible covering. Most of them, however, have a shell composed of two valves or, more commonly, of thin plates of cellulose fitting together in a mosaic. The naked ones are extremely delicate and colorful, and the shelled species are wonderfully ornate.

Most dinos have a small red "eye spot," which enables them to determine if they are moving toward or away from light. All species possess two flagella by which they can, to some degree, keep themselves in areas where light and dissolved nutrients are favorable. One ribbonlike flagellum sets in a deep groove that encircles the body like a girdle. The other is threadlike and trails out behind like a tail. The girdle flagellum turns the creature round and round, while the lashing of the tail pushes it forward. Thus these strange creatures literally screw themselves through the water.

Dinos reproduce mainly by dividing in half, without a decrease in size. Practically none of the dinos cling together in permanent colonies, as do some diatoms. Many species are luminescent, and as night approaches countless millions of

A Silicoflagellate

Tri Horned
Ceratium

Gymnodinium

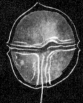

Dinoflagellate

Noctiluca

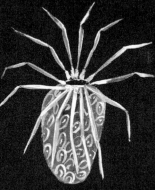

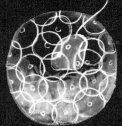

Coccolithus
fragilis

Coccolithophore

these marine fireflies often cause the sea to glow with a uniform ghostly-green light. Some light emitters are identified by such generic names as *Noctiluca* (night light) and *Pyrocystis* (flaming cyst).

In daylight, highly-colored dinos present in vast number sometimes color the sea green, yellow or red. Extraordinary "bloomings" of the naked dino *Gymnodinium brevis,* known unofficially as "Jim Brevis," sporadically turn the water of the Gulf of Mexico a brilliant yellow or yellow-green. During normal times Jim Brevis measures about 1,000 per quart of Gulf water. During spectacular blooms there may be as many as 90 million cells per quart and the water takes on a syrupy texture. As the oxygen is used up, individuals die and release a poison that affects the nerves of marine animals. Fish take in the poison through their gills and die by the millions. An outbreak of this misnamed "red tide" off the west coast of Florida in 1946-47 resulted in the death of at least 50 million fish and uncounted numbers of invertebrates. Poisonous vapor evaporated from the water produced severe irritation of the eyes, nose and throat in humans and brought on attacks of crying, coughing and choking.

Another single-celled plant floating in large numbers near the surface is *Halosphaera.* It and a near relative are the only plants in the open sea that possess the same bright green color as land vegetation. *Halosphaera viridis,* less than $\frac{1}{25}$ inch in diameter, inhabits all parts of the Atlantic from the tropics to high latitudes. In cold antarctic waters shunned by dinoflagellates, this species is second in importance to diatoms. In the Mediterranean, where they occur abundantly, these miniature spheres are known to fishermen as "punti verdi" (green points).

If the lenses of our microscope ship were powerful enough, we could see organisms yet smaller than the diatoms, dinos and green points—very tiny plants known as *coccolithophores* or "little bearers of seed stones." Seed stones (coccoliths) are minute shields or plates of lime that cover and protect the soft parts of these plankters. Some plates are oval and perforated, others are round or hexagonal and have short, club-shaped spines. When these little pieces of shell were first dredged up with the ooze from the ocean floor, scientists were at a loss to explain what they were. Finally, in the 1870's, Sir John Murray, an English naturalist, discovered that they are the external skeletons of flagellates less than $\frac{1}{5,000}$ inch in diameter.

Living coccolithophores were first discovered entangled in the feeding apparatus of small plankton animals, having until that time escaped notice because they slip through the meshes of even the most closely woven nets. Then in the early part of this century Hans Lohmann used a centrifuge to separate them from the water. His work opened up a yet smaller world of marine life and made possible more detailed exploration of the oceans.

Although most common in the tropics, coccolithophores may occasionally be so numerous in the North Sea they give the water a milky appearance. Fishermen call this "white water," and generally consider it a good sign of the presence of herring which feed on them. There is no doubt that these plants are also an important source of food for many planktonic animals.

Below the lighted zone, living diatoms and dinos are rare or absent. But down to at least 13,000 feet, various coccolithophores and blue-green algae make up a remarkable deep-sea or "shade" flora. In the Atlantic and Mediterranean, between 7,000 and 240,000 cells of *Coccolithus fragilis* were found in quart samples of water brought up from 3,000 to 10,000 feet. Because no photosynthesis can take place at that depth, they must absorb organic material through their body walls. Undoubtedly, coccolithophores serve as food for deep-living as well as near-surface plankton.

Lohmann introduced the term *nannoplankton,* meaning dwarf or centrifuge plankton, for those organisms less than $\frac{1}{5,000}$ inch in size. If the lenses of our microscope ship could magnify everything 250 times, the largest nannoplankters would appear to be about twice the diameter of a period on this page. This dwarf plankton is composed of diatoms, coccolithophores, bacteria, some protozoans and a group called *silicoflagellates*. Silicoflagellates, frequently found in the digestive spaces of one-celled animals, are persistent members of floating communities in all colder seas. They have delicate open shells of silica with radiating spines that give them a starlike appearance. These shells, as well as those of the other phytoplankton, make up a large part of the sediments that carpet the ocean floor.

Cruising the World Ocean in our special ship, we would see many more individuals of the centrifuge plankton than of the larger plants. It would probably surprise you to learn that the dwarfs exceed the other plankters in both number and volume. In the sea, as a rough general rule, the smaller the size of living things the greater will be their volume.

Besides algae, there are some 30 species of flowering plants, or *angiosperms*, living in salt water. These higher plants did not originate in the sea but invaded it by way of fresh water. The eelgrass, *Zostera*, the most important member of this group, is found along the coasts of North America, Europe and Asia from the tropics to the arctic. Others worth mentioning are the turtle grass *Thalassia*, which lives in quiet, shallow waters, and *Phyllospadix*, which grows on the open, wave-battered shores of western North America. Many animals find food and homes in the submarine meadows formed by these "grasses." Actually, they are not grasses at all but owe this popular name to their long, green leaves. Such plants have true roots and grow completely submerged in depths up to 50 feet. These plants are pollinated by the currents; the threadlike pollen grains have the same weight as water and are easily carried from place to place.

Fertility

Besides light, plants need carbon dioxide, oxygen, nitrogen and phosphorus. Except in isolated areas, plenty of carbon dioxide and oxygen is available, even at great depths. Nitrogen and phosphorus, present in mineral salts called nitrates and phosphates, are small in supply but large in demand. In thickly vegetated areas they may become depleted or exhausted. When their concentration falls below a certain level, growth stops and the population begins to dwindle.

The sea will bloom again only when a fresh supply of nitrates and phosphates is brought up from below by upwelling.

For good health and normal growth various marine plants demand different amounts of such elements as sulphur, iron, manganese, zinc, copper and even arsenic. In the ocean as on land, growth is limited by the factor present in the smallest amount. All other conditions may be favorable, but if a shortage of, say, iron exists certain plants will be absent.

Also there is evidence that some unknown substance must be present before plants, and therefore animals, can live. Artificial seawater has been made which contains precisely the same chemicals in the same proportions as present in nature. But sea plants will not grow in it unless small amounts of natural seawater or seaweed extracts are added. This mysterious *élan vital* may act as vitamins do in our own diet. Vitamin B12 (cobalamin), which occurs naturally in seawater, has been found necessary for the growth of various types of plants. Other species need B1 (thiamin) in addition to B12.

One of the liveliest debates among marine biologists involves the question of whether the ocean's primitive plants produce as much food as the higher, more concentrated flora on land. Does plant production in the sea equal or exceed the staggering yearly increase of plant matter in grasslands, farms, forests and jungles?

From 1950 to 1952 Danish biologists attempted to answer this question during a world cruise in the ship *Galathea*. They determined plant productivity in many places by what was then a new technique. The water was "salted" with small amounts of radioactive carbon. Geiger counters measured how much of this carbon the plants took up in photosynthesis. This provided an index of how much growth was taking place. According to the Danes, about 40 billion tons of organic matter is produced in the World Ocean every year—roughly the same as the annual production of plants on land.

When light and nutrients occur in ideal combinations parts of the sea produce as much living matter as a rich Iowa cornfield or dense Brazilian jungles. When conditions are not so favorable watery areas can be as barren as the tundra or the semi-arid plains of western United States. Since the World Ocean contains about 70 percent more acreage than the land, one would think that production there would average out much higher. But as Dr. John Ryther points out, luxuriant growth in the sea occurs for only a matter of days or weeks each year. On land vegetation occupies a much smaller area, but it is a thousand times greater in bulk and can maintain high productivity for years.

4.

The Wanderers

"Some looked like fringed, fluttering spooks cut out of cellophane paper, while others resembled red-beaked birds with hard shells instead of feathers. There was no end to Nature's extravagant inventions in the plankton world. . . ."
— HYERDAHL

LIKE a calm, watery island surrounded by swift flowing streams, the Sargasso Sea rotates lazily within the ring of currents that fringes the North Atlantic. This strange oceanic sea, or at least the area where the golden weed is found, is oval in shape. It reaches from the seaward edge of the Gulf Stream off Florida to the Azores and extends about 1,000 miles in a north-south direction. In cross-section it is a lens-shaped mass of warm water, 3,000 feet thick at its deepest part, lying atop a body of cold water that is roughly five times as deep. Overhead, winds are light and variable, skies bright and clear, and weather fair and sunny most of the year.

The abundant sunshine causes much water to be evaporated from the surface. But the salts remain behind, making surface waters briny and heavy. There is little rainfall to dilute the briny sea, and ocean currents cut it off from river outflow. As the salt load increases, water begins to sink slowly and carry life-giving nutrients below the lighted zone. No vertical mixing replenishes this loss and only a small inflow from surrounding currents brings in new supplies.

54

Without this food there can be no luxuriant plant growth and consequently no large animal population. For this reason the Sargasso has been called "the great desert of the sea" and has been compared to the vast land deserts of Africa, Arabia and Iran, which lie in the same latitudes. Its clear blue tone—an indirect sign of a paucity of life—is often referred to as "the desert color of the sea." Where water is rich in plankton it becomes turbid and colored green, brown or yellow according to its microflora. These hues predominate in coastal waters and with all their varying shades are known as "the colors of life."

But scientists aboard the *Galathea* and others who have investigated the ocean's fertility say no deserts exist there, at least not comparable to the sandy wastes and sterile ice caps on land. They point out that plankton, "the greatest of all living worlds," is present everywhere. Every patch of *Sargassum* is a floating jungle inhabited by miniature

SARGASSUM FISH

Marineland of Florida

shrimps, worms, crabs, octopuses, sea horses, pipefish, and the eggs and young of innumerable other creatures.

Many of these beasts are specially adapted to the weed worlds, varying in shape and color according to the species of plant on which they live. Some are soft, shapeless, shell-less snails with flowing brown bodies mottled with dark circles and fringed with flaps and folds of skin. As they glide through the weeds in search of prey, they can scarcely be distinguished from their background. Streaked and mottled with brown and gold, the small, rapacious sargassum fish, *Histrio histrio,* has branching, leaflike extensions of skin that match those of the *Sargassum.* To complete its camouflage, *Histrio's* rich colors and patterns change as it moves from weed to weed. This big-headed "tiger" of the Sargasso Sea can capture and eat prey almost as large as itself.

The eggs of flying fish, which nest in the weed, look much like the "berries" or bladders that keep *Sargassum* afloat. Some creatures even include white designs that mimic worm tubes in their disguise. The actual tubes are made of lime, and worms hang their heads out one end to catch food from the weeds and water. Then there is the water-walker *Halobates*—the only insect that lives in the open sea. This seagoing bug runs across the surface of the tropical Atlantic and Pacific on six thin, hairy legs. In the Atlantic, the islands of *Sargassum* offer a refuge and resting place for these extraordinary beasts.

Much life thrives below the surface of this ocean sea. A rich community of zooplankton, fishes and squid live between 3,000 and 5,000 feet. In many places a more or less permanent thermocline lies 1,300 to 1,600 feet down. This layer provides a sort of "false bottom," slowing the sinking salts, decomposed creatures and pieces of weed. The resulting concentration of food supports another sizeable population. The number of shrimplike crustaceans at this depth far exceeds that found at the surface.

While no really desolate areas exist in the World Ocean, the Sargasso Sea cannot support a large plant and animal population. On the *Galathea* Expedition this was found to be true of all the central ocean areas, particularly in the tropics. Crossing the open Pacific from New Zealand to California and the Atlantic from the West Indies to the English Channel, production of plant material was found to be low and "astonishingly uniform." (Exceptions were areas of divergence and coastal waters.) This is because nitrates and phosphates sinking below the lighted zone are not replaced by horizontal or vertical mixing. In the tropics a pronounced and persistent thermocline forms a semipermanent barrier to upwelling. Production remains low year-around and life is mostly confined to deeper waters.

Pattern of Seasons

Farther north and south in temperate latitudes, fertility varies from season to season. During winter, surface waters are cooled to the point where they become heavy enough to sink. Winter winds and high waves help mix the ocean to depths of 1,000 to 1,500 feet—well below the lighted zone. Thermoclines are destroyed, and rich stores of nutrients pour into the near-surface layers. But the moving waters also carry many tiny plants downward, forcing them to spend considerable time in darkness. This, together with the low level of light during winter, prevents any prolific plant growth.

But with the coming of spring, changes so evident on land can also be observed in the sea. Mixing subsides, and a thermocline forms. Plants in the euphotic zone remain there and have access to large stores of food brought up by mixing. As the sun gets higher and more light is available, the phytoplankton begin a tremendous orgy of reproduction. Diatoms divide in half every 18 to 36 hours. In a week their numbers may increase a hundredfold, in two weeks ten-thousandfold, until many tons of vegetation float on an acre of ocean. As green shoots appear and buds unfold on land, a tide of new life sweeps across the sea. The sparkling blue or dull gray winter waters turn green and brownish-green as vast areas become transformed into lush pastures. This is the characteristic "spring bloom" of temperate seas.

Unlike its counterpart on land, this rush of life is short-lived. As plants in the top layers multiply, they block light from those below. In the open sea, the lighted zone may decrease from 300 to 15 feet or less. The shallower the photosynthetic zone, the smaller the supply of food available, and this food is rapidly depleted as the population continues to increase. During a period of fine calm weather in March or April, spring flowering may run its course in a day or two. But storms, cold weather or anything that promotes mixing, can prolong it for one or two months.

Spring is also spawning time for many species. Every day swarms of eggs and young rise from shoals, shelves and deep breeding grounds. The waters come alive with baby crabs, worms, jellyfish, fish fry and forms that resemble no living adult. These beasts are born hungry and immediately gorge themselves on the abundant vegetation and each other. Some gluttonous little creatures eat their own weight every two days. One copepod that is hardly big enough to see, *Eurytemora hirundoides,* may gulp down as many as 120,000 diatoms daily. Some plankters eat more than they can digest and continually void fecal pellets containing partly digested plants.

Even the prodigious reproductive rate of diatoms cannot keep pace with this steady devourment. A fivefold increase in grazing animals can wipe out a population of a million cells per quart of water in five days, even though the plants are doubling their number every day. Under the pressure of ravenous grazing and the diminishing supply of nutrients, pastures are laid bare, and animals dominate the scene.

There may be other brief population explosions, involving diatoms or other phytoplankters. All plants do not increase or decrease together. Shelled species may give way to shell-less, larger plants to smaller, as the supply of silica and food dwindles. Because of their slower growth rate and lower nutrient requirement, dinos frequently displace diatoms as food becomes scarcer. Also, some plants may release substances into the water which injure other species and speed their disappearance.

No matter what the succession of species the intense, vivid pace of spring inevitably slackens to a summer torpor. Once the store of nutrients is used, life is maintained by recycling of the organic material between surface and thermocline. Dead bodies and wastes are decomposed by the action of bacteria, which increases with temperature, and the ingredients are redistributed among the surviving organisms.

Life goes on at a low, lethargic pace until fall, when cooling and higher winds again mix the water. The thermocline is pierced and nutrients flood into the lighted zone. With plenty of light still available, a second outburst of life takes place. This fall flowering is less intense than that of spring and equally short-lived. The food supply quickly diminishes, after which the plant population drops off sharply. Many little grazing animals die. The young of creeping, crawling and attached creatures have grown up and settled down on the ocean bed.

As winter gales roar across the temperate seas, chilling and subsidence turn over the surface waters like plowed land. They became uniformly cold and enriched with nutrients. However, the number of organisms falls to the lowest level of the year because mixing is too violent and there is not enough light. Turbulence fertilizes the upper layers, but a calm period must follow so plants can reside in the lighted zone long enough to utilize the nutrients and grow.

There can be no spring growth on land unless plowed ground is seeded. By the same token, there will be no renewal of life in the sea unless some plants cells are present to take advantage of favorable spring conditions. To survive the harsh winter many organisms go into a sort of hibernation or suspended animation. Some copepods spend the winter in deeper waters, or sleep it away in bottom mud. They live, like hibernating bears, on a store of fat built up in times of plenty. Many creatures form what are known as *resting stages* or *resting spores*. The protoplasm of certain diatoms becomes condensed into a compact mass around which is secreted an extra thick wall of silica. In this state they wait out periods of inadequate food, darkness or unfavorable salinity. Diatoms living in polar regions may spend the winter frozen in sea ice. When the spores germinate during spring melting, plants are often present in such numbers they stain the ice and water brown.

In polar regions, the spring bloom and fall flowering may merge into a single midsummer outburst. Due to constant upwelling, the concentration of nitrates and phosphates in the Antarctic Ocean is probably higher than in any unpolluted surface area in the World Ocean. Here the spring bloom usually starts in October, and by November the brownish water is crowded with armies of shrimplike euphausids, seals, penguins, fishes, petrels, squid and the largest population of whales in the world. At the other end of the globe, during the northern hemisphere summer, dense swarms of copepods graze on the abundant vegetation. Huge schools of mackerel, herring and other fishes, clouds of sea birds, and a multitude of whales and seals feast on copepods, swimming snails and each other.

When considered over the whole year, or over a period of years, fertility probably does not vary greatly between high and low latitudes. In polar regions productivity is crowded into a few months of vigorous and spectacular growth. In the tropics activity is low to moderate, but it is fairly constant all year long.

Little Nomads

To the plankton belong the largest number of living organisms on Earth, and the zooplankton make up an assemblage of creatures more diverse and widespread than any other realm of life. Nearly every major division (phylum) of the animal kingdom is found here. Almost every creature in the sea lives as a plankter at one stage or another during its life. Considered together with the plants, then, the major portion of living things on our planet exists as an almost invisible dust scattered through the ocean.

If you dip a sample of plankton out of the sea and magnify it you can see immediately that all are not helpless drifters. Some swim freely and move many times their own length. They are so small, however, little actual distance is covered. Also they do not keep on a steady course, but swim jerkily in all directions. Only under certain conditions, such as when moving toward or away from light, do they make

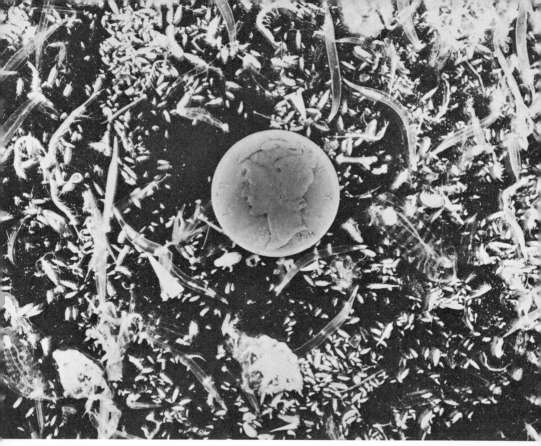

University of Miami

PLANKTON as viewed under a microscope. The transparent, eel-like creatures are arrow worms. The oval, antennaed beasts are copepods. The banded, transparent organism to the right of the dime is a salp.

consistent, though restricted, progress. Unlike plants, animal plankters are found at all depths down to the ocean floor, but they are not, as was once believed, uniformly distributed either vertically or horizontally.

Most zooplankters are permanent nomads. They spend all their lives drifting passively. Mingling with these permanent drifters are the eggs and young of bottom-living and actively swimming adults. Such temporary plankters are most abundant in coastal waters. "Blue water" plankters, or those that live in the open sea, are mostly permanent types.

The smallest marine animals and the simplest zooplankters are the one-celled protozoans ("first animals"). Their single-celled bodies are often encased in shells of extraordinary beauty and complexity, which they secrete themselves. Protozoans are generally microscopic in size, but some of them can just be seen without the aid of a lens. Many of these larger ones live in kidney shaped or spiral shells made of lime. Some have ornate shells or external skeletons of silica; some make bell- or urn-shaped shells of organic material, bits of sand, etc. Yet others flow around the sea naked.

Sponges, which make up the phylum Porifera or "pore bearers," are not very important in the plankton. For the most part, they live in colonies attached to the ocean floor or to solid objects. They send up eggs which when fertilized develop into free-swimming larvae, but these young live as plankters for only a short time.

Members of the phylum Coelenterata, to which jellyfish, coral polyps, siphonophores and sea anemones belong, are very prominent in floating communities. Included in this group are the largest wanderers. Some jellyfish may be as much as 6½ feet in diameter and have tentacles 115 feet or longer. These beasts and their near relatives possess a variety of insidious devices to poison, paralyze and ensnare weaker and smaller creatures. Jellyfish often congregate in such numbers that the sea seems covered with a quilt of delicately shaded circular patches.

Other jellyfishlike coelenterates called *siphonophores* keep afloat by gas-filled bladders. The Portuguese man-of-war *Physalia,* whole fleets of which often travel north with the Gulf Stream, belongs to this group. So does the by-the-wind-sailor *Velella* which has a beautiful blue, purple or lemon-yellow float with an elevated crest. When wind catches this "sail," *Velella* moves through the water like a ship sailing before the wind. Under its "keel" dangles a mass of tentacles, ready to grasp any creatures unlucky enough to be in its path.

Comb jellies or sea walnuts bear close resemblance to jellyfish and siphonophores. However, detailed studies reveal basic differences in anatomy so comb jellies are placed in a phylum of their own called *Ctenophora.* Among the most exquisite and delicate of marine creatures, ctenophores live only as plankters and they boast prominent membership in both surface and deep communities. Despite beauty and a fragile appearance, these animals play a sinister role in the economy of the sea. Fearsome and voracious, they often sweep the water clean of young, commercially valuable fish or crustaceans on which the fish fry depend for food.

One insatiable ctenophore is the sea gooseberry *Pleurobranchia*. Full-grown, this pirate is the size and shape of a large gooseberry, or about one inch in diameter. It has a mouth at its lower end and two tentacles about ten times longer than the gooseberry part. The tentacles have immense numbers of fine, hairlike processes. These are covered with knobby *lasso cells* which exude a sticky substance when touched. Propelled forward by rows of comblike plates along its sides, like an old paddle-wheeled steamer, *Pleurobranchia* drags the water with this horribly efficient fishing gear. No creature small enough to be captured ever escapes. Victims try desperately to free themselves, but the more they struggle the more they become entangled with lasso cells. The muscular cores of the tentacles contract, pulling the prey toward the gooseberry's protruding lips. These beasts capture young fish twice their own size, and individuals have been found with as many as five herring fry in their stomachs.

Other gluttonous eaters in the plankton include a large assortment of worms—flatworms and ribbon worms, round worms and wheelworms, tube worms and arrow worms, and annelids or segmented worms. Of these only the ribbon worms, round worms and arrow worms have many permanently planktonic species. The most characteristic are arrow worms, which belong to the phylum Chaetognatha—the "bristle mouths." These worms live only as plankters and one species or another inhabits every part of the World Ocean. The most common group, those you are most likely to see in a sample, is the genus *Sagitta*. About an inch long, these transparent beasts look like tiny glass rods with two sets of side fins and a horizontal tail shaped like an arrowhead. They have two small black eyes and can look in all directions without turning their heads. They can even look down through their own transparent bodies. On either side of the head are stout, curved bristles which act like powerful jaws, and make these creatures the dragons of the plankton world.

A little dragon lies motionless in the water until a victim comes within striking range. Then, with violent up and down movements of its tail, it suddenly darts forward. An arrow worm can cover a distance five or six times its own length in a wink. With strong bristles it seizes and devours young herring as big as itself, copepods and even other *Sagitta*. As with comb jellies, the only time glass worms are easily visible is when they have partially digested victims in their transparent stomachs.

Arrow worms and all zooplankters taken together are vastly outnumbered by the shrimplike copepods. There are probably more of these tiny crustaceans than all other multicellular animals in the sea combined. Their numbers are exceeded only by the plants on which they depend for food. A net towed for 15 minutes in the Gulf of Maine, between Cape Cod and Nova Scotia, has captured as many as 2½ million individuals. There are some 750 different species of copepods which make up about 70 percent of the zooplankton. These range in size from a pinhead to a grain of rice. *Calanus hyperboreus,* a giant among the group, reaches a length of one-third inch.

Like shrimp and lobsters, copepods are built in segments and enclosed in jointed shells which they shed periodically. These protective coats are horny and transparent like the coverings of shrimp. Typical species have one eye in the middle of their head which can look forward, upward and downward at the same time. Italian fishermen once called these copepods "occiussi" or eye-bearers.

The name "copepod" comes from two Greek words meaning "oarfoot"—a title given them because their limbs are flattened like the blade of an oar. They leap actively in the water and move haphazardly in a series of jerky hops. Like all crustaceans, copepods have two pairs of antennae, three pairs of "head" limbs and a varying number of trunk and abdominal legs. The first pair of antennae are usually much longer than the other appendages and equipped with a profusion of feathery bristles to help keep the bearer afloat.

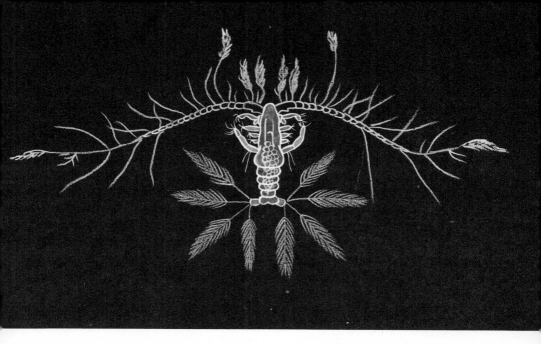

COPEPOD *(Calocalanus pavo)* has feathery, spinous limbs that spread its weight over the water and help keep it afloat. When resting, such plankters stretch out their limbs and hang vertically downward.

Many species habitually "tread water" by vibrating or "fanning" their front limbs as fast as 600 times a minute. This rapid movement keeps them in a fixed position or raises them to a level where light and feeding conditions are more favorable. At the same time, fanning draws water toward the copepod's mouth. The fifth pair of limbs has curved, whiskered spines which form a sieve and chamber just beneath the mouth. As the creature slowly moves forward a stream of sea "soup" is forced through these "chin whiskers," and plants and other food collect on the fine hairs. When a good portion accumulates in the food chamber, another pair of legs pushes it into the craw.

Other copepods have strong "mouth" legs adapted for seizing and holding prey. These beasts eat their smaller vegetarian brothers, fish fry and diverse plankters. However, the majority of species are *filter feeders* and subsist on plants they strain out of the water with their chin whiskers. In the sea, these tiny copepods fill the same niche as cows, sheep and other vegetarians do on land. They graze on the ocean

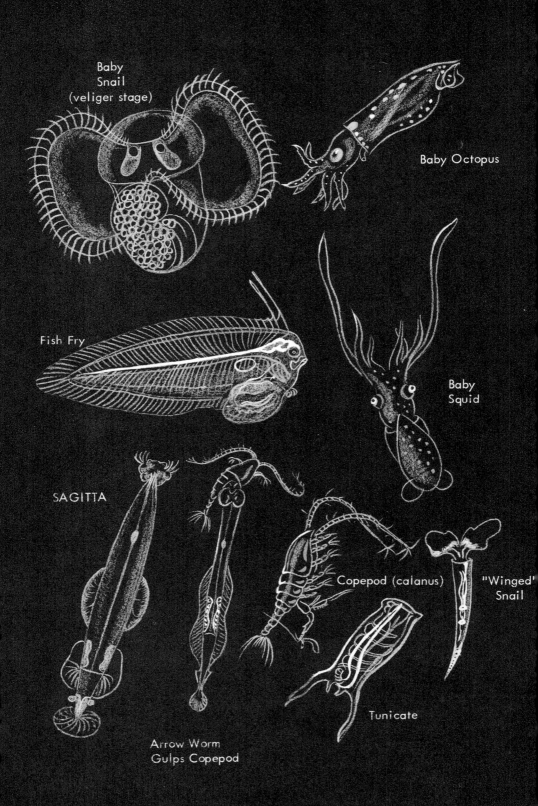

Baby
Snail
(veliger stage)

Baby Octopus

Fish Fry

Baby
Squid

SAGITTA

Copepod (calanus)

"Winged"
Snail

Tunicate

Arrow Worm
Gulps Copepod

pastures and turn plant material into animal protein, which in turn nourishes the flesh eaters. No other zooplankters play a more vital role in the economy of the sea.

Copepods reproduce rapidly and profusely. Females are carrying fertilized eggs only 14 days after they themselves hatch. Then both mother and babies may produce one or more broods that year. During spring bloom in Cape Cod Bay there may be as many as 2,000 of these shrimpers in a cubic yard of water. Herring, mackerel and other creatures swim through these dense masses gulping down prodigious numbers. As many as 60,000 copepods have been found in the stomach of a single herring.

"Fringed, Fluttering Spooks"

Many zooplankters look more like whimsical trinkets than animals. Examining a plankton sample under a microscope, you may see spiny, cellophanelike creatures resembling fantastic insects with large black eyes, or intricately carved glass figurines or impossible flowers designed by extravagant artists. There are grooved, glassy spheres encircled by bristly girdles; transparent "urns" with graceful, outsized handles; clear globs with hairy, earlike flaps. Some resemble decorated coolie hats, plumed football helmets or twisted, tentacled tubes. Nature appears to have been in a flamboyant mood when she designed this miniature menagerie. But each part of every design is some plankter's answer to the problems of staying afloat and reproducing its kind.

The forms that seem most outlandish and unfamiliar are those that lead a drifting life only during their early youth. In fresh water, newly-hatched snails, worms, clams and insects crawl out of eggs or parental pouches and take up life near their parents. In the sea, oysters, lobsters, starfish and other bottom-dwellers hatch out as free-swimming larvae and become scattered by the currents. Many of these youths look so completely unlike their parents even experienced zoologists do not know they are the same animal. In numerous cases larva and adult remained classified as separate species for years.

The two are dissimilar because they occupy totally different surroundings and must adapt to different modes of life. The youths must remain afloat as long as possible to distribute the species as widely as possible. At the same time, they must grow up quickly and sink to the bottom before falling victim to some hungry predator. The shape and structure of every baby represents special adaptations to, and a compromise between, these rival requirements.

Prime prerequisites for staying afloat, whether for a short time or a lifetime, are to be small and light. Also, needle-like spines and long feathery limbs and tails spread an animal's (or plant's) weight over a large area and increase its resistance to sinking. A high water content both reduces weight and contributes to transparency. The more transparent a creature the harder it is to see, an obvious advantage with a multitude of voracious predators always on the prowl. Having some power to swim, no matter how feeble, is an important means of keeping afloat. The simplest and most effective way for very small animals to move about is by the beating of numerous *cilia,* or fine hairs. For these reasons, then, many temporary and permanent plankters are small, hairy, spiny and transparent.

When ready to become adults, larvae change form completely before they switch their mode of life. Some youths do this gradually, while others undergo a rapid and dramatic transformation. Many worms and mollusks emerge from their eggs as a transparent sphere with a ciliated girdle. Movement of the cilia twirls the sphere around like a spinning top. As this whirling trinket waltzes through the water, currents created by the cilia continually draw food and water into its tiny mouth.

The young of segmented worms develop a series of ciliated rings below the original sphere. The first hairy ring can support only limited weight, but as new segments are added they assist in holding up the gradually increasing bulk of the larvae. Some of these baby worms grow long stiff bristles which serve, as do the sharp spines of young crustaceans, to make them too awkward to be swallowed.

Other larval worms carry their rear segments tucked up into a cavity formed by the folding over of those in front. This has been compared to the "top of a stocking turned inside out and drawn back over the foot." When it is time to take up residence on the bottom, the youth suddenly straightens out in a violent metamorphosis that takes only seconds. Hairy rings and other float structures no longer needed are eaten by the worm. Its first meal on the ocean floor is itself.

Some ragworms hatch out with three pairs of muscular limbs that enable them to swim. These babies look very much like the young of copepods and other crustaceans. This is the main reason zoologists believe crustaceans descended from "wormy" ancestors. Adults that differ greatly in appearance but have similar babies or larval stages are descended from similar or the same ancestors.

A baby crustacean is a tiny, lucid triangle with six legs. This little creature grows in size and repeatedly bursts out of its chitinous shell. At each molting, it gains legs and changes form until it finally takes on the appearance of a miniature adult.

Snails go through what is known as a *veliger* stage before they begin to look like the parents. During this time the larger part of their internal organs is twisted through a U-turn in relation to the rest of the body. Familiar species of sea snails then settle down to the bottom, but there are snail-like mollusks that remain with the permanent plankton. Called *pteropods* or sea butterflies, these creatures have bodies drawn out on either side into winglike lobes. They swim by "flapping" these lobes like wings. Some pteropods lie naked in the sea, while others have light shells shaped like a snail spiral or a long, slender cone.

The Echinodermata or "spiny skins"—sea urchins, starfish and relatives—spend all their adult lives creeping along, burrowing into or attached to the ocean floor. They are represented in plankton communities only by temporary residents, which are famous for leading "dual lives." After hatching and passing through a number of intermediate stages,

starfish and sea urchin young develop a fluid-filled sac or
coelom on their left sides. This sac resembles a tumor or
malignant growth. Around it, tissues become arranged into
the shape of an adult. If it is a starfish, a little star forms
complete with a mouth and nervous system. The larva on
which it hangs also has its own mouth, nervous system and
hairy bands for locomotion.

For a while the two live happily together, each going about
its own business. But the more organized "tumor" soon begins to feed on the larva that bore it. Eventually the larva
is consumed completely. Then the echinoderm sinks and
takes up life as an adult.

Another group of animals found in the plankton—the
tunicates—are mixed up in the evolutionary transition from
creatures without backbones to creatures with backbones.
The best known tunicates are the bottom-living sea squirts
or ascidians. They resemble a sack with two openings at the
top, one for taking in food and water the other for eliminat-
ing wastes.

Ascidians send up a remarkable tadpolelike larva. Less
than an inch long, it has some of the characteristics of much
more advanced backboned animals. This led the late Professor Walter Garstang, an English planktonologist, to advance the theory that all fishlike and higher creatures evolved
from little tadpoles much like these. He did not say that
man and his stiff-backed relatives developed from present-
day sea squirts, but rather from some animal that resembles
their young and which lived in the distant past.

To carry the theory back further, this ancient creature
and the spiny-skinned echinoderms both descended from the
same yet more ancient ancestor. In other words, some unknown creature, now lost in time, gave rise to both the starfish clan and sea squirts. The former never amounted to
much, but the latter developed a swimming baby that gave
rise to all backboned beasts.

Garstang thought it happened this way. An ancient and
distant relative of modern ascidians sent up planktonic
young, just as sea squirts send up little "tads" today. The
forces of natural selection acted upon this larval form and

changed it to better meet its two rival needs—staying afloat and reproducing quickly. Over many generations the tads developed a muscular tail and became better swimmers. At the same time, their reproductive organs developed faster than the rest of their body. Eventually the tads became able to reproduce while still swimming in the plankton. With the birth of their first offspring, a bottom-living adult stage was eliminated and a new line of free-swimming tunicates appeared.

There is evidence that copepods evolved in the same way from an ancient bottom-dweller resembling modern crabs and lobsters. Comb jellies, siphonophores and even insects may have arisen from floating babies which matured before they settled down.

Garstang thought that the vertebrate line began in this way. He envisioned an evolutionary giant step from a sedentary, attached creature to one that was active and free-swimming. This swimmer in turn may have been the progenitor of new races that led to new species and finally to some 45,000 different backboned creatures. This is, of course, only a theory. Backboned beasts may just as well have arisen, as other biologists believe, from gradual changes in adult forms.

Garstang's main point was that evolution does not affect adults alone. He showed that natural selection acts just as powerfully on the young, preserving those variations that make them better fit for survival in their surroundings.

5.

Spineless Creatures

"When you were a tadpole and I was a fish,
In Paleozoic time."—LANGDON SMITH

ACCORDING to a rough rule-of-thumb in biology, an unborn infant repeats the evolutionary history of its parents. The sequence of development, which took its ancestors millions of years to complete, is condensed into a few days, weeks or months in the egg or womb. The human embryo develops gills like a fish, a kidney like that of a shark and a stiff rod of cartilage (notochord) which is characteristic of primitive chordates. Comparable structures occur in every species of the animal kingdom. This idea should not be taken too literally because when examined in detail many missing links occur, and there are links that do not match. Nevertheless, the similarity between stages of a developing embryo and the increasing complexity of higher and higher animals is truly amazing.

Human sperm cells resemble flagellates, and female eggs (ova) are much like one-celled animals living in the bodies of copepods and other creatures. When the fertilized egg begins to divide the new cells form a colony that is not unlike a sponge. The embryo next develops two layers of cells, like an inner and outer skin, which resembles the body walls of a jellyfish. Then comes a third or middle layer such as

72

appears in flatworms and spiny-skinned sea urchins and starfish. A body cavity or coelom then develops within the middle layer. The first animals on the evolutionary scale to have such a cavity are segmented worms, which are more advanced than flatworms. At this stage of development both human embyros and segmented worms also have a nervous system and a simple heart that pumps colorless or red blood.

Plant and animal kingdoms merge in the flagellates. Protozoans and higher animals may have evolved from flagellate-like cells that lived in the plankton of ancient seas. Perhaps these cells resembled *Noctiluca,* a modern dinoflagellate entirely animal in nature. Individuals are about the size of a pinhead and under a microscope look like rubber balls with a short, stout elastic strand. This thick strand serves as a tentacle to seize prey and push it into the mouth opening. They usually eat diatoms but can capture and devour animals the size of baby copepods.

Noctiluca dinos have a pink or reddish body and when present in large numbers turn the sea the color of tomato soup. Their name means "night light," and each luminescent creature glitters in the night sea like a nautical firefly. When vast crowds of them congregate the separate lights merge into an eerie, sometimes brilliant, green glow. Any breaking wave, ship's bow or animal that ruffles the glowing water suddenly comes ablaze with cold, fiery light. Since this can be a distinct disadvantage during war time, the U.S. Navy has invested a lot of money in the study of bioluminescence.

When considered animals, dinos and their close relatives are placed in the class Flagellata ("whipbearers"), a group including all protozoans that move by means of threadlike flagella. Other seagoing protozoans get around by waving cilia in unison (Ciliates), or streaming extensions of themselves in one direction and flowing the rest of themselves after it (Rhizopods). Another group has no means of locomotion and lives in the bodies of other animals as parasites.

The best known Rhizopod is the amoeba, a clear, jellylike blob often found in large numbers near the surface of fresh water bodies. In the open sea amoebae are rare and their class is dominated by Foraminifera and Radiolarians.

"Forams" are cosmopolitan and live in both cold and warm water, on the ocean bottom and as plankters. The bottom dwellers build little apartments around themselves by cementing together bits of sediment and hard parts of decomposed organisms. They resemble tiny wet jawbreakers that have been rolled in sand and crushed shell. No one knows exactly how they do it, but the plankton species remove salts from solution in the sea and build them into hard, limey shells. These forams have been around for at least 500 million years, and since different species prefer different temperatures their fossilized shells are important in tracing the history of the Earth's climate.

As they outgrow their shells some species secrete a succession of larger and larger chambers, then flow part of themselves into each chamber. Such forams take the shape of miniature snails, kidneys, rice grains or golf balls. Some have a large opening at one end, others are perforated with many small holes through which thin strands of protoplasm are thrust for locomotion and feeding. *Globigerina* streams out slimy "feet" which branch out to form a sticky net. When diatoms and others blunder into the net, digestive juices surge through every strand. The victim is digested outside the shell, and its dissolved substance flows back along the netting to the insides of the foram.

Radiolarians or "rayed ones" secrete delicate and fanciful shells of silica that resemble fantastically ornate glass models of shining stars, rayed globes, spiny vases and three-cornered helmets. They are to the sea what snow flakes are to the land, decorating it with some 4,400 exquisite and striking designs. Their protoplasmic strands radiate from a central mass along needlelike spines or filaments. These are sticky, and when a hapless creature touches them two or more come together to seize it. Then streams of protoplasm flow out along the rays and carry the victim back to the central mass where it is digested. Radiolarians live only as plankters. They and planktonic forams drift at all depths down to 16,500 feet, but all are most numerous in the upper 650 feet. Countless billions of them have been coming to life and dying for hundreds of millions of years. Their lifeless remains carpet all but the deepest parts of the ocean floor with an organic ooze that makes a rich feeding ground for bottom-dwellers.

Sponges

Instead of making their way through life alone, some flagellates band together in colonies. When a single cell joins a colony its environment changes radically. The cell can best adapt to the new surroundings by specializing, perfecting one of its functions to perform a single vital service for the whole colony. Any essential activities it neglects in doing this are taken up as specialties by others. Some cells get food and oxygen, others act as skin, still others provide support. Division of labor and greater mass enable the group to withstand stresses from the outside better than would any individual cell.

Flagellate "societies" bear strong resemblance to sponges, the most specialized and successful of cell colonies. Inert and plantlike, sponges show little evidence of being alive beyond the slow opening and closing of orifices at their "head" end. It was not realized that they were animals until as late as 1825.

A sponge consists basically of cells arranged into a vase-shaped wall of living tissue that encloses a hollow space. The extremely thin wall, or skin, has two layers which are peppered with thousands of perforations. These give sponges the scientific name Porifera or "pore bearers." The pores are canals lined with flagellate-like cells that wave their tiny whips to move water from the surrounding sea into the hollow interior. These cells also take food and oxygen from the water as it flows by and pass it to other cells in the colony. The moving water then picks up waste material, carrying it into the hollow center and out the opening or openings at the top. A single sponge the size of a fountain pen can move five gallons of water through itself a day.

Within the animal's skin free-moving amoeba-like cells run a "Sponge Colony Pickup and Delivery Service." They move through the living tissue, helping to distribute bac-

teria and algae food and picking up the wastes for transport
back to the canals. Sandwiched between the two layers of
cells, which form an inside and outside skin, is a gelatinous
substance. Imbedded in this are thousands of spines of lime
and silica. Shaped like straight or curved needles, rayed stars,
tiny clubs and umbrellas, these interlace to produce a rigid
framework that braces the sponge against the forces of moving water. The natural sponges that people use in bath-
room and garage have skeletons of a resilient organic material called *spongin,* rather than rigid spicules.

Sponges live in almost every sea, inhabiting depths from
the shallows to 30,000 feet. Some are small enough to live
in the shells of snails; others, like Neptune's Cup, are big
enough to sit in. They come in a wide variety of shapes
and colors: gray, figlike masses; white or coral red encrustations; orange-yellow branches that look like deer antlers.
There are huge, brown goblet-shaped species, round yellow
"sea oranges," pale-green paper-thin bread crumb sponges,
and brilliant scarlet red–beard sponges. Bath sponges can
grow to the bulk of a cow, and are black and evil-smelling
when harvested from the bottom. Spicules of ancient species
have been found in rocks more than 600 million years old.

Sharp spicules, bad taste and disagreeable odor make
sponges unappetizing to all except some sea slugs and sea
spiders. Because they are immune to attack, all manner of
small creatures find refuge in their pores and passages.
Worms, brittle stars, barnacles, shrimps, crabs, octopuses
and small fish wander through their evil-smelling tunnels
and scrape food from the walls. As many as 16,000 small
snapping shrimps have been found in a single loggerhead
sponge as big as a washtub. Certain shrimp find their way
into the central cavity, then grow so large and fat they cannot get out. Sponges growing on shells inhabited by hermit
crabs dissolve the shell away, then the crab takes up residence in the sponge cavity.

No matter how specialized sponge cells become they never
lose their ability to lead an independent life. Any cell can
separate itself and start a new colony when conditions are
right. If you grind up a sponge and squeeze it through a fine

silk cloth, the cells that are still alive will regroup and grow into a new sponge. This is the essential difference between colonial and multi-cellular animals. In the latter, cells become so specialized they can no longer survive by themselves.

Multi-cellular creatures did not evolve from sponges. After sponges made a beginning toward specialization nature seems to have gone back and started over, leaving sponges in an evolutionary blind alley. Nobody knows for sure how multi-cellular animals got started. They could have originated when a single cell divided and redivided, the daughter cells remaining together instead of separating. Or they may have arisen from a single cell that became partitioned by internal walls. At least one noted biologist thinks multi-celled animals could have evolved from multi-celled plants, like those that capture insects.

Jellyfish and Their Relatives

The simplest multi-cellular beasts are coelenterates or "hollow guts." These creatures come in two basic varieties: flowerlike *polyps* and bell-shaped *medusae*. The former, represented by sea anemones, corals and hydroids, usually live attached to something. The latter are free-swimming and include jellyfish and siphonophores. Some species alternate between the two forms, which are merely different variations of the same body plan. An anemone is squat and cylindrical with one or more rings of tentacles around the top. If it could be turned upside down, flattened out and the tentacles moved to the outer rim, the anemone would be transformed into a jellyfish.

In both cases, one opening into the gut serves as a mouth and an exit for waste, eggs and sperm. The body walls are made up of two layers with a jellied substance sandwiched between. The inner skin has cells that secrete potent digestive juices into the hollow gut. Muscles contract the body walls, expelling undigested material in much the same way deodorant is squeezed from a plastic bottle.

The outer skin contains thousands of stinging cells most of which are located on the tentacles. A tiny trigger hair projects from each stinger. The slightest contact with these hairs releases a volley of sharp, barbed threads that pierce a victim's skin. Then, with explosive force, slender hypodermic-like tubes shoot through the threads and into the wound. Each injects a drop of paralyzing poison. Some species have long, sticky hairs on their tentacles to hold prey while batteries of minute rapiers deliver the *coup de grâce*.

The stingers of some species like the lion's mane jelly, *Cyanea,* can inflict a painful and dangerous sting on human bathers. These brutes, the largest jellies known, grow to at least six feet in diameter. The biggest ones live in the arctic, and are so hardy they come alive after being solidly encased in ice for hours. Bathers in temperate and tropical Atlantic waters usually encounter only smaller individuals, one or two feet in diameter. These can be distinguished from the bluish moon jelly *Aurelia*—the most common jellyfish species in the Atlantic and Pacific—by their reddish color, thin tentacles as much as 30 feet long and voluminous lips that hang like tattered curtains. *Cyanea* feeds by using its tentacles as a poisonous net; *Aurelia* catches small plankters on bands of sticky mucus on the upper and lower surface of its umbrella. These bands are moved by cilia toward the rim of the umbrella where four tonguelike extensions of the lips lick off the food.

Occasionally, storms or persistent onshore winds drive great fleets of that curious dreadnought, the Portuguese man-of-war *Physalia physalia,* onto Atlantic beaches. Their stingers cause a burning, irritating sensation, or in some cases cramps, nausea, breathing difficulties and, rarely, death. Recommended first-aid consists of bathing the affected part with alcohol, lighter fluid or other organic solvents. A doctor should be contacted as soon as possible.

Instead of an umbrella, the man-of-war has a float topped by an irregular, inflated sail. At a distance, a convoy of them moving along the surface of a calm sea looks like a profusion of colorful bubbles. In sunlight the floats often shine with a blue iridescence that merges into mauve and pink at the top of the sail. Occasionally one sees a dab of orange or a splash of peacock green. Underneath this colorful headdress,

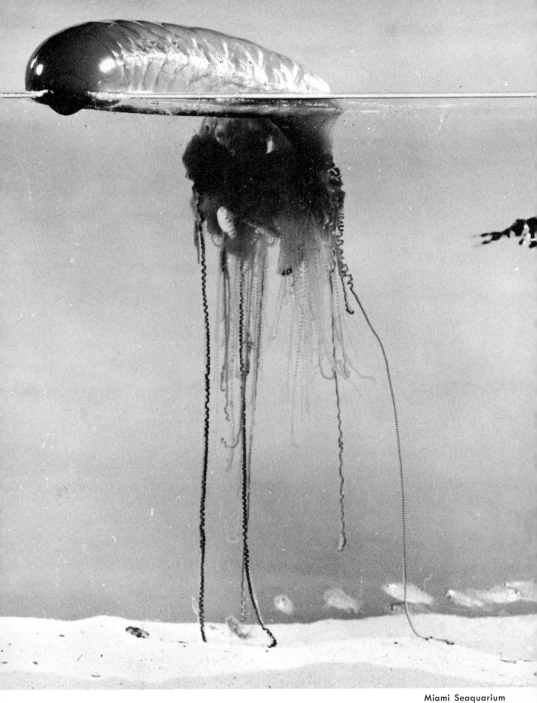

Miami Seaquarium

PORTUGUESE MAN-OF-WAR and MAN-OF-WAR FISH. Usually this colorful colonial creature drifts in the open seas of the tropics, but occasionally fleets of them invade Atlantic coast beaches as far north as Cape Cod. Man-of-war stings have sent bathers to the hospital in shock, and in 1964 severe stinging triggered a heart attack that killed a Florida bather.

a deadly tangle of elastic tentacles, as long as 30 feet, silently finger the water for prey. Averaging about 7 inches across, *Physalia* captures mackerel as large as itself, and it is an awesome sight to watch a fish being hoisted slowly toward the sacklike mouth.

Man-of-war is a siphonophore and, like all members of this group, is not a single animal but a colony of multi-celled individuals. A number of different medusa (jellyfishlike) and polyp (anemonelike) "persons" live together and function as one individual. One person forms the quart-sized float or bladder which *Physalia* blows up with gas of its own manufacture. The stomach is made of a mosaic of polyp persons that cover the food with their open mouths. Polyp persons carry the stingers, and adults give birth by budding off tiny, fully formed medusae.

Physalia and *Cyanea* often have one or more finger-long fishes living among their deadly tentacles. The fish are not immune to the poison but highly resistant to it. Sometimes the fish, *Nomeus gronovii,* which shelters under the man-of-war takes a wrong turn and gets fatally stung. In turn for protection, then, these creatures must spend their lives deftly twisting and dodging among the ribbons of a poisonous curtain.

Crowds of small medusae, ranging in size from one-half to seven inches across are characteristic members of the plankton. They swim by rhythmically opening and closing their umbrellas. Some species expel a stream of water from under their bells with such force they are literally jet propelled. The parents and children of many of these small medusae are not free swimmers but live as attached polyps.

This group of jellies vomits sperm and eggs into the water and these unite to produce oval young covered with cilia. Instead of growing into miniature copies of their parents, the babies sink to the bottom and become polyp persons. Each polyp then develops by budding off side branches until a tiny colony is formed that looks like a fragile fern or encrusting moss. A close look reveals two types of persons among the branches. Feeding polyps, looking like diminutive flowers, extend their petal-like stinging tentacles from the branch tips in search of food for the whole colony. At

COLONIAL HYDROID. The tentacles of the individual animals stretch out to grasp and poison smaller passersby. Victims are stuffed into a tiny body cavity which connects with all other cavities in the colony by means of a hollow stem. Some species bud off miniature jellyfish.

the base of the branches, sexual polyps become covered with buttonlike medusae of various sizes. The larger ones near the top jerk free, climb through a narrow opening in the urnlike protective sheath surrounding the polyp, and swim away, with a jerky rhythm. These newborn medusae grow into free-swimming jellyfish that give rise to another generation of sedentary polyps.

Sea anemones have no jellyfish stage. They reproduce by splitting up into new individuals, budding offspring off their sides or, most frequently, by the union of sperm and eggs. In many cases sperm enters the female via water currents and fertilization is internal. The hairy babies grow and swim in the hollow gut of the parent before being disgorged into

SEA ANEMONE.

Marineland of Florida

the sea. After swimming around awhile, they settle down to a sedentary life on rocky bottoms, coral reefs, the shells of other animals or any hard surface. Adult anemones can move by gliding along on their bases, "cartwheeling" with their tentacles, or releasing their hold entirely and letting currents carry them to a new spot.

Anemones live in all seas. Among the most common fixed animals on the deep ocean bottom, specimens have been dredged up from depths as great as six miles. Ranging in size from less than an inch to about three feet across, they are among the most colorful creatures in the sea. Their brilliant greens, reds and oranges, rich browns and delicate blues rival the beauty of land flowers. Generally anemones have a short, broad trunk capped by a chrysanthemumlike "blossom" that waves enticingly at passing creatures. This blossom consists of rings of tentacles that grasp and poison. Any victim that blunders too close is seized and stuffed into a hidden mouth that stretches to accommodate animals so large they push the trunk out of shape. Shrimps, crabs, fishes, snails, even spiny sea urchins and stones disappear into its greedy gullet. Anything not digested is ejected back into the sea, an anemone sometimes turning its stomach inside out in the process.

Certain fish shelter among the tentacles and lure other creatures to the poisonous stingers. Anemone and fish then share the feast. One sheltering species, the clown fish, darts in and out of the anemone's mouth and helps itself to food in the host's stomach. Except for a king-sized species in Indo-Pacific waters, anemones do not have stingers virulent enough to produce more than a slight tingling sensation when touched by humans.

All other coelenterates possess the same basic body plan as anemones. Reef corals live in colonies and are minute versions of anemones that secrete a hard, limey apartment around themselves. When the polyps die their vacant apartments remain intact and succeeding generations keep adding new, occupied floors atop the remains of their ancestors. Over millions of years these creatures build sizeable land masses—coral reefs, islands and atolls—where no land existed previously.

Coelenterate flower animals also contribute to vari-colored and multi-formed marine gardens of dazzling beauty. Bushy sea whips form dense strands of shrubbery sometimes as tall as a man. Meadows of sea pens, their purple, red and yellow "quills" full of minute polyps, wave gently like fields of strangely-colored wheat. Soft corals vary from squat, spongy masses to erect, treelike colonies. Red, violet and iridescent sea fans build delicate, lacelike apartment houses, and a thousand tiny tentacled heads appear at the windows to sieve plankton from the water.

Beauty and Beasts

From some of the most attractive invertebrates we pass to those that some people consider the most repulsive: worms. Worms are everywhere in the sea. They live by themselves, in groups, on plants and inside animals. Worms even live inside other worms. They swim, crawl, creep, glide and burrow. Actually, "worm" is an all-inclusive term that encompasses a multitude of beasts, some of them quite unwormlike in appearance.

There are free-living flatworms that resemble fleshy leaves gliding gracefully over seaweeds, other animals or the ocean bottom. Many are drab gray or dull brown, but others rival the beauty and brilliance of butterflies. Some can swim, and one "flies" through the water with elegant, wavelike motions. Flatworms often eat other worms. A flatworm slips its frilly mouth over the tail of a segmented worm four times its own length. The living mouth gradually dissolves and swallows until there is nothing left but the head of the bigger worm. If a flatworm cannot find a meal, it absorbs its own internal organs, becoming smaller and smaller until it expires.

Flatworms never grow more than six inches long, but one of their relatives, a ribbon worm known as *Lineus longissimus,* is the longest of all spineless creatures. *Longissimus* grows to 75 feet—longer than many whales—but is only as thick as a piece of string. This creature is as stretchable as a rubber band and possesses a very long "tongue" or proboscis. The tongue secretes a sticky mucus and sometimes has a poisonous hypodermic at the tip. The worm shoots it out at prey, entangling them as in a sticky lasso.

Ribbon worms or *nemerteans* were the first group to evolve a digestive tract and circulating fluids (blood) which carry food and oxygen to every nook and cranny of their bodies. Swimming and burrowing nemerteans are found from the polar regions to the tropics and in both shallow and deep water. Brilliant scarlet and orange species live at depths of 10,000 feet, or you might come across a 35-foot long, flesh-colored *Cerebratulus lacteus* while digging for clams along the east coast of the United States.

There are some tiny round cousins of parasitic hook-worms and pinworms—the *nematodes*—that wiggle freely in surface waters, crawl over and inside other animals and squirm through decaying detritus on the bottom. Nema-todes are the most diversified and numerous group of multi-celled creatures living at the bottom of the sea.

Wormlike *phoronids* live in limey, sandy or transparent tubes on shallow bottoms and filter food from the water with a spiral whorl of tentacles extending from the open end of the tube. Besides being classified with worms, phornids are distant relatives of the Bryozoans or moss animals—colonial creatures resembling hydroids and corals. Bryozoans live in horny or limey apartments that form small bushy tufts, rigid lattices, lacy leaves and thin encrustations on hard objects from the tide line to deep water.

Swift planktonic arrow worms live far out at sea and at great depths in all latitudes. Those inhabiting near-surface waters are completely transparent, while species living be-tween 3,000 and 6,500 feet are bright red.

The best-known, most-advanced worms are the *annelids*. "Annelida" means "ringed ones," and the bodies of these beasts are divided into rings or segments each of which may be thought of as an incomplete organism. Earthworms and sandworms are familiar land-dwelling types. The most im-portant marine annelids, *polychaetes* or "many bristled ones," have one or more species living in almost every part of the World Ocean. Polychaetes usually have a pair of

bristles or "feet" on each of their segments, and these serve
as limbs for locomotion and food-getting, gills for breathing
and fingers for digging.

Some annelids, the vividly colored fan and feather duster
worms, possess a crown of delicate, plumelike tentacles which
act as gills. These tentacles also have sticky mucus and cur-
rent-creating cilia for capturing food. The strong hooklike
mouths of some species inflict a painful bite. Others are
equipped with detachable bristles capable of piercing skin
and causing a distressing burning sensation. *Tomopteris* has
its feet modified into twin-lobed paddles. It appears to run
through the water like a centipede runs along the ground,
throwing its transparent or crimson body into a series of
serpentine undulations.

Spiny Skins and You

Sharing the nutritious bottom mud with worms and in
some cases providing homes for them, are the echinoderms
or "spiny skins." This diverse and abundant phylum includes
starfish, brittle stars, sea urchins, sea cucumbers and sea lilies.
The great majority of these creatures creep over the oozy
bottom pastures, gorging themselves on mud to get the bits
of organic food mixed with it.

Sea urchins are like undersea porcupines. They are much
spinier than starfish, the skin of which is usually studded
with rounded knobs. Starfish in turn are spinier than sea
cucumbers. All have a flexible outer skeleton made either
of limey plates more or less rigidly joined together and imbedded in the skin, or of small plates and spines scattered
through the body wall. Echinoderms have not changed their
appearance in hundreds of millions of years, and no one is
sure who their direct ancestors were.

Starfish usually have five arms, but there are species with
four, six, seven, eight, ten or more. The basket star has arms
that subdivide again and again until their number defies
counting. Starfish take on a variety of vivid colors: pink, blue,
red, brown, purple, orange and the more familiar yellow.

Miami Seaquarium

STARFISHES devour a parrot fish. The suckered tubes or tube feet lining the center of their arms are used for moving along the bottom and grasping prey.

The largest known species, the sunflower star, has up to 24 arms and a span of more than 2 feet.

Starfish, sea urchins and sea cucumbers get around by a water pumping system and "tube feet" that look like pale rubber tubes with suction discs. Starfish have rows of tube feet lining deep grooves extending from the mouth to the arm tips. A water-filled bulb at the inner end of each foot contracts to pump water out and extend the tube. Suckers on the ends of the tubes firmly grasp the surface under the star. Muscles then expand the bulbs, pulling water out of the tubes. This causes them to contract and as they shorten the animal is pulled up to where the feet are fastened.

Starfish move no faster than a few feet an hour, but to co-ordinate all the feet on all the arms takes a nervous system more complicated than the telephone exchange of a large town.

The suckers also come in handy to "shuck" oysters, clams and other shellfish. A star humps over its victim in a tent-like manner. The tube feet grip the two shells and force them apart. If you have attempted to open a good-sized clam or oyster with your fingers, you know how difficult this is. But an average star can exert a force of more than 100 pounds for a short time and apply a much smaller but continuous pull for as long as two days.

Under this steady pressure the prey's muscles eventually tire. If the shells part only a slight bit the slow, silent battle is over. The star can pass almost all of its stomach through its mouth and push it into an opening only $\frac{1}{25}$ inch wide. The thin saclike stomach flows around the soft flesh of the helpless mollusk which is digested alive.

Marauding starfish inflict tremendous damage on natural and cultivated clam, mussel and oyster beds, costing shell fishermen millions of dollars every year. Plagued by these depredations, oystermen on the east coast of the United States hired men to chop them in two as they were brought up with the catch. On the Pacific coast, citizens hacked up every star they could find to prevent them from exterminating mussel populations. But if echinoderms could laugh, starfish would have the last one. Because of their amazing regenerative powers almost every piece that was thrown back into the water probably grew into a completely new animal. Whole starfish can grow from only a small part of the central disc or, in some cases, from a piece of arm only two-fifths inch long. The five arms of the slimy, dark-colored *Astrometis* sometimes walk away from the center part and each becomes a complete animal. When cut in half brittle stars become two whole animals in about three months. The arms of brittle stars break into pieces when they are handled or disturbed; that is how they got their name. They move by wiggling their limbs like so many cooperating snakes, and some species even swim in this fashion. Tube feet help them get around somewhat but are mainly used for touching, tasting and breathing.

Brittle stars have only one bottomside opening that serves as both mouth and anus. Sea urchins, like starfish, have a bottomside mouth and an anus on the topside. Externally, starfish and urchins bear little resemblance but their internal organs are much the same. If you brought the arms of a starfish upward and fused them together to form a dome over the central disc, you would have the body plan of a sea urchin. Then, all you need to do to make a complete urchin is lengthen the spines and put a gnawing, crushing device, called "Aristotle's Lantern" into its mouth. These intricate jaws consists of 40 bones operated by more than 60 muscles. The pieces are arranged in five toothed segments which converge on prey like five-jawed pincers.

Acres of richly-colored urchins cover rocks and reefs in shallow water, their purple and red spines looking like fancy hatpins crowded into many pincushions. These marine porcupines live on all types of bottoms, at all depths and in all seas. They move about by means of long, slender tube feet that reach beyond the spines. Those species having flexible spines use them to "walk" or "run" along the bottom.

The needlelike spines of some species can pierce flesh, gloves or even shoe soles. Some contain poisonous glands. *Diadema,* common in all warm seas, has brittle spines that break off in the skin. *Aerosoma* has a sting as painful as a Portuguese man-of-war. Normally, the spiny armor makes urchins unappetizing, but triggerfish break off spines bit by bit and get their dinner without being stabbed.

To ward off the horde of larvae and little beasts looking for a place to settle, urchins and starfish have microscopic pincers scattered between their spines and tube feet. These crush larvae that try to roost, nip tiny intruders and capture small prey. Some are poisonous.

If you could stretch a sea urchin into a tube shape, remove its spines and soften the body walls, you would have essentially a sea cucumber. About all you would need do is move the mouth to the front end and surround it with a ring of tentacles. These are used for feeling, tasting and sweeping

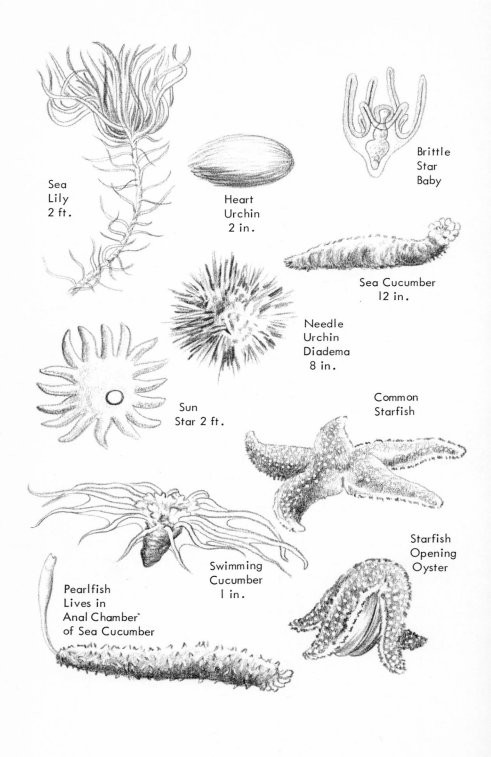

Sea
Lily
2 ft.

Heart
Urchin
2 in.

Brittle
Star
Baby

Sea Cucumber
12 in.

Needle
Urchin
Diadema
8 in.

Sun
Star 2 ft.

Common
Starfish

Starfish
Opening
Oyster

Pearlfish
Lives in
Anal Chamber
of Sea Cucumber

Swimming
Cucumber
1 in.

ooze into the mouth. Resembling their namesakes in the vegetable markets, cucumbers have tube feet for locomotion but lack pincers. Their skeletons consist of limey spicules and plates scattered throughout and deeply imbedded in the skin. A few bottom-dwellers rise off the sea floor by wiggling up and down like leeches. Three or four species swim by waving long tentacles or undulating leaflike fringes around their mouths or bodies.

Some of the larger cucumbers play host to a small, transparent pearlfish, *Carapus affinis,* which wiggles tail first into their anal opening. Cucumbers breathe, or take in oxygenated water, through this opening. A chamber just inside of it makes a good place for the small fish to live because it is protected and well supplied with fresh water. The fish can often be seen sticking its head out of this refuge, but it leaves only at night to search for food.

When attacked or molested some cucumbers eject their insides through their mouth or anus. Viscera may even rupture through the side of their body. Part of this evisceration is a mass of mucus threads which swell up and form a sticky net which entangles lobsters, crabs and other predators. Apparently none the worse for this experience, the cucumber grows a new set of internal organs in six to eight weeks.

Despite their unappetizing appearance and unsavory habits, sea cucumbers are a delicacy in China and other parts of southeast Asia. They are eaten under the names *trepang* or *bêche-de-mer.* The body walls, boiled then dried, are sold by Chinese merchants in the United States, where they have the reputation of being an efficient aphrodisiac.

Spiny skins live at all depths and are among the most common animals found on the deep ocean floor. Living as far down as 27,000 feet are plantlike echinoderms which resemble many-armed starfish attached to the bottom, mouthside up, by long stalks. These are sea lilies or feather stars. They spread their plumy arms to feed, directing food-laden currents into their mouths by the motion of cilia. Shallow water species remain anchored during youth, but as adults they break away and swim from place to place by waving their feathery arms.

As unreasonable as it seems, echinoderms win the biologists' vote as the spineless animals most closely related to you and me. Said more precisely, these unimpressive beasts appear to be the closest living relatives of the chordates, which include all backboned creatures. Although they bear little external or internal resemblance to any backboned beast, spiny skins are linked to them in an impressive number of ways.

Proteins in the bloods of both groups show definite relationships; their muscle and nerve chemistry is similar. Echinoderm larvae are almost indistinguishable from the larvae of primitive chordates. For a long time the young of one of the least advanced chordates was thought to be a baby starfish. Neither larva looks like either adult, but the fact that the young resemble each other means the adults must be related. Also, spiny skins and vertebrates develop their middle skin or third layer of body cells in the same way. This is different from the way in which worms, mollusks and crustaceans form their third layer. Bones, muscles, genital organs, circulatory system, respiratory system and part of the intestines of vertebrates are all derived from cells in this layer. The fact that spiny skins and vertebrates evolved it in the same way is another indication that we are more closely related to echinoderms than to any other invertebrates.

This does not mean that man descended from a starfish any more than Darwin meant man descended from a monkey. Rather, it suggests that spiny skins and backboned animals, like men and monkeys, have a common ancestor.

The missing link in both cases is still unknown. The common ancestor of vertebrates and echinoderms may have been a stalked, sessile creature like a sea lily, or an active, free-swimmer like a starfish larvae. This unknown beast may exist only as a fossil, or its direct descendants may still live in the sea. In any case, the best place to look for a solution to the mystery of our ancestry is in the ocean or in the layers of rock and sediment under its bottom.

6.
Lobsters, Crabs
and Shrimps

" 'Tis the voice of the lobster: I heard him declare 'You have baked me too brown, I must sugar my hair.' "—LEWIS CARROLL

IN MARCH 1963, France and Brazil were on the brink of war over lobsters. Brazilian warships chased six French lobster boats fishing 60 miles off the Brazilian coast. Brazil claimed that creatures walking along the continental shelf adjacent to her shores are part of the country's resources. France disagreed in the form of a destroyer dispatched to protect her fishermen. "De Gaulle's *force de frappe* Thermidor," sneered a Brazilian official and Brazil ordered its fleet ready to sail. When it looked as though a naval battle was imminent, a Brazilian newspaper suggested: "Since both Brazilian and French gourmets delight in lobster, let us solve this crisis at the dinner table." The French must have thought this was a good idea because they recalled their ships and bloodshed was averted.

Animal protectionists, who generally ignore coldblooded beasts, have also taken an interest in lobsters. In 1937, a group in Norway tried to get a law passed making it illegal to kill lobsters and crabs by plunging them into boiling water. They championed the method of cooking widely used in Great Britain—placing the crustaceans in warm, salted water and applying heat gradually. Today, housewives and chefs still debate about which method is easier on the lobster and which yields the more palatable meat.

Besides being delightful eating, lobsters are the largest and best known of the arthropods—creatures characterized by jointed legs. This group includes about 90 percent of all animal species living on Earth today. In a few fertile square miles on land there are more flies, bees, ants and other insects than there are human beings on the entire planet. In the sea copepods, isopods, lobsters and their relatives outnumber all other multi-celled beasts.

No other class of multi-cellular animals exhibits such great diversity. Descended from annelids, they have segmented bodies, usually with one pair of jointed limbs on each section. These limbs are modified into feelers, jaws, feeding whiskers, clawed hands, walking legs and swimming arms. Arthropods possess well developed eyes, hearts in their backs, nerve cords in their stomachs and are the first phylum to evolve a respiratory system. The vast majority of water-dwelling arthropods belong to the class *Crustacea,* which includes shrimps, crabs, barnacles, water fleas and a horde of other shrimplike and "buggy" beasts.

Most crustaceans have compound eyes, which are made up of a large number of tiny tubular eyes each pointing in a slightly different direction. This gives them an extremely wide field of view but one that is split into a mosaic of small pieces. Crustaceans thus get only a fuzzy generalized picture of the outside world. Movement is detected by changes in the pattern of light and shade on the mosaic. Some species, particularly plankters, have eyes mounted on short stalks and these animals can look in every direction at once. This is a decided advantage when enemies may be above, below, behind or beside.

Arthropods have an outside covering of horny organic material called *chitin.* Crabs and lobsters extract lime from the ocean and add it to the chitin for strength. Unlike the internal skeleton of vertebrates, this external skeleton cannot grow with the animal. Crustaceans and their insect cousins must periodically molt, or "burst out of their skins" when they become too tight. Lobsters and shrimps split their shells along the top and the creature backs out through the opening. A crab shell cracks around the middle and the soft bodied animal steps out, pulling each leg from its shell sheath.

Watching this process makes you wonder how lobsters and crabs can free fleshy claws as much as four times the diameter of the joints through which they must pass. To accomplish this, blood flows out of the claws prior to molting and causes them to shrivel. Then lime in the joints dissolves and softens, making it easier for crustaceans to draw their shrunken limbs through small passages. Nevertheless, claws and whole limbs sometimes are lost during molt. Crustaceans usually can regenerate small replacement limbs immediately. These gradually grow to full size during the next several molts.

Without armor, crustaceans become especially vulnerable to attack. They often retreat to a secluded hiding place until their soft, wrinkled skin hardens into a protective shell. For a lobster this takes from six weeks to three months. During this time they often eat their own shells or weaker lobsters to obtain the necessary lime. Molting is particularly trying for blue crabs who in an unarmored condition are known and relished as soft-shelled crabs.

Lobsters and crabs will eat anything they can get a claw on—animal or vegetable, living, dead or dying. Cannibalistic by nature, they prey on their weaker brothers and sisters. If their planktonic babies were not scattered by currents, lobsters would be in jeopardy of eating themselves into extinction.

The succulent Maine lobster is known to scientists as *Homarus americanus*. It ranges from Labrador to North Carolina, but has been caught mostly in a strip 30 to 50 miles wide and 6 to 600 feet deep off Nova Scotia and Maine. The average *H. americanus* you eat has molted about 25 times and is 5 years old. The largest Maine lobster ever caught weighed 47 pounds and some people claim it was at least 50 years old.

As winter approaches, *H. americanus* wanders from shallow rocky bottoms toward deeper water in search of comfortable temperatures, food and a mate. The average female lays between 8,000 and 10,000 eggs. She carries them glued under her abdomen until they hatch. The largest number of "berries"—as lobstermen call the eggs—ever found on a female was 97,400. These eggs take from 10 to 11 months to hatch. Young hatchlings drift with the plankton for 3 to 5 weeks, then settle to the bottom and make their way toward rocky regions close to the shore.

Mother lobsters give birth to prodigious numbers of offspring for the same reason as other prolific species—to assure

SPINY LOBSTERS (Florida crayfish) tread the bottom lightly on "toes" and tails, tangling their clublike antennae with the tentacles of a LION'S-MANE JELLYFISH. Recently large populations of Maine lobsters were discovered living offshore from Cape Cod to Delaware Bay at depths of 300 to 1500 feet.

Marineland of Florida

the survival of enough individuals to perpetuate the race. Five-day-old lobsterlings are half-inch replicas of their parents, just the right size to provide many small predators with a lobster dinner or large ones with delicious hors d'oeuvres. Cod are especially fond of lobsters and, after man, are their most voracious enemies. Tautog, skate and dogfish also take a heavy toll.

Instead of claws, spiny lobsters or crayfish have long, heavy antennae which they use to strike down prey or ward off enemies. The antennae and the surface of their shells are covered with numerous short, sharp spines which give these creatures their popular name. The Pacific Coast variety, *Panulirus interruptus,* reaches a weight of about 30 pounds; but individuals more than 6 pounds are rare and 2 to 3 pounds is average. The southern crayfish *P. argus* loves the nooks and crannies of coral reefs in the Caribbean, Gulf of Mexico, Florida waters and off the Bahamas. It averages ten inches in length. Every fall in the shallows off the Bahamas, males and females form migrating chains 3 to 30 lobsters long. The head of each overlaps the tail of the animal ahead. Proceeding at a speed equal to the swimming pace of a man, these processions move long distances to spawning grounds in deeper water.

Instead of resembling their parents, baby crayfish look like squashed spun-glass spiders. At first glance, it appears as if a pair of eyes is swimming by itself. A closer examination reveals that the eyes are on the end of stalks attached to a spidery baby as thin and transparent as a piece of cellophane. Investigating further you can see the workings of its internal organs and the beating of a tiny heart. But the only hint of its parentage is a tiny, lobsterlike tail.

Fiddlers, Fighters and Hermits

Such exotic offspring as baby spiny lobsters are often mistaken for separate species. One queer, shrimplike creature with huge black eyes; long, sharp "nose," and a high, curved spine in back of its head was called a "zoea" when first discovered. Another big-eyed beast that appears to be part lobster-part crab was christened "megalopa." A long time and many observations passed before scientists realized that zoea and megalopa were not separate species but two larval stages that common crabs pass through while growing up. As they drift with the plankton, these babies undergo a change in appearance with each molt until they come to resemble their parents.

Adult crabs can be thought of as flat, rounded lobsters with tails reduced to a small flap or apron neatly tucked under their bodies. Pugnacious and active, crabs are found the world over. There are about 1,000 different kinds, ranging from wheat-grain size to 15 inches or more across the back. They live from the tide line to depths of over 13,000 feet.

EDIBLE CRAB growing from a transparent, planktonic youth to a scampering, snapping adult was mistaken by scientists for 3 different animals. After hatching (top) the baby goes through zoea (right) and megalops (left) stages before it can be recognized as a crab.

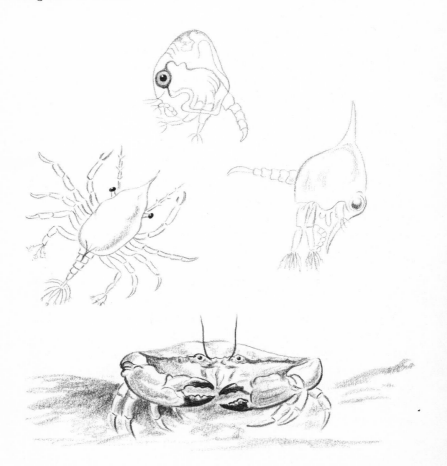

Swift, gypsy-eyed ghost crabs dig burrows above the breakers on warm sandy, shores. Blind, pallid *Ethusa* crabs, with insidious parasites and orange eggs dangling under their tails, scamper along dark, deep-sea bottoms on long, spidery legs. About the size of its namesake, the tiny pea crab lives in the mantle cavity of clams, in the anal opening of the "sweet potato" sea cucumber and in the burrows of ghost shrimp. Mottled with colorful patterns, male fiddler crabs have an oversized claw that they move back and forth like a fiddler using his bow. It is used as a trap door for their mud burrows, for fighting and for attracting females. The tropical boxer crab *Lybia tesselata* defends itself by wielding a stinging sea anemone in each claw.

Spider crabs place bits of seaweed, distasteful sponges and stinging anemones on their bodies to camouflage themselves and discourage predators. These disguises often continue to grow, and hungry crabs sometimes make a meal out of the gardens on their backs. One species, the delicious king crab *Paralithodes camtschatica,* inhabits the cold offshore waters of the North Pacific. Spectacular individuals measuring 12 feet between outstretched claws have been found off Japan, and 15-pound kings with 5-foot leg spreads are common off Alaska.

Many crabs spend all their adult lives on the bottom, but some possess hind legs modified into paddles for swimming. The delectable blue crab *Callinectes sapidus,* found from Cape Cod to Mexico, swims sideways. It cocks the elbow of one large claw so it cuts the water like a ship's prow. Because their gangling legs extend from the sides of their bodies, it is easier and faster for crabs to scamper sideways than to walk forward. Legs on the leading side pull them ahead while trailing legs push from behind. Ghost crabs (*Ocypode*) running sideways at full speed can turn their bodies completely around while continuing to move in the same direction.

All crabs are entertaining to watch but the hermits rate star billing. Having soft, unprotected rears, they scurry around looking for empty snail shells to back into for protection. House hunting for these comical creatures is a care-

Marineland of Florida

HERMIT CRAB with a sea anemone on its borrowed shell. The anemone's stinging tentacles provide protection and disguise, in turn for which the flowery beast gets transportation and scraps from the crab's meals.

ful and meticulous affair. Each potential shell is turned over and over and inspected to be sure it is clear of debris. Like a woman shopping for a girdle, a hermit may wiggle into a half dozen shells to find one whose whorls match the right-hand twist of its abdomen. The crabs outgrow these borrowed shells, and when this time comes they must go on another shopping expedition. Hard pressed for a house, hermits will camp almost anywhere, including worm tubes, pieces of bamboo, and in one case, the bowl of a discarded pipe. Roving carnivores, they fight over food and shelter sometimes dispossessing snails and other hermits by violently yanking them out of their shells.

Most Valuable Catch

While crabs and lobsters like to live alone on the bottom, shrimps are social creatures, swimming and congregating on the sea floor in large schools. Lacking heavy armor and powerful claws they would rather flee than fight. Their favorite foods include weaker crustaceans, worms, small fish and sea scraps. Swimming shrimps move forward by using their abdominal legs, or dart backward by quickly flipping their fanlike tails under their bodies in the same manner as lobsters. They range from mosquito size to a maximum length of about 12 inches. The larger ones are often called *prawns,* particularly in Great Britain and Europe.

Shrimps living near shore are pale in color to match the sandy bottoms over, on and into which they swim, walk and burrow. Offshore, vivid scarlet and blood red varieties swim in deep temperate and tropical water to depths exceeding 16,000 feet. Some deep dwellers are translucent, rose-pink or peppered with red spots; many are brilliantly luminescent. A few deep species are blind. The short paddlelike limbs and long, strong legs of deep dwellers indicate a powerful swimming ability.

On the sea floor off the United States Pacific coast, pistol shrimp of the genus *Crangon* have an oversized claw with which they make a loud snapping sound. During World War II, thousands of these "gunmen" snapping their claws on the sea bottom off California's coast panicked sonarmen and rendered submarine listening devices useless. When a small fish or other prey wanders into the vicinity of a *Crangon* burrow, the shrimp quietly creeps up behind it and suddenly fires a "shot." This stuns the victim which is then dragged into the burrow and devoured.

The species most commonly seen in North American markets are the white (*Penaeus setiferus*), brown (*P. aztecus*) and pink shrimp (*P. durorarum*). The inedible head or front part of these creatures houses the heart, stomach and other vital organs, and comprises about 40 percent of their bulk. The tail or abdomen is the only edible part and a pound of these contains 400 to 500 calories and a high proportion of vitamins A and D.

In spring and summer shrimps travel from shallow coastal waters to the saltier, deeper sea to spawn. Females lay from 500,000 to a million eggs directly into the water, rather than carry them on their abdominal legs like lobsters and crabs. Barely visible, the round eggs hatch in less than a day on or near the bottom. The hatchlings, which resemble tiny mites, swim feebly and drift with the currents for many weeks while they undergo changes in form. Those not gobbled up by hungry predators reach shallow inshore grounds where they settle down to grow to maturity. When mature they move out to sea again. Shrimp live to a ripe old age of between one and two years.

Various species are fished from Alaska and Maine to Chile and Argentina. For many years seasonal fishing in water no deeper than 60 to 75 feet was the practice in the United States, and American shrimpers trawled only during daylight hours. Then in 1949, by accident, one shrimper set his trawl at night over grounds that produced nothing during the day. He was flabbergasted when the nets came up filled with large, tasty individuals. This discovery precipitated a shrimping boom off southern Florida in the 1950's. Today shrimpers work year-round in depths up to 300 feet and shrimp is firmly established as the most valuable United States catch, far exceeding its closest rivals, salmon and tuna.

While shrimpers rushed to the new Florida grounds in 1950, U.S. Fish and Wildlife Service biologists discovered appreciable numbers of giant royal red shrimp (*Hymenopenaeus robustus*) living in the Gulf of Mexico. Among the largest of the deep sea prawns, royal reds grow to a foot or more in length. When cooked they have a color and taste not unlike lobster. These creatures live 50 to 125 miles out and from 1,000 to 2,000 feet down. In the late 1950's some boats fished for them in 1,200 feet of water off the east coast of Florida, but they could not make a profit. The depths and distances involved require heavy and expensive gear, and there are plenty of shrimp within easier reach. The fishery has since been abandoned, but specially outfitted boats from Texas made impressive exploratory catches in the western Gulf recently. One Texan who is building boats specifically designed for going after these deep sea delicacies predicts they will be as common as other shrimps in the markets before too long.

Krill and Kin

Closely related to shrimp and looking very much like them are the handsome *euphausids*. The name, which means "shining light," refers to their remarkable luminescence. A dozen euphausids in a glass jar will give off enough bluish-white light to read by. These shrimpers reach a maximum length of about two inches and one or more species is found in every ocean. Although most live between the surface and 3,000 feet, some range to depths of 6,500 feet. Euphausids are mainly transparent or colorless, but some have spots or washes of pink or red. They prefer colder seas, and at times congregate in northern seas and the Antarctic Ocean in such dense swarms the water turns red.

Those that live in warmer, deeper water are meat eaters, but most others strain floating plants out of the sea. They set up a backward-flowing current by rhythmically moving their abdominal legs, then they filter out the vegetables with the feathery hairs on their front legs.

Euphausia superba, the largest species, grazes on the rich summer crop of diatoms in Antarctic waters. Tons of these shrimpers in turn are consumed by toothless whales, some of which are the largest creatures on Earth. Whalermen working cold northern and southern seas have long known that the appearance of "krill"—as they call euphausids—means whales will soon be sighted.

Along with krill, shrimps, crabs and lobsters, the crustacean class includes a horde of other shrimplike and insect-like beasts. All have the same general body plan, modified according to how and where the creatures live. There are bottom-dwelling *stomatopods* or mantis shrimp, so called because they resemble the praying mantis in shape, savagery and method of eating. They possess a unique jackknife claw which pops out like a switch blade. With it a mantis can slash a ghost shrimp in two so fast you can hardly see the movement.

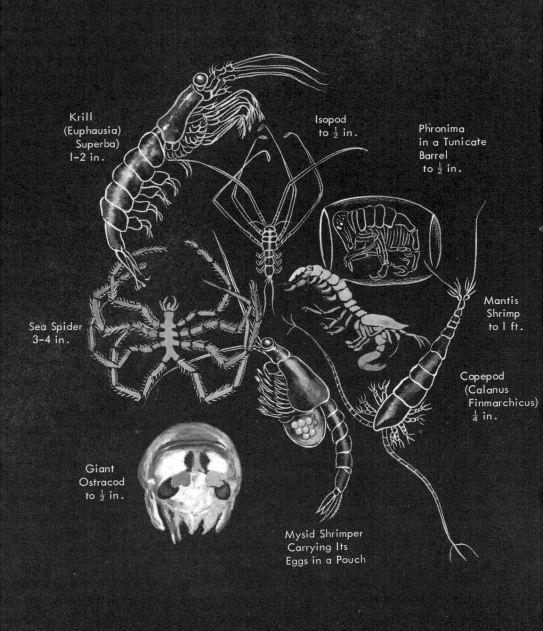

Krill
(Euphausia)
Superba)
1-2 in.

Isopod
to $\frac{1}{2}$ in.

Phronima
in a Tunicate
Barrel
to $\frac{1}{2}$ in.

Sea Spider
3-4 in.

Mantis
Shrimp
to 1 ft.

Copepod
(Calanus
Finmarchicus)
$\frac{1}{4}$ in.

Giant
Ostracod
to $\frac{1}{2}$ in.

Mysid Shrimper
Carrying Its
Eggs in a Pouch

The bug-eyed *amphipods* or scuds, which look as though they have been squeezed flat by pinching from the sides, resemble fleas more than they do shrimp. Rarely reaching an inch in length, they swim and walk, run and jump over the surfaces of seaweeds and rocks. Most carry their young slung under their bodies in protective brood pouches, but one warm water form uses what is probably the strangest baby carriage in the ocean. The amphipod *Phronima* attacks a drifting tunicate, eating the individual and taking over its transparent barrel-shaped float for its own home and nursery. This flealike creature can be seen pushing a barrel full of its babies around the sea like a mother wheeling her children on an afternoon stroll.

Amphipods have some louselike relatives called *isopods* which are flattened from top to bottom instead of side to side. The most widespread of the crustaceans, they live in almost every part of the sea, on and in the bodies of other creatures, on land and in fresh water. A gigantic black species 12 inches long and 4 inches wide, lives in deep water. Another spends its life lying across the abdomen of a shrimp. One isopod, the common gribble *Limnoria lignorum,* causes extensive damage by boring into wooden hulls and pilings and chewing through insulation on submarine cables. Another species is parasitic on a barnacle that is parasitic on a spider crab.

Zoologists thought barnacles were some outlandish kind of clam until it was discovered, in 1883, that they gave birth to joint-legged young. Now biologists describe barnacles as crustaceans that lie on their backs in clamlike shells and kick food into their mouths with their feet. Each adult is a shrimplike beast fastened to the inside of its shell by what would be the back of its neck. Long feathery feet extend through the shell opening and sieve food particles out of the water. As the animal pulls its legs back, comblike mouth parts scrape off the food.

Barnacles live attached to solid objects like ships and pilings or as parasites on whales, crabs, turtles or other barnacles. All are hermaphrodites, that is, both male and female. Each deposits sperm in the bodies of its neighbors by means

of an extensible, thread-thin organ. Solitary barnacles probably fertilize themselves. To prevent drying out, shoreline
barnacles seal a bit of sea in their shells by means of little
plates that close like shutters. As the tide ebbs over a colony
of these counterfeit clams, the soft, snapping sounds produced as they shutter their shells has been called "the whis-
pering talk of barnacles."

Barnacles have some relatives, the *ostracods,* that look like
round, microscopic clams. Some of these are bottom dwellers
and some are plankters. The latter swim like water fleas,
that is, by means of antennae extending through the opening between shell halves. The Gargantua of this group, a
form called *Gigantocypris,* is almost a half inch across, deep
orange in color and has huge headlightlike eyes. Rapid swimmers despite their improbable appearance, these midget
monsters live in the depths and hunt such active beasts as
copepods, arrow worms and small fish.

Striders and Spiders

Just as few crustaceans have come ashore, so almost none
of their cousins, the insects, have returned to sea. Of all
the "bugs" only *Halobates*—the water strider—has adapted
to life in the open ocean. Even this remarkable air-breathing
beast does not enter the water, but runs across the surface
the way its landlubber brothers scurry over ground. How
these fragile creatures survive the weather and waves of the
open tropical Atlantic and Pacific without any shelter is another perplexing mystery of the sea.

Some 400 different kinds of sea spiders, five species of
horseshoe crabs and numerous nautical mites are placed in
the class Arachnida. The spiders inhabit all seas and some
carry a bubble of air for breathing when they sink below the
surface. They subsist by sucking the body juices from anemones, sponges hydroids and sea squirts. The daddy-long-legs
of the deep sea is the giant red spider *Colossendeis colossea.*
This beautiful nightmare, which has been photographed
standing on the bottom in 6,500-foot depths, is blood red
in color and has legs nearly two feet long. About 400 million

years ago, its scorpionlike ancestors, some of which had leg spans of ten feet, became the first animals to venture onto land.

Scorpions do not live in the sea today but boast some marine relatives known as "horseshoe crabs," although they are not crabs at all. Zoologists are not really sure how to classify them. Their popular name stems from the shape of their shells—like a horse's hoof to which a daggerlike spine has been added. Up to two feet in length, horseshoe crabs crawl slowly along shallow, sandy bottoms in many parts of the world, especially in temperate waters between 12 and 36 feet deep. They plow up sediments hunting for sea worms and other small tidbits. These are grasped with six pairs of clawed legs, then chewed by means of hard spines located on legs near the crab's mouth. Sometimes called "living fossils," these enigmatic beasts are the only remaining members of a large group of extinct animals, and they have survived virtually unchanged for some 250 million years.

7.

Squid, Octopuses and Others

"Such monstrous things, they say, now sleep
Within the caverns of the deep."—T. MILLER

THE imagination can hardly picture a more terrible object than one of these huge monsters brooding in the ocean depths, the gloom of his surroundings increased by the inky fluid which he secretes in copious quantities, every cup-shaped disc, of the hundreds with which the restless tentacles are furnished, ready at the slightest touch to grip whatever is near. . . . And in the center of this network of living traps is the chasmlike mouth, with its enormous parrot-beak, ready to rend piecemeal whatever is held by the tentaculae. The very thought of it makes one's flesh crawl."

Giant Squid

Thus British seaman-author Frank T. Bullen described the largest, swiftest, most terrifying invertebrate on Earth—the giant squid *Architeuthis princeps*. Immortalized in literature as "the mighty Kraken," this bizarre beast would make many of the fearsome dinosaurs of prehistory look like underfed alley cats. In short bursts of speed it can outdistance most fish. It grows as long as many whales, and engages in mortal combat with the largest toothed leviathans in the sea.

It is difficult to imagine that such ferocious and agile predators belong to the same group of animals as the sluggish, shell-encased snails and clams. Yet despite the startling differences in habits and external appearance, they possess many characteristics in common, including a remarkably similar internal anatomy. These characteristics place them in the phylum Mollusca, a fabulous menagerie of some 60,000 species of squids, octopuses, snails, clams, oysters, scallops and other shelled creatures. "Mollusca" comes from the Latin word meaning "soft" and refers to their supple, unsegmented bodies.

All mollusks have a muscular organ called a *foot* which has been modified for different uses during evolution. In squids and octopuses it serves for propulsion and may have been formed into the tentacles. In certain planktonic snails the foot is converted into a pair of winglike paddles for swimming. Clams use it as a shovel for digging and as a means of locomotion. Snails and chitons plaster their foot firmly against a surface, then move by a succession of rhythmical waves that progress slowly from rear to front. Each wave moves the animal forward a fraction of an inch. Snails can travel as fast as 3 inches a minute this way.

A mollusk's vital organs are enclosed by a blanket of tissue called a *mantle*. In squids and octopuses this takes the form of a bullet-shaped cylinder of tough flesh. In snails and other armored mollusks it covers the top and sides of the body like a loose, sleeveless overcoat, and contains cells which secrete the limey shells. In all cases, the mantle creates a cavity or chamber which holds the heart, liver, kidneys, stomach, gills and reproductive organs. This cavity is constantly flushed with oxygenated water.

Squids, octopuses, snails and chitons possess a tonguelike rasping device called a *radula*. This consists of many sharp, horny teeth set in a tough, elastic ribbon. It is used to scrape algae off rocks, to hold prey and to tear food into shreds. Some predaceous snails and octopuses use it to bore through the shells of other mollusks and crustaceans, rasping in one place for hours until they drill a neat feeding hole. Snails like the oyster drill and king conch have a radula on the end of a stretchable, trunklike proboscis. Thrust into the feeding hole, it "chews" the soft parts of oysters, clams and others. Octopuses inject a paralyzing venom through the hole, together with digestive fluids which break up the tissues so that they can be sucked into the inkfish's small mouth. Octopuses also dislodge shellfish and shuck them with their powerful arms.

Snails range in size from smaller than a pinhead to two feet in length. Each species has a shell different from all others, and this variation reflects differences in how and where the creatures live. The small or pointed end is the rear and oldest part of the shell where the beast lived in its youth. Snails constantly add to their shells as they grow older, building wider and deeper chambers or whorls. Some large species add as much as an inch and two full spines to the shell in 18 days. The animal lives in the biggest, newest whorl and sticks its foot, head, fleshy feelers and siphons out the opening.

Primitive eyes, located on the feelers, can distinguish only light and dark. Snails have good "noses" though and react strongly to the odor of enemies and the opposite sex. Feelers or tentacles can be retracted, or regenerated if lost. Some species pull all their soft parts into the shell and seal the opening with a horny or limey lid on the end of the foot. In others, the shell is too small to accommodate the soft parts.

Some snails have a chisel-like tooth on the shell lip with which they pry open clams, mussels and barnacles. *Naticas* or moon shells burrow into mud and sand in search of clams, wrap their foot around the victims then drill the fatal feeding hole. *Nassarius fossatus* wraps its foot tightly around its meals then rolls over on its back, holding the food above the sea floor so other snails that have the scent will not find the morsel.

Dog whelks, cone shells and others use their radula to inject poison. If a live *Conus* punctures your skin, venom from its salivary gland can cause quick death. You don't have to worry about cone shells in North America but some species living in the tropical Indo-Pacific are extremely dangerous.

The most primitive snails—the limpets and abalones—scrape plant material from rocks with their radulae or eat dead organic matter. Limpets make themselves permanent homes by wearing depressions into rock which conform exactly to the shape of their shells. The abalone has an oval caplike shell that resembles a large human ear. Its foot, when sliced into steaks and pounded tender, makes superb eating. Abalones live in many parts of the world, but the Pacific coast, especially California and Oregon, is noted for an abundance and variety of these creatures. California has made the delectable mollusks wards of the State and protects them with stringent laws, but abalones continue to become increasingly rare.

One of the largest marine snails in American waters, the beautiful queen conch *Strombus gigas* reaches a foot or more in length and a weight of over 5 pounds. Sometimes this scavenger's massive shell provides a retreat both for the snail and for the one-inch conchfish. The latter takes up residence in the snail's mantle cavity. Queen conch shells, with their broadly flaring lips, are lined with a brilliant pink substance secreted by the mantle. This material builds up in layers around particles that drift into the shell and occasionally forms handsome rose-colored pearls of great beauty and moderate value. Delicate pink cameos are cut from these shells, but the white and deep chocolate linings of the helmet snails are much preferred for this because they do not fade.

Shell-less and Winged Snails

Not all snails have shells. Sea hares, some of which resemble a mass of spotted, colored jelly the size of a fist or

CONCH. The snail sticks its head out to look around for a meal. The fleshy feelers have eyes on the end, and a siphon extends down between them.

football, have only a thin remnant of a shell under their flesh. These creatures were named for their rabbit-shaped bodies and two cone-shaped flaps of skin or tentacles that resemble bunny ears. They feed mostly on plant material, and some individuals attain weights as great as 15 pounds. Large hares of the genus *Aplysia* emit a smoke screen of harmless fluid the color of cranberry juice when molested; others repel attackers with a cloud of sulphuric acid.

Sea slugs have no shell at all. Among the most gaily colored creatures in the sea, they resemble seaweed fronds flowing along the bottom, or enormous flatworms with clusters of brightly hued plumes on their backs. The plumes are gills by which the animals breath, and when extended they often resemble a tiny garden of exotic flowers. Sponge and sea weed-eating slugs often camouflage themselves by adopting the same shape and color as the species on which they feed. Some voracious flesh eating species prey on their weaker brothers, gulp down anemones with poisonous tentacles and bite the stinging heads off hydroids (who quickly grow new ones). Not only have these slugs evolved a technique to prevent discharge of the coelenterates' explosive cells, but some species store the ingested firearms in their plumes and use them against their own enemies. Hungry fish that swallow such slugs quickly vomit them back into the sea, after which they shake their heads as if experiencing extreme discomfort. On both land and sea it is common for such noxious animals to wear gaudy and conspicuous colors as a warning to would-be predators.

The remarkable blue-purple snail *Janthina janthina* hangs upside-down from a raft of bubbles made out of a glycerine-like mucus that it secretes. The bubbles harden into a clear, celluloid-type substance that is surprisingly difficult to puncture and easily supports the weight of *Janthina's* light shell. Riding under its raft, the colorful snail ventures far from shore in practically all warm seas. One of *Janthina's* favorite meals is the by-the-wind sailor Velella, but before it begins to eat the poisonous tentacles the snail puts its victim to sleep with a purple liquor exuded into the water.

Purple SEA-SNAIL *Janthina janthina* hanging upside down from its bubble raft.

William M. Stephens

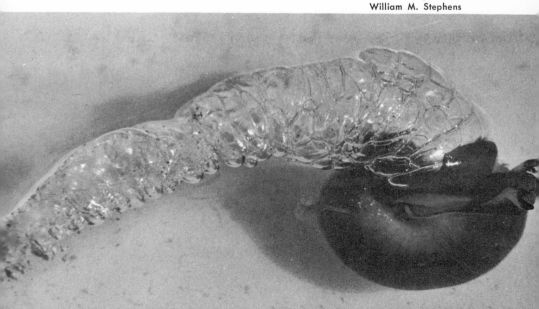

In the open sea, along with *Janthina,* are billions of curious little "winged" snails known as *pteropods* and *heteropods* or "sea butterflies." The edges of their tiny feet are drawn out into thin paddles or winglike lobes. By flapping these wings, they can swim horizontally or move upward on a broadly spiraling course. But even when remaining still they must beat their wings constantly in order to stay afloat.

Rarely more than a half inch long, some pteropods have transparent paper-thin shells while others swim around naked. The shells are either slender, straight-sided cones or squat spirals. The wings protrude from the open end. Pteropods occur in astronomical numbers in the plankton of temperate and tropical seas. Like diatoms and protozoans, so many have died and fallen to the bottom over the past millions of years that large parts of the ocean floor are carpeted with an ooze characterized by their remains. Called *pteropod ooze,* it is white to light brown in color with a reddish, pink or yellow tinge.

Hatchet Foots

Instead of a one piece shell like snails oysters, mussels, clams and scallops have a shuck consisting of two *valves,* held together at the top by an elastic hinge. Muscular force must be exerted at all times to compress the hinge and keep the shell closed. When the muscles relax, or are exhausted by the counter pull of a starfish, the valves then spring open.

No two species of this highly edible class of mollusks have shells exactly the same. Like snails' shells, each has been modified by natural selection so as to give the creature inside some advantage in its particular habitat and way of life. Successful adaptation to their surroundings has freed them from any necessity to change, and fossils show that these mollusks look much the same today as their ancestors did hundreds of millions of years ago.

Mussels anchor themselves to rocky bottoms by tough threads secreted by the foot. Oysters cement their shells to hard bottoms; scallops lie on gravelly or sandy beds. Clams swim; walk along the sea floor; or burrow into mud, sand, hard clay, wood and even solid rock.

Lacking radulae, these creatures feed by filtering microscopic food particles from water which enters and leaves the rear of the shell through two tubes or siphons. The beating of cilia moves incoming water over leaflike gills. Strands of mucus, also driven by cilia, entangle food particles in the water and carry them to the mouth. A tough three-chambered heart pumps blue, red or colorless blood through the gills where it absorbs fresh oxygen. Deoxygenated water, indigestibles and wastes leave through one of the siphons. An oyster pumps and filters through itself as much as 27 quarts of water an hour.

The siphons of nonburrowers are usually not visible. In burrowing clams they extend through the opening between valves and are popularly referred to as the "neck." Clams are thus topsy-turvy beasts; their neck is at the rear and their "head" is where the foot is.

Clams, mussels, oysters and scallops belong to the molluskan class *Pelecypoda,* the word "pelecypod" meaning "hatchet foot." By some stretch of imagination, the foot, which extends between shell halves like a tongue between two lips, can be said to resemble a hatchet tip. It is pushed out the front part of the shell when the animal forces blood into a network of internal cavities. Pumping blood out of these tiny spaces, together with muscular action, contracts the foot. Jackknife clams can jump across the sea floor a foot or two at a time by rapidly expanding and contracting their foot muscles. But the more usual method of clam locomotion is to slide the foot as far ahead as possible then draw the rest of the body up to it.

Oysters, which attach themselves to the bottom by the outside of one valve have a curious sex life. Never completely male or female, they alternate from one to the other throughout their lives. Their sexual products, discharged into the sea, unite fortuitously. A single female may produce from 15 million to 115 million eggs at the spawning. If all survived, the offspring of a few dozen oysters would, in a short time, be sufficient to feed the entire world.

Oysters thrive best in enclosed bays, sounds and river mouths where salinity is reduced by an influx of fresh water. They are better balanced from the point of view of nutrition than almost any other food. Whether raw or cooked their soft bodies contain essential vitamins and minerals, proteins of high nutritive value and starch in a readily digestible form. But if these pelecypods have filtered water polluted by human waste, they can cause infectious hepatitis—a virus borne disease of the liver that confines the victim to bed for 8 to 12 weeks.

If you believe oysters should only be eaten in "r" months (September to April), you will be surprised to learn that North American oysters are usually at their best in May and June. The "r" month idea came from Europe where oysters are usually sold raw and shucked. Before modern refrigeration, they naturally kept better in colder or "r" months. Again, the babies of European species hatch and grow minute shells before leaving their parents' mantle, making some adults gritty and undesirable during summer months. However the "r" idea also stems from the fact that, in summer, toxic bacteria and protozoans may become plentiful in certain waters. Eating oysters or clams that have fed on such creatures has the same paralyzing effect on the nervous system as gulping strychnine.

During summer, the California mussel *Mytilus californianus* and some species of clams along the American west coast dine on the poisonous dino *Gonyaulax*. The poison accumulates in the mollusks' liver and humans that consume them are stricken with paralytic shellfish poisoning. Therefore, you should not eat mussels and clams that grow along the open Pacific coast during summer and early fall. Oysters, the small wedge-shaped mussel *M. edulis* and clams growing in sheltered inshore waters are not affected and can be eaten year-around.

Mussels grow in tightly-packed beds that are also populated by marauding starfish and snail drills, barnacles, colorful worms, flat little crabs, squat isopods, encrusting sponges and a horde of others. The spaces beneath and between mussel shells provide shelter and serve as traps for sea scraps on which many of these beasts feed. One teeming bed off the United States Pacific Coast yielded 4,711 animals from an area 10 inches square; only 625 of these were mussels.

Clams are more active than mussels or oysters. Those that burrow do so by working the pointed end of their foot down into the sediment. This tip is expanded in such a way it serves as an anchor. Then muscular contraction draws the rest of the clam toward its foot, or head first down into the mud or sand. The razor clam *Siliqua patula* buries its thin, 6-inch-long shell in less than 7 seconds.

Burrowers and borers bury themselves until only their siphon-equipped posteriors are exposed. Clams with thin shells generally have longer siphons, are more active and bury themselves deeper and faster than do hard-shelled species. Hard-shelled *Venus mercenaria,* which lives along the American east coast from New England to Texas, is called a "quahog" in New England and a "little neck" further south. "Quahog" is an old Indian name, and small ones are known as "cherrystone clams." The soft-shelled *Mya arenaria* or "long neck," which New Englanders claim is the only "true" clam, is chiefly found north of Cape Cod. A hardy beast, *Mya* ranges all the way to the Arctic where walruses, polar bears and seals find it a tasty morsel.

Clams up to 12 pounds in weight and 8 inches long (*Panope generosa*) grow along the American Pacific coast. But even this species is small compared to the enormous *Tridacna gigas* which reaches a weight of 500 pounds and a width of three feet. Native to the Indo-Pacific, *Tridacna's* body lies upside down within its shell, and the edge of its brilliantly-colored mantle harbors growing algae which the clam sometimes eats. One individual taken off the Philippines yielded a 14-pound pearl. *T. gigas* is the villainous "man-eating" clam that entraps so many movie and television divers. But the beast is not a people eater and authenticated records of its trapping humans do not exist.

"Shipworms" are actually clams with long, wormlike siphons and small shells sharp enough to bore through wood. During the years 1917 to 1920 *Teredo navalis* destroyed much of the piling in San Francisco Bay, causing wharves to collapse and pitching warehouses and loaded freight cars into the water. In Los Angeles harbor, the boring clam *Pholadidea penita* drills into rock and concrete so hard you need a sledge hammer to break into its burrows.

Some clams, like *Lima dehiscens,* swim by a primitive type of jet propulsion. Scallops, the most alert and active of the pelecypods, get around this way. When they detect an octopus or starfish approaching they quickly clap their valves together, causing a jet of water to shoot out the open bottom edge. This propels them along hinge first. Scallops also swim forward (bottom edge first) by squirting water through openings on either side of the hinge. In both cases movement is awkward and jerky. It takes them out of reach of starfish, but is of no avail against the vigorous octopus.

Scallops espy enemies by means of a fringe of crimson, finger-length tentacles. These project between the shell halves and are capable of feeling, smelling and distinguishing light from dark. Scallops open and close their corrugated shell by means of a single large muscle or "eye." (Oysters have one such muscle while clams and mussels have two.) When you eat scallops in the United States, you eat this eye; the rest of the flesh is discarded. People in European and other countries consider this wasteful and rightly so. They consume the entire scallop and regard it as a delicious and nutritious food.

Chambered   Squid   Pteropods
Nautilus   (much magnified)

          Octopus   Scallop
                               Swimming   Sea Hare   Sea S

The Head Foots

Although we think of jet propulsion as a modern innovation, mollusks have been using it to get around for hundreds of millions of years. The undisputed masters of marine jet transportation are squids, octopuses and their famous relative, the chambered *Nautilus*.

Giant nerves activate powerful muscles in the squids' torpedo-shaped mantle, causing it to expand then contract. This acts as a pump, forcing water in and out of a cavity containing two feathery gills. Water enters through slits along the side of the neck, flows backward over the gills, then forward and out through a funnel-shaped siphon in the position of the "Adam's apple." When alarmed or excited squids work their mantle muscles rapidly, ejecting water from the siphon in a jet that propels them backward at surprising speeds. Normally, the siphon points forward so the animal darts through the water stern first. The tip of this tube can also be curled back on itself so as to thrust the creature through the water head first. Maximum speed, however, is obtained when the arrowlike tail end cuts the water and the serpentlike tentacles trail out behind in a streamline fashion.

By quickly reversing their siphons squids shuttle back and forth through schools of herring, mackerel or other fish, stuffing victim after victim into their fiendish craws. Often

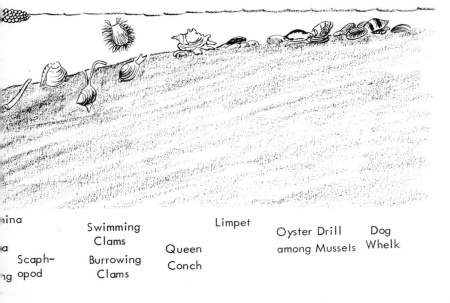

ina

Swimming
Clams

Limpet

Oyster Drill   Dog

a   among Mussels   Whelk

Scaph-   Queen

ng opod   Burrowing   Conch
              Clams

they take only one bite out of a hapless creature before reaching for another. Cannibalistic and pugnacious, mobs of these rapacious mollusks frequently engage in murderous orgies, seemingly killing far beyond their needs. Well did Michlet term them "the insatiable nightmares of the sea."

For leisurely head-first swimming or hovering, squids slowly flap the two triangular or lobe-shaped fins near their rears. During rapid tail-first dashes, these serve for steering and stabilization. Some small species build up enough speed to shoot out of the water and use their fins to make long, gliding flights like flying fish. The crew of Kon-Tiki, who drifted part way across the tropical Pacific, reported that small schools of glittering squid sailed over their raft at a height of 4 or 5 feet and made soaring flights of 50 yards.

Being less streamlined, the bulbous, saclike octopuses are inferior swimmers. Interrupted jetting causes their movements to be jerky and rather awkward. A few species spend their lives swimming at mid-depths, but most types content themselves with scuttling along the bottom on their arms.

Huge nerves, as big around as a wooden match in some species, enable squid to sense a situation and act faster than other invertebrates. Sensory impressions travel to and motor impulses go from their brains as much as 220 times faster than messages moving over a jellyfish's nerve net. Experiments have shown that squids have the ability to learn and can profit by experience. They associate one event with another and remember the significance of the association.

Their large brains have centers for controlling and co-ordinating the tangle of suckered, pythonlike arms in the acts of feeling, grasping, crawling and copulation. It used to be thought that these arms formed from the foot when, during the course of evolution, it grew forward and became divided into a ring of tentacles surrounding the head. This is how this class of mollusks got the name Cephalopoda or "head foots." Today, however, some biologists believe the frightening arms may have originated as direct outgrowths from the head.

Octopuses, as "octo" indicates, have eight tapered tentacles joined by a web near the base. Their whiplike tips coil, uncoil and twitch almost constantly. Each horrendous arm has a double row of suckers with remarkable holding power. They flee from, rather than attack humans, but there have been instances of large ones holding divers underwater until they drowned.

In addition to eight arms, squids have two extra long tentacles which have no equal in the animal kingdom. The rubbery limbs of giant squid can stretch out to 35 feet or more, as long as a 3-story building is high, or snap back until they disappear among the nest of other arms. The ends of these living cables are flattened like open palms. Stalked suckers with hard, saw-toothed rims line the tentacles and are concentrated on these "hands." As an added diabolic touch, some of them also have sharp hooks which can be extended like cat claws.

When the English troopship *Britannia* went down in the Atlantic on March 25, 1941, one survivor, clinging to a life raft, felt something grab his leg. While a dozen of his ship-mates watched in helpless horror, a large squid wrapped its tentacles around the sailor and pulled him, screaming, to his death.

One can only hope he drowned before being drawn to the devilish jaws hidden in the center of the head arms. Shaped like an upside-down parrot beak and as big as a man's head in some species, these horny jaws can reduce a giant tuna to shreds in a short time. Bullen called this hideous beaked head "as awful an object as one could well imagine in a fevered dream."

Octopuses use their curved beaks when fighting each other, but they are not known to employ them as freely and fero-ciously as squids. A person must exercise caution in handling any of these creatures since their bites are poisonous. In one rare case, an Australian pearl diver, who let a small octopus crawl over his arms and shoulders, was bitten on the back of the neck and died within three hours.

Cephalopods see victims and enemies very well. As big as beach balls in giant squid, the highly developed eyes give you the uncanny feeling of being watched. No one knows what they actually see, but in theory the unique eyes of squids and

Common OCTOPUS (*Octopus vulgaris*).

octopuses have a wider field of clear vision than humans do.

Good eyesight, fast reflexes and high speed do not prevent them from falling prey to various fishes, sea birds, seals and whales. Schools of cod cut broad swathes through battalions of small squids as they jet along in precise, military formation. Squid is the favorite food of the sperm whale. This swift colossus dives to 3,000 feet for a squid dinner and has been known to swallow 35-foot, 400-pound individuals whole.

The nemeses of octopuses are the savage moray and conger eels. They stalk their prey by poking tooth-filled, snakelike snouts into likely caves and crevices. If an octopus is too big to swallow whole, the moray twists off an arm by spinning the full length of its long body. The inkfish may be eaten tentacle by tentacle in this manner, but should it manage to escape the missing limbs can be regrown.

Another voracious enemy, man, takes about a million tons of octopuses and squids out of the sea every year. In Spain inkfish are a national dish, and stuffed octopus flavored with chocolate is a supreme delicacy. Ancient Romans baked octopuses in big, spiced pies; modern Italians sauté squids in olive oil and eat fried octopus sandwiches. Portuguese cook them in their own ink. In other areas of the Mediterranean coast, whole baby octopuses are served hot on a fork like hot dogs. The Japanese consider octopus eyes an epicurean delight and relish raw octopus hors d'oeuvres. Cold octopus salad has a rare, subtle flavor, and those who have never tasted squid properly tenderized and prepared have missed a savory, inexpensive dish.

Besides speed, cephalopods command a couple of unique ways to avoid gracing the dining table and to protect themselves against morays and other enemies. Best known is their habit of emitting a cloud of dark ink. Manufactured by a special gland, this fluid is blown out the siphon. When an octopus or squid jets away, the ink remains as a blob which forms a decoy; when released from a standing position it acts as a "smoke screen." Inkfish that live in the eternal blackness of deep waters discharge a bright, luminous cloud that confuses attackers as much as a sudden darkening in sunlit waters.

Cephalopods also "disappear" or blend into the background by changing color and the pattern of their marking in the wink of an eye. No creature in the animal kingdom can match their amazing speed or repertoire of designs—the chameleon is slow and unimaginative by comparison. *Sepia officinalis,* a squat, bottom-hugging squid, wears a light mottled frock when resting on the sandy sea floor but changes to a strongly contrasting cloak of black and white when swimming over dark stones and light shell.

Different color pigments carried in tiny, transparent sacs cover the surface of their bodies. When muscles attached to the elastic walls of these sacs relax, each snaps down to a pin-point and no color appears. Muscular contraction pulls the walls of the bags outward so each forms a star-shaped patch of color. These drawstring bags of color are embedded in the skin in a layered arrangement, for instance a yellow, red then blue layer. By combining colors from various layers, opening some sacs and closing others, all manner of hues and patterns can be produced.

A frightened octopus often contracts all its sacs and turns livid white. When angry or in the excitement of killing, many squids and octopuses blush reddish brown. Touch or frighten a squid (be sure it's a small one), and it may turn pale and watery. Provoke *S. officinalis* and you will see a remarkable succession of black stripes flicker over its pallid body, followed by the rapid appearance and disappearance of black spots. A male of this species displays alternating purple and white bars during courtship.

Upon seeing such a pattern, a female in mating condition keeps quiet and waits. The male inserts a specially modified and enlarged arm into her mantle cavity. This arm deposits sperm wrapped in small packets. The wrapping unravels and the released sperm fertilize eggs as they pass to the siphon on the way out. Male argonauts (a type of octopus) leave the entire copulating tentacle in the female's mantle cavity and grow a new one. When first discovered, zoologists thought this arm was a new species of parasitic worm and they named it *Hectocotylus.*

Mother octopuses lay from a few dozen to 45,000 eggs then tend them diligently. They keep small creatures and particles off the eggs by constantly working their suckered arms over them like a vacuum cleaner and hosing them down with jets of water. Squid mothers dispense with this maternal care since their eggs are embedded in protective jelly, and are inedible. Squid hatchlings are fierce-looking, thumbnail-sized replicas of their parents. Those not eaten by predators grow into adults of all sizes from an inch to spectacular lengths of 57 feet and perhaps more. The most common squid, *Loligo,* grows to about 1½ feet.

Squids jet around at all latitudes and from the surface to depths in excess of 11,500 feet. According to some zoologists, their bulk exceeds that of any other two creatures on land or sea. This may be an exaggeration but there is a tremendous number of these molluskan nightmares in the World Ocean.

Marineland of Florida

Common SQUID, *Loligo*. The mosaic appearance of its body is caused by color sacs in various stages of expansion and contraction.

The largest known squid is a specimen of *Architeuthis princeps* washed up on a New Zealand beach in 1888. This giant measured 57 feet, 35 of which was tentacles. Such monsters rarely appear at the surface, and some zoologists believe even bigger ones live in the depths. They talk of behemoths 75 feet long with 50-foot arms. An ailing captive whale regurgitated two *Architeuthis* tentacles 42 feet long. Inkfish experts figure these limbs belonged to a prodigiosity that weighed 85,000 pounds and was 66 feet long. A 50-foot squid leaves 4-inch sucker marks shaped like bottle cap imprints on the hides of sperm whales. But some captured sperms wear sucker scars 18 inches across. Could these have been inflicted by mighty krakens 200 feet long that lurk in the unexplored abyss?

Compared with such giants, octopuses are small, a 110 pounder with a 28-foot arm spread being a Gargantua. Comparing the two in disposition is like matching a tiger and a kitten. Squids attack anything, including inanimate objects and other squids. Although they share the name "devilfish" with the batlike manta rays, octopuses are shy and timid. However you should always keep in mind that large ones are less shy than small ones.

Squids, octopuses and other mollusks evolved from limpet-like creatures that crept along the sea bottom as long ago as 500 million years. Primitive cephalopods gave rise to two lines of descendants. One line retained the external shell and the only members that have survived to modern times are three species of pearly or chambered *Nautilus*. Immortalized in the poem of Oliver Wendell Holmes, "The Chambered Nautilus," they dwell around reefs in the southwest Pacific and range to depths of 2,000 feet. Each has about 90 short, suckerless arms that protrude from the open end of a delicate, colorfully ornamented shell which is tightly coiled like a ram's horn. The creature, which lives in the largest and last formed of 33 to 36 chambers, has a parrot beak and can swim by jet propulsion but lacks an ink sac and highly developed eyes. The empty back rooms of the shell are filled with gas that keeps the animal afloat.

In the other line, the shell became enclosed in the body and gradually reduced. In cuttlefish like *Sepia* this skeleton has diminished to a limey slab or cuttlebone which finds wide use in bird cages. Other squids have only a fragile pen-shaped internal shell composed of horny material. Octopus skeletons consist merely of a pair of vestigial hard parts to which muscles are attached.

This loss of shell played a major role in the success of cephalopods. The heavy shucks retained by their cousins, snails and pelecypods, provide protection and other advantages, but deprive them of mobility and block off sensory impressions from the outside world. As squids and octopuses lost their cumbersome shells, they gained mobility and developed special organs to deal with increased inputs from their surroundings. The resulting large brains, keen eyes and rapid reflexes have made them the most agile and advanced of all invertebrates.

8.

Sharks

"Now although Oikopleura *sits by himself
In the midst of his house on a jelly-built shelf,
He's firmly attached in front by his snout,
And never lets go till his house wears out."*
—PROF. W. GARSTANG

THESE lines are part of an ode to a curious little
plankter who lives in a wonderful jelly-bubble
house and is somehow mixed up in the evolution of backboned creatures. Looking like a
pollywog tadpole but about half as long as a book match,
Oikopleura spins a house around itself and moves it through
the sea by jet propulsion. The transparent abode has two
screened windows on top and a front and back door on
bottom. It is actually an elaborate feeding device that ranks
among the most marvelous adaptations in the animal kingdom.

The little "tad" secretes a jellied envelope around its
body. Then undulating motions of the tail pump a stream
of water into the envelope, inflating it like a bubble. The
constantly flicking tail, which accounts for most of the body
length, sets up a current that flows in through the windows.
Screens block the passage of all but such tiny creatures as
flagellates and coccolithophores. (Toward the end of the last
century the German planktonologist Hans Lohmann, while
carefully examining Oiky's filters, became the first man to
see living coccolithophores.) These minute tidbits flow to

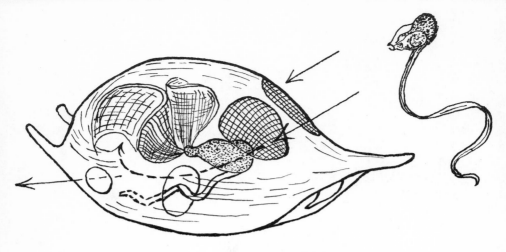

OIKOPLEURA

the front of the house and two funnel-shaped nets that lead
into the animal's mouth. Filtered water is expelled out the
front door so fast it propels *Oikopleura* through the water.
When the screens become clogged, or in times of danger
when the house is an encumbrance, the little tad slips out the
back door and with a twitch of its tail darts away to safety.

What has *Oiky* got to do with sharks and other backboned
creatures? Running through the middle of its tadpole tail,
Oiky has a tough, flexible rod known as a *notochord* (back
string). This gristly rod is the forerunner of backbones.

Abundant and cosmopolitan in surface waters, *Oikopleura*
belongs to the class *Tunicata,* a group named for the
celluloselike envelopes or tunics which enclose many of the
species. The most common tunicates are sessile sea squirts,
or ascidians—vase-shaped sacks of tough tissue with two openings at the top like the siphons of clams. They feed by taking
in water through one opening, straining it through gills then
discharging it from the other orifice. Often brilliantly colored and found attached to rocks below the low tide mark,
they have the habit of squirting water when handled.

Squirts send up planktonic young that have a notochord
in their tails and resemble *Oikopleura* adults *sans* the bubble
house. In fact young squirts probably evolved into free-
swimming adults which in turn gave rise to *Oikopleura*.
Both possess a hollow nerve chord which lies above and
parallels their notochords. This distinguishes them from all

animals mentioned thus far, which have a solid nerve cord running below the gut. A nerve column above the gut represents a definite advance since the digestive system does not pass through the middle of the most delicate and complex portion of the nervous system.

Because they possess a notochord, topside nerve cord and gills to strain food out of the water, characteristics not found in any invertebrates, tunicates are placed in the phylum (or superphylum) Chordata. This huge menagerie is named for and embraces all creatures that have a notochord at some time in their lives.

Higher animals, from fish to man, have a notochord in the egg or womb. As they develop, sections of gristle or bone are added for strength, and these form a series of connected segments (vertebrae) collectively called the backbone or spinal column. These vertebrae enclose the notochord and to a greater or lesser extent, depending on the species, replace it. They also enclose and protect the nerve cord. All chordates possess gill slits at some time in their developments. (You and I have them in the womb.)

As stated before, chordates and echinoderms evidently descended from the same ancestor. This missing link could have been a stalked bottom dweller or an active swimmer. If the latter is true, it may have resembled the swimming larvae of starfish. Such babies are similar to those of the *acorn worm,* a wormlike animal that burrows into shallow bottoms as an adult and has gill slits and traces of what might be a notochord. If the ancestral vertebrate was a swimmer then, it might have given rise to the backboned line through acorn worms.

Acorn worms are grouped with small, primitive, plantlike creatures called *pterobranchs,* which grow in colonies attached to the bottom. Individual members of the colonies project like diminutive flowers from the ends of branching tubes. If the chordate/echinoderm ancestor was sessile, it might have been like a pterobranch. By development of a gill system these creatures might have evolved into the ancestors of sea squirts. Then by means of young which became sexually mature while still plankters, such primitive chordates could have gained a new-found mobility and freedom from the bottom. Retention of this freedom and continued development of the tadpole tail for locomotion would have led to an increasingly active life. This in turn would result in the evolution of higher and higher animals.

Oiky and other tunicates, acorn worms and pterobranchs lie in the shadow zone between invertebrates and vertebrates, just as viruses lie in the shadow zone between the non-living and living. There is a third group of primitive chordates whose position on the tree of life is better known. Called *cephalochordates* (head chords), they are direct, bona fide ancestors of the backboned clan, having a notochord extending from the front of the head to the tip of the tail throughout their adult lives. The group is represented in today's seas by the obscure little sea lancelet *Amphioxus*.

These translucent, eel-like creatures rarely grow more than two inches long and spend most of their lives buried in clean sand up to their necks. They live along shallow coasts in the tropics and temperate zones and strain food out of the water with fingerlike structures in their mouths. On certain southern California beaches at very low tide, stomping on the sand will cause a number of them to pop completely out

American Museum of Natural History

LAMPREY mouth (a model). Sharp, horny teeth around rim enable this eel-like creature to fix itself to a victim. The powerful toothed tongue (center) then rasps away scales, skin and flesh.

of their burrows. They writhe about for an instant then hurl themselves back into the sand head first, burrowing as rapidly as many fish swim.

Except for a specialized array of 50 or more pairs of gills, this primitive beast is probably much the same as the head chords that burrowed into the sea bottoms a half billion years ago. Like modern *Amphioxi,* these ancients had no nose, ears, limbs, skeleton or brain. A mighty undistinguished ancestor for the powerful sharks, swift fishes and proud men. Yet, many paleontologists believe ancient lanceletlike creatures were the central ancestors of all higher animals. According to Dr. Edwin H. Colbert of the American Museum of Natural History, "in *Amphioxus* we see in effect our chordate ancestor of 500,000,000 years ago."

Blood Suckers and Hags

There are a number of striking similarities between *Amphioxus* and the young of the most primitive living vertebrates—lampreys and hagfish. Young lampreys, blind, eel-like creatures about one-quarter inch long, bury themselves neck deep in the quiet, soft bottoms of rivers and streams and sieve food from the water like *Amphioxus.* After two to five years of this kind of life, these formerly harmless creatures undergo a startling change. They develop large, staring eyes, hideous sucker-mouths and rasplike tongues. Now four to seven inches long, they wiggle their soft, scaleless bodies out of the mud and swim downstream to the sea where they take up a life of bloodsucking parasitism.

Lampreys invaded the Great Lakes sometime before 1829, and by 1950 they had destroyed 95 percent of the trout (whitefish) in Lakes Michigan and Huron and ruined a five million dollar fishing industry. Their round mouths are rimmed with sharp, horny teeth by which they fix themselves to the body of a hapless fish. Then the powerful tongue, riddled with horny teeth, begins to rasp through skin and scales. Sometimes several lampreys will attack one fish and feed upon its blood, body fluids and flesh. The shredded flesh is dissolved by a powerful substance in the saliva called

HAGFISH or slime-eel mouth (a model). They eat their victims from inside out.

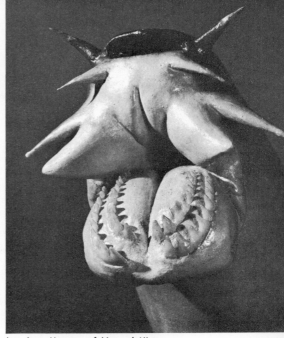

lamphredin. This chemical keeps the fish's blood from clotting, and doctors are studying it in the hope of learning what prevents clotting in hemophilics or bleeders.

Hagfish or slime eels have even more disgusting eating habits. They hatch in the sea from large, sticky eggs, then grow to a maximum adult size of about two feet, somewhat smaller than lampreys. Their mouths, surrounded by four fingerlike feelers, lie in a groove on the underside of their heads. With rasping tongues they bore through the neck or enter the mouth, anus, gills or open wounds of dead or dying fish. Hagfish eat from the inside out until nothing is left of their victims but a skinful of bones. Over a hundred of these sea vultures have been taken from the body of a single fish. Their menu also includes all manner of bottom-dwelling invertebrates.

Like lampreys, these repulsive creatures yield a substance that may be of immense benefit to man. From the hearts of hags living at 1,200 to 1,800 feet off the California coast, scientists have isolated a chemical that has corrected faulty heart beats in frogs and dogs. Applied to a human heart, this substance may restore a normal beat when it has been interrupted or delayed as a result of serious disease.

By studying these beasts, zoologists get a partial picture of the first vertebrates on Earth. Like larval lampreys and *Amphioxus,* these were probably small, sluggish creatures that wiggled across the sea floor, sucking up mud and straining it through their gills to obtain food. Fossils indicate that these ancients, instead of being soft-bodied were covered with an armor of bony scales. During the long course of evolution they lost this armor, and competition from other creatures forced them to take up specialized feeding habits in order to survive. Lampreys and hags developed a toothed tongue and began feeding upon the bodies of others. As often happens with parasites, their bodies degenerated, taking on an eel-like form supported by a feeble, poorly developed skeleton of gristle instead of bone.

Lampreys and hags, then, are modified survivors of the first vertebrates on Earth. Their ancestors were the first to possess an internal skeleton. They evolved eyes, a heart and red blood independently of the invertebrates. By closely studying their modern descendants and combining this information with that derived from fossils, scientists can visualize some of the steps in the evolution of more advanced creatures like sharks and rays.

Evolution and Man-Eaters

Among the most hated and feared animals in the sea, sharks represent an enormous advance over lampreys and hags. Watching sharks in an aquarium, you cannot help being impressed. Among the most beautifully streamlined of all fishes, they slip through the water with graceful, menacing ease, driven by seemingly effortless sweeps of their powerful tails. In contrast, lampreys and hags, lacking the paired fins that stabilize and smoothen the sharks' motion, move awkwardly and swim ineffectively. Instead of rasping tongues and weak jawless mouths, sharks have steel-trap jaws full of knifelike teeth for slashing large chunks out of their victims.

This superior design, the essentials of which were evolved hundreds of millions of years ago, has enabled sharks to solve the problems of changing conditions and fierce competition for food and living space without greatly changing themselves. Hence, modern sharks are generally similar to the first sharks that swam in the oceans 300 million years ago. As one scientist put it, watching a shark is like looking down the corridor of evolution into the distant past.

In today's seas, sharks are so successful they have very few enemies, and almost no friends. In fear and ignorance, man has cloaked them in mystery and misinformation. At one and the same time, they are portrayed as fearless killers and bullying cowards, as aggressive predators and dull-witted, self-propelled garbage cans.

What are sharks really like? No one can give an accurate answer. Zoologists who have devoted lifetimes to studying them cannot even generalize about their behavior or personality. After thousands of observations and hundreds of attacks on humans, man is not yet sure why they attack people and under what conditions.

This enigmatic beast comes in some 250 varieties or species. Most of them live in the comfortable tropical and subtropical seas; a few, like the Greenland shark, inhabit arctic waters. Sharks range in size from 6 inches to 45 feet or more, from the little green dog shark to the biggest fish in the sea. The overwhelming majority are seagoing creatures, but some frequent brackish and even fresh waters. Sharks have assaulted people as far up rivers as 150 miles. One species has established residence in a Nicaraguan lake where it has killed a number of bathers.

Evolutionarily speaking, the characteristics that set sharks and kin apart from lampreys and hags are jaws and paired fins. The characteristics that set them apart from other fishes are lack of an air bladder and a skeleton of gristle or cartilage instead of bone.

"Invented" some 400 million years ago, jaws are a big thing in the evolution of vertebrates. Their development freed fishes from a life of mud-sucking and enabled them to seize bigger prey, to better defend themselves, and to crush hard-shelled mollusks and crustaceans. Such vast new possibilities were opened up by their evolution that jaws contributed greatly to the dominance of fishes over invertebrates.

A modern shark's maw is uncomfortably large in proportion to its body size, the jaws of a big tiger shark being ample
enough to girdle two men standing back to back. Add row
upon row of razor-sharp teeth set in a grim crescentic mouth,
and you have a picture of a man-eater. Unlike the teeth of
humans and other vertebrates, which are anchored to the
jawbone by roots, shark dentures are merely imbedded in
the skin or gums. There are four to six rows of teeth which
move steadily forward as they grow or increase in size. After
being used awhile the front teeth fall out, but are quickly
replaced by those moving up from behind. Over a 10-year
period, a tiger shark may produce, use and shed as many as
24,000 saw-edged teeth.

In most species, the mouth lies well back on the underside
of the head beneath the shovel-edged snout. This is an ideal
position for grabbing food off the ocean floor, and has led
to the old belief that sharks must turn on their backs or
sides to bite. If you have ever watched a shark feed in an
aquarium you know this is not necessarily true. They frequently attack from below, angling their snout upward and
out of the way so the mouth can easily slide over the prey.
The powerful jaws snap shut and the shark shakes its body
violently from side to side, tearing loose as much as 10 or
15 pounds of flesh.

Shark bites have a tell-tale crescent shape, are jagged and
often very deep. In attacks on humans a major artery is frequently severed, and a person may bleed to death before he
can receive aid. There are reports of sharks playfully tossing
mutilated bodies into the air, but more likely the victim
was thrown out of the water by the force of the shark's rush
from below.

Even a light brush with these beasts can cause painful
lacerations. Shark hides are covered with tiny, hard, closely-
packed scales which resemble short teeth with a sharp apex
pointing backward. Run your hand along a shark from head
to tail, and the creature feels quite smooth. Rub a shark the
wrong way, from tail to head, and you may pull back a cut
and bleeding hand.

A shark's rasplike scales and its teeth are actually the

same. The outer skin folds into the mouth to form its front lining, and the scales on this skin become enlarged into teeth much like human dentures. In fact, the latter have evolved from the scales of fishy ancestors.

Sharks have vertical and horizontal fins which give them great stability and moderate maneuverability. The large pair of pectoral fins at the front of the body, and the smaller pair of pelvic fins at the rear, steer the body up and down. Vertical fins, usually two dorsals on the back and one anal fin on the belly, prevent rolling and reduce side slip. The large tail propels sharks forward by back and forth sculling motions, and it also turns them left or right.

Because their paired fins are fairly rigid, sharks cannot swim as fast or maneuver as well as bony fishes. They use the pectorals as brakes but they cannot come to a sudden stop or back up. Sharks usually swerve aside to avoid an obstacle, and once their heads pass the food they must circle back to take it. Bony fishes fold their flexible fins against their sides to attain greater forward speed, and many fishes can "turn on a dime" by thrusting one pelvic fin straight out and giving a flip of the tail.

Many bony fishes possess gas-filled bladders, which make them the same weight as the water and enable them to stay at certain depths without effort. Lacking such a bladder, sharks tend to sink. At least one species, the sand tiger, remains suspended by inflating its stomach with air. But most sharks have to keep moving to take advantage of the lift offered by their winglike pectorals. Literally, they must swim or sink.

To assist them in this never-ending effort, many species have an enormous liver full of lighter-than-water oil. The vitamin A in these livers supported a prosperous shark fishery in the United States until 1950 when an inexpensive artificial substitute was produced. But the oily organs may again come into demand. Recently it was discovered that tiger and lemon shark livers contain a fatty substance which increases resistance to cancer, retards tumor growth and increases the life span of certain cancerous animals.

Having a skeleton of cartilage, instead of heavier bone, is another weight-saving device, and it raises a tricky question. One group of scientists thinks cartilage evolved first, then as animals became more advanced, it was abandoned in favor of bone. Another school feels it is just as likely that bone came first. Instead of representing a primitive condition in sharks, cartilage may be a degenerative one or an advanced specialization to save weight.

This question casts some doubt on the general belief that sharks are more primitive than bony fishes. Fish fossils appear before those of sharks in ancient rocks. Brain areas controlling thought and reason in sharks, though still rudimentary, are more advanced than those of most bony fishes. A shark's sex life, too, is more highly organized, and in this respect he is more like people than other fishes.

Males and females copulate, whereas many bony fishes discharge their sex products into the sea and leave them to unite fortuitously. Some primitive sharks lay eggs and abandon them to hatch in the sea. But most species hatch eggs within their bodies and give birth to live young. Depending on the species, a litter may be anywhere from one to eighty, one baby weighing as much as 100 pounds. The pups, which may be carried two years, come into the world fully formed and able to swim. Many leave the womb with a mouthful of teeth, fully prepared to defend and feed themselves in an adult world. All are born hungry, so the never-ending search for food must begin immediately.

Scientists, working with captured sharks and observing them from ships and planes in the open sea, have only recently figured out how they find their next meal. A quarry is first detected by the vibrations or changes in pressure it sets up as it moves through the water. The vibrations from an animal as far away as 600 feet are picked up by nerve endings arrayed along an open groove or closed canal, extending along a shark's sides from gills to tail. The pulses that impinge on this *lateral line,* as it is called, may register in the shark's brain as sound. However they are too low in frequency to be heard distinctly by humans.

Once the shark has heard the dinner bell, he brings into play a keen sense of smell. These bloodhounds of the sea can sniff an ounce of blood in thousands, even millions of gallons of water, or detect a scent as far away as a quarter-

mile in a strong current. The shark follows a corridor of
smell or vibrations, or both, like an airplane homing in on
a radio beacon.

At about 50 feet, eyes come into play if the water is clear
enough. Although notoriously near-sighted, sharks see well
in dim light. Their eyes are designed to detect movement
rather than distinguish shapes. At about 10 feet they usually
begin to circle slowly, warily. After an inspecting pass or
two, they may turn away indifferently or begin feeding.
When attacking in a pack, sharks describe tighter and
tighter circles around prey, swimming faster and faster until
one moves in for the first bite.

Once body juices or blood flow into the water, sharks
become agitated and may go into what is called a "feeding
frenzy." Then nothing short of death stops them. They will
bite at anything that moves, and their thrashing, whipping
bodies often churn the sea into a bloody froth. If a shark
is accidentally bitten in the mad melee or slashed by another's fins, the pack will turn upon and devour him with
the same ferocity as an unrelated victim.

Sharks are infamous for their ravenous appetites and
catholic diet. Although almost all species prefer fresh, oily
fish, they also gobble squid, seals, sea birds, other sharks,
turtles, crabs, lobsters, garbage, humans and in one case, a
crazed elephant that ran into the sea. Porpoises and others
that swim too fast for them when healthy are enjoyed when
disabled, dying or too young to defend themselves. The
stomachs of captured sharks have given up grass, wooden
crates, tin cans, sacks of coal, the skull of a cow, the hind
quarters of a pig, the head and forelegs of a bulldog, horse-
flesh, and a broken alarm clock.

Sharks just bite and swallow without bothering to chew.
They can store food in their stomachs for days without digesting it. In one famous Australian murder case a big tiger
shark, eight days after its capture, vomited a human arm
so well preserved that police could identify the victim by
the tattoos on the limb.

On the night of November 28, 1942, the troopship *Nova
Scotia* was torpedoed off the east coast of South Africa. A

thousand of the Italian war prisoners on board lost their lives, many of them to sharks who presumably did their ghastly work in a feeding frenzy. According to an account by J. L. B. Smith of Rhodes University, "The sharks apparently preferred to attack whole living men rather than partly dismembered bodies."

Yet in 1944 a U.S. Navy training manual intimated that practically all stories of man-eating sharks were fictitious. Suitably rephrased, this droll manual appeared in a popular national magazine as an article entitled "The Shark Is A Sissy." During the same year the story was published, a Navy pilot downed off Guadalcanal was almost eaten alive by a shark.

Between 1917 and 1961 there were over 560 shark attacks on humans all over the world, nearly half of them fatal. Since records have been kept, 78 attacks occurred along the United States east and Gulf coasts, 26 of them fatal. This is a very small number indeed considering the millions of bathers, skin divers, etc., but it demonstrates that a real danger exists. Stewart Springer of the U.S. Fish and Wildlife Service suggests that many attacks on humans are made by "rogue" sharks or "bank loafers," solitary sharks who have become separated from the main concentrations of their species and wandered into shallow water.

V. M. Coppleson, an Australian scientist who has been studying the activities of sharks since 1919, says that once sharks have dined on human flesh they may acquire a taste for it. Examining records of sea temperatures at the time and place of attacks, Coppleson noticed that the vast majority took place in water warmer than 68° F. This led him to the conclusion that sharks will not attack in water colder than this.

However, Dr. Leonard P. Schultz of the Smithsonian Institution points out that bathers seldom enter waters colder than 68° F., and the times of attack coincide with swimming seasons. In other words, a high concentration of bathers, not water temperature, is responsible for shark statistics. Schultz notes that three divers were attacked off California in 55° F. water, and he believes that as more and more suit-protected divers enter colder water the temperate ranges and areas of attack will expand.

Aquarium tests show that shark appetites do go up and down with water temperature. Lemon sharks in captivity fed less and less, then quit entirely when water in their tank dropped below 68° F. Some individuals ate nothing from mid-December until mid-February when the water warmed and remained above 70° F.

Amateurs and experts have come up with all sorts of methods to protect people against sharks, including wire fences, noise makers, electric and sound barriers, poisons and even coordinated aircraft and ship raids. All these devices have one thing in common—they don't work. Despite the announcements by certain resort and hotel managers that curtains of bubbles rising from punctured air hoses are "absolutely impenetrable," research shows that sharks completely ignore bubbles once they get used to them.

The only successful method of beach protection developed to date has been "meshing," anchoring heavy gill nets parallel to beach areas. Meshing was first tried off Australia's shark infested east coast in 1937 and has been used off Durban, South Africa, since 1952. No shark attacks have occurred on protected African beaches since, and the number of assaults on meshed Australian beaches dropped to two in eight years.

To protect shipwreck victims or those from downed aircraft, the United States armed forces, as a result of a crash program begun during World War II, came up with a concoction optimistically called Shark Chaser. Most authorities believe its greatest value has been as a morale booster, the name being worth, as one scientist put it, "all the money spent in its development." This repellent has prevented lone sharks from closing in on swimmers, and seems to repel curious or circling sharks of most species if they are alone and not in a feeding frenzy. However, Australian scientists were astounded to discover Shark Chaser not only did not chase some sharks but was eaten by them as fast as it was thrown in the water. The consensus seems to be that it is better than nothing but shark repellents, like sharks, should not be trusted.

What to Do in Case of Attack

There is plenty of advice around about what to do if you find yourself in the water with a shark, much of it unreliable. You are probably not enough of an expert to tell whether your swimming companion is a dangerous species or not. (Chances are you are not going to look too closely, anyway.) So your best recourse is to consider them all dangerous and get out of the water as quickly and quietly as possible.

Above all, try not to panic. Move away rapidly but swim as rhythmically and smoothly as possible. One of the old standby bits of advice, often repeated to servicemen and civilians, was that sharks could be frightened by violent kicking and splashing. Experts have now decided that this is like ringing the dinner bell. To sharks threshing swimmers sound just like a struggling or wounded fish and both could easily meet the same fate.

If a shark moves in before you can get out of the water, your best, and only, recourse is to fight back. Charge the shark and smash it on the snout with anything you have handy. Use your fists only as a last resort. The sandpaper hide may cause bleeding abrasions and blood will certainly spur the attack.

Never give up hope. The Navy flyer mentioned earlier was repeatedly attacked while floating without clothing in a life jacket off Guadalcanal. Each time the shark charged he hit it with his fists on the nose and eyes. Although severely injured in the struggle the pilot came out with his life and limbs.

To lessen the danger of attack, the Shark Research Panel of the American Institute of Biological Sciences offers the following advice:

Always swim or dive with a companion.
Don't swim or dive in the evening or at night; most species are more active and feed at that time.
If you receive a bleeding wound, get out of the water.
Remove speared fish from the water immediately.
Don't trail arms and legs from a float or raft.
Avoid bright or contrasting bathing suits and shiny

jewelry. More attacks have been made on swimmers wearing shiny white or brightly-colored suits and on those
whose suits contrasted markedly with skin color.

Never—never—tease, grab, spear or try to ride even a
small shark. The likelihood of attack is less than that of
being struck by lightning, but the odds increase immensely
if you deliberately provoke a shark.

Rogue's Gallery of Man-Eaters

Not all sharks eat people. Of 250 species, more or less,
only about a dozen have been caught in the act. But the vil-
lain is not always identified, so others may be added to the
list at any time.

By far the most infamous man-eater, one that seems to
have developed a taste for human flesh, is the swift, powerful white shark *Carcharodon carcharias*. Unquestionably the
most dangerous, aggressive and voracious of all sharks, this
brute has more attacks on people and boats to its credit than
any other species. Its name derives from a dirty-white belly;
its back is grayish, brownish or bluish. The largest specimen
ever caught was 30 feet long, but 12 feet is closer to average
size. In the most famous shark incident recorded in the
United States, an 8½-foot rogue white killed four persons
in ten days off New Jersey, including a ten-year-old boy who
was ripped to death at Matawan Creek, 20 miles from the
ocean. The attacks occurred in July 1916.

Another dangerous pair are the sharp-nosed mako or
bonito sharks, *Isurus oxyrinchus* and *I. glaucus*. Faster than
the whites, they may be the swiftest sharks in the sea. Up
to 12 feet long and 1,200 pounds in weight, they are well-
known for the spectacular habit of hurling this impressive
bulk completely out of the water. Their dark blue-gray or
blue backs have a large dorsal fin, bellies are whitish and
bodies are like a streamlined ellipse with tail lobes of nearly
equal size.

The largest family of man-killers is the appropriately-
named requiem group: tiger, lemon, blue and ground
sharks. Most "typical looking" of the sharks, they have tails
with the upper lobe longer than the lower and, like the

whites and makos, range through all tropical and temperate oceans.

The tiger shark, *Galeocerdo cuvieri,* is the most voracious and common member of this family. There is almost nothing it won't eat from offal to humans. Only small ones, up to five or six feet, have the "tiger" markings, dark brown blotches or stripes on a grayish background. The largest individual ever caught measured 18 feet long, but tigers frequently reach 20 to 30 feet in adventure magazines. They are the most common large species in the Caribbean.

Lemon sharks (*Hypoprion brevirostris*) have a yellowish belly and two back fins about the same size. Strictly inshore inhabitants, they cruise bays, sounds and river mouths from New Jersey to Brazil. Reaching 11 feet in length, these fish have a mean and erratic disposition.

Greedy, streamlined and beautiful, the blue shark (*Prionace glauca*) prefers the open ocean where it is feared by sailors and cursed by whalers. Its slim, graceful body, indigo blue above grading to white below, reaches a length of 30 feet in men's magazines but only 13 feet in nature. Like all sharks, blues seem to feel little pain even when badly injured. Severely wounded, even mutilated, by whalers' cutting spades, individuals have continued to feed on a whale carcass until attacked and eaten by brother sharks. One captured blue was gutted and thrown back into the water. He began feeding immediately and was then recaught on a hook baited with his own intestines.

The oddest looking man-eaters are the hammerhead or bonnet sharks (*Sphyrna*). Their weird T-shaped head resembles a flattened blacksmith's hammer. This unreal-looking creature has nostrils on the outside or "striking" part of the hammer, while its eyes are on the front edge near the nostrils. Such wide spacing gives the beast better vision and allows it to pinpoint the source of a scent more accurately. Hammerheads are often the first to arrive when blood is spilt.

The thresher shark (*Alopias vulpes*) has a peculiar tail instead of a peculiar head. The upper lobe is drawn out into a scythe-shaped extension which may be as long or

Basking
Shark
to 45 ft.

Thresher
to 18 ft.

Hammerhead
to 18½ ft.

Blue Shark
to 12½ ft.

Dogfish
5 ft.

Mako
to 12 ft.

Tiger Shark
to 18 ft.

Sea Turtle

Shark
ft.

Lemon Shark
to 11 ft.

White Shark
to 21 ft.

longer than the rest of the body. (One 14-footer had 7½ feet
of tail.) They swim around a school of fish in tighter and
tighter circles, all the while threshing the water with their
tough, flexible tails. When the frightened fish are herded
into a small, compact group, the threshers attack. The flailing
tail may also stun the fish by loudly slapping the water or
by clubbing them directly. Threshers are as long as 18 feet
and occasionally leap clear out of the water.

Sharks count among their ranks the largest fish in the
ocean: the whale and basking sharks. You might expect these
creatures to be ferocious dragons of the sea, but actually
they are placid, plankton-eaters, and so inoffensive that
swimmers have ridden on their backs. But they have attacked boats when provoked and their enormous size and
power makes them potentially dangerous.

The basking shark *Cetorhinus maximus,* largest fish in
temperate waters, grows to 45 feet in nature and 60 feet in
popular literature. However, 30 feet is a more common size
for these thick-bodied, short-snouted sharks whose long gill
slits cleave their entire flanks and almost meet on the back.
In spring and summer the grayish-brown backs and high
dorsal fins of *C. maximus* can be seen in the open ocean
from North Carolina to Iceland and from California to
Canada. They disappear in autumn to breed, but where
they go no one knows, perhaps to deeper water. It is difficult
to believe such a huge, docile beast could develop the speed
or motivation to fling its four-ton bulk completely out of
the water. Yet this is what they sometimes do. It is an un-
forgettable sight. While in mid-air they twist around, then
all that ponderous mass lands on its side with a thundering
smack that can be heard for miles.

Basking sharks feed by swimming slowly ahead with their
immense mouths agape. As water passes to the gills, small
fishes and plankton become caught in "hairy mats" that
entwine across the gill openings. These fine comblike sieves
are called *gill rakers,* and the big basker simply swallows
food that accumulates on them.

The whale shark (*Rhineodon typus*), the basker's counterpart in tropical waters, feeds the same way. Instead of being

tucked under a short snout, the whale shark's mouth is at the extreme front end of the body for easy feeding. Gentle back and forth swings of the powerful tail propel the rigid body through the water at two to three miles an hour. If the gigantic fish cruised any faster, it would merely push a slug of water ahead of itself instead of filtering as much as 400,000 gallons an hour. Inadvertently, all sorts of unwanted objects find their way into this moving sea cave, including old shoes, driftwood and large fish that follow small fish right into the shark's mouth.

Whale sharks have white to yellow bellies and gray-brown or greenish backs embellished with white or yellow spots and narrow, irregular stripes. There are three peculiar curved ridges running along their back and sides. These lumbering behemoths are so gentle biologists have used these ridges as hand holds while clambering aboard to inspect the beasts. Although repeatedly reported to reach a length of 60 feet or more, 45 feet is considered a maximum by the U.S. Bureau of Commercial Fisheries. Whale sharks generally outweigh baskers, so are more deserving of the title "largest fish in the ocean."

Skates and Rays

A few of the shark's flattened, evil-looking cousins, the skates and rays, appear on lists of dangerous beasts, but generally they are a harmless, inoffensive lot. Although some look formidable and ferocious and others can stab, poison or shock a man, none are known to launch unprovoked attacks on humans.

One that would scare anybody out of the water is the powerful, heavily-armed sawfish, a wicked-looking fellow that commonly reaches a length of 16 feet. Its cartilaginous snout is extended in a long, flat "saw," equipped with sharp scales or denticles which have been enlarged into teeth on both sides. Big species, which can attain a length of 22 feet, may have a saw 6 feet long. This prehistoric-looking creature charges into a school of small fish, swinging its nose sword from side to side and impaling victims on the teeth.

SAWFISH. Sluggish but powerful, this sharklike ray will not attack swimmers unless provoked. Young sawfish make good eating.

They are then rubbed off on the bottom and eaten. The bottom dwelling sawfish also use their serrated snouts to probe the sediments for crabs, scallops, sea urchins and other invertebrate delicacies.

Sawfish have a sharklike shape and swim by sculling with their tails. But because their gills are on the underside of the body, scientists class them as rays, not sharks. Most other rays are more flattened, and their pectoral fins have been broadened and lengthened into "wings" which merge into the head and sides of the body. Skates and rays resemble gigantic butterflies or sea bats more than fish, especially in the way they swim. They create undulating waves that travel smoothly along the margins of their fins from front to back. The curved surfaces of these "wings" push against the water and the ray flows forward in graceful, rippling movements.

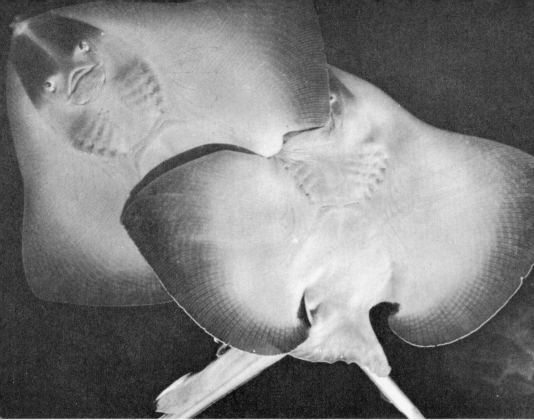

SKATES mating. View of the underside of these "winged" creatures.

When sting rays want to move fast, they flap their wings like birds and "fly" through the water. Eagle and manta rays always swim this way, moving through the water like bats swimming in slow motion.

Skates and rays sacrifice high speed for greater mobility and a more convenient shape for bottom life. Many use their wings to dig into mud and sand after clams, worms and other burrowers. Some swim above more active prey like shrimps and crabs then drop down on them like a living blanket. Their small, often blunt teeth are arranged in pavement fashion for crushing the armor of mollusks and crustaceans. Rounded torpedo rays spring off the bottom in a burst of speed and envelop a fish with their wings. The jaws close on the prey as wings, snout and tail curl around it in a death-hug.

Lying like a rug on the sea floor, resting or waiting to ambush its dinner, a ray's underslung mouth is pressed against the bottom ooze. The animal could not breathe without gulping uncomfortable and gill-damaging sediment were it not for two holes (called spiracles) in the top of its head. Water enters these holes, passes down a short tube to the throat and is forced out the gills on the underside. The five to seven pairs of open gill slits characteristic of sharks were fixed at five in the rays and forced to the underside of the body by the overgrowth of the pectorals. Spiracles are actually gill slits that became displaced when the columns or arches behind the front slits moved forward to become part of the jaws.

Splayed out on the bottom, lying perfectly still, skates and rays are extremely difficult to spot. Pale and patternless on the underside, their backs are dark and often take on a design that blends in with the bottom. In addition, skates and some rays stir up sediment with their wings, letting it fall back and partly bury them. They often while away their days asleep under a thin blanket of sediment. Then at night they rise from their oozy beds and go off in search of food.

Skates and rays are found the world over but, like sharks, the majority live in tropic and subtropic waters. There are some 400 different species, ranging in size from South Sea rays a few inches wide to the giant devilfish which may be 22 feet from wing tip to wing tip.

Electric rays or torpedoes grow from one to six feet in length and weigh up to 200 pounds. Their rounded wings are too thick and heavy for swimming, so most species scull along slowly with their sharklike tails. Located in the wings are two large, bean-shaped "batteries," which weigh as much as nine pounds in a 55-pound animal. These organs contain tubes filled with flat, disc-shaped cells that remind one of the plates in a car battery and function in much the same way. They are modified muscle fibers which exaggerate the ability of all living tissue to generate minute amounts of electricity. During the course of evolution, these cells abandoned their capability to bring about movement and specialized in generation of electricity. The giant Atlantic torpedo, *T. no-*

biliana, can produce a current of 50 amperes at 60 volts, enough to electrocute a large fish or knock down a full-grown man.

The shock, really a series of very short pulses, is used to ward off attacks by predators such as small sharks and conger eels. It is also an excellent device for overcoming such active and faster-moving prey as salmon, flounder, pollack and cod. In an aquarium a 3-foot torpedo was seen to pounce on a 20-inch cod and instruments recorded a strong shock the instant the ray folded its wings over the fish.

The ancient Romans draped torpedoes over the legs and head of people suffering from gout, chronic headaches and even mental illness. The treatment supposedly originated when Emperor Tiberius trod on a torpedo while bathing and discovered that the shock relieved the pain of his gout. Unwittingly, the Romans were using electroshock therapy, a technique that 2,000 years later was to find important applications in "modern" medicine.

Sting rays defend themselves with poison daggers rather than with electricity. All of the barbed spines on their long ratlike tails contain poisonous tissue which is often torn loose and left in a wound. Such spines vary from thorn to

Stingaree
to 14 ft.

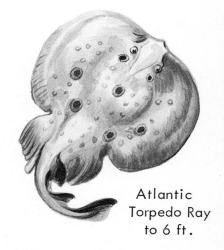

Atlantic
Torpedo Ray
to 6 ft.

sword size, and the ray drives them home by lashing the victim with its whiplike tail. This weapon does not always work. Ray-eating hammerheads have been seen with as many as 54 spines sticking out of their head, jaws and body. without any apparent discomfort.

Humans are not as tough. Stepping on a stinger causes agonizing pain often followed by swelling, inflammation, cramps and, in rare cases, gangrene and death from shock or heart failure. The sting of some small species like the two-foot-wide round rays (*Urolophus*) is as dangerous as that of the much larger rhombic-winged stingarees (*Dasyatis*). Therefore, even the smallest rays should be accorded proper respect.

Eagle rays are armed with one or more poisonous tail spines, but these are too near the body to be wielded effectively. Although normally inoffensive, these powerful beasts are treacherous to handle when hooked or harpooned. One

The graceful SPOTTED EAGLE RAY or LEOPARD RAY attains a maximum wing span of almost 8 feet.

Miami Seaquarium

spotted eagle ray (*Aetobatus narinari*), only five feet in wing span, surprised its attackers by towing them and their 22-foot boat through the water. These rays sometimes leap completely out of the water and ripe females give birth to their living young one at a time while in mid-air.

Why they employ such an unusual and spectacular method of birth is unknown, but the technique must have some advantage because it is also used by the little devilfish *Mobula hypostoma*. In addition, pregnant females of this latter species often leap into the air and forcibly eject their embryos when harpooned. The little devil's big, batlike brothers, the manta rays, jump out of the water, too, not to give birth but to escape enemies, to dislodge fish lice and other parasites and when frightened. John Oliver La Gorce of the National Geographic Society harpooned a 22-foot-wide, 3,000 pound manta (*M. birostris*) that hurled itself out of the water several times. It came down with a roar and splash that he compared to the explosion of a depth charge.

This family of big rays shares the popular name "devil-fish" with octopuses. "Manta" means blanket in Spanish but these rays were christened "devilfish" because of their horns—3- or 4-foot-long fins that project upward and outward from either side of their flat heads. Despite this satanic name, an awesome appearance and villainous roles in magazines and movies, mantas are not predatory or aggressive. The biggest things they eat are small fish. They do not launch unprovoked attacks on humans. However, harpooning a large manta for "sport" can unleash a fury of power that may see small boats dragged under or smashed to splinters by sledge hammer blows of the powerful pectorals. After La Gorce's party sank three harpoons into it off Bahama, the 22-foot devilfish fought for five hours and towed their 25-foot boat, loaded with six men, at *motor speed* for several miles!

Spookfish

In addition to sharks and rays, the phylum of gristle-skeletoned beasts boasts another class, the goblinlike *chimaeras*.

Chimaera

These bizarre creatures have a tapering body, grotesque in shape but beautifully iridescent in color. Most have big eyes and a long ratlike tail which earned them a second name— ratfish. Like rays, they no longer use their tails for propulsion so these have degenerated into long, stringy appendages. Chimaeras are most abundant in cooler, deeper waters along continental slopes. Ranging from about one to six feet in length, they feed on bottom-living invertebrates and swim along the sea floor by flapping fanlike pectorals.

The ghoulish ratfish are remnants of a once numerous and diverse group, some of which were giants compared to modern species. Their lineage goes back 300 million years to what were golden days for gristly fishes. Some paleontologists have suggested that the abundance and variety of sharks and kin in those ancient seas may have been as great as that of the bony fishes in today's oceans. But by 230 million years ago many of these sharklike creatures had become extinct due, perhaps, to overspecialization. At the same time the evolution of bony fishes was continuing in an ever-expanding fashion.

Sharks, however, held their own. Some 150 million years ago the modern species began to appear. They increased in number and variety until, by 50 million years ago, all the presently existing families of gristly fishes had evolved. They have changed little since. The unique solutions sharks have worked out to the problems of survival enabled them to cope with sea-climate changes; variations in food supply; and competition from prehistoric marine reptiles, multitudes of bony fishes and the highly-intelligent mammals. Although not as numerous or advanced as other marine vertebrates, sharks have been around longer and must be considered among the most successful inhabitants of the water world.

9.

Fishes

"Master, I marvel how the fishes live in the sea."
—SHAKESPEARE

SOME 450 million years ago a tiny tadpolelike animal wiggled its muscular tail and freed back-boned creatures from a life of creeping and crawling at the bottom of the sea. This first swimmer gradually added incompressible cells packed with water to its tail and developed a jellylike notochord. As this spine stiffened the little tad began to move more vigorously, if somewhat aimlessly. It grew to a few inches and at some point became encased in a bony armor. A heavy skull and shell-like mail of bony plates or scales were necessary protection against such formidable predators as eight-foot long scorpionlike *eurypterids*. These monstrous "bugs" had oar-like legs and could probably move as fast as the early fish who swam clumsily by lashing their bodies from side to side, much like modern lampreys and hags.

With time, swimming speed increased and one group evolved jaws that enabled them to seize and crush predators and prey. Having such a tremendous advantage, these *placoderms* or "bony skins" grew aggressive and came to dominate the water world. They developed into species rang-

156

There are some 20,000 different kinds of fishes, including the spiny, inflatable PORCUPINE FISH (top left), the swift, voracious BARRACUDA (top right); the slender, needle-nosed GAR FISH, and the bloated, poisonous PUFFER.

ing from minnow-sized, sharklike fishes to 30-foot dread-noughts with enormous armored heads. Before becoming extinct some 250 million years ago, placoderms gave rise to both gristly sharks and bony fishes.

This picture of the origin of fishes is a vague one put together with fossilized fragments of bone and with clues from the structure of living things. Evidence is indirect; interpretations vary. Perhaps sharks arose from species that made the sea their home, while bony fish descended from fresh water ancestors. Some evidence exists that fishes, or at least many species of them, evolved in rivers then later invaded the sea.

From the fossil record we see that fishes underwent a population explosion once they were well established. They evolved in all directions, multiplied and diversified. Today, their numbers are as countless as the stars but their variety is much more dazzling. There are more species of fishes than all other backboned animals combined. The fish you put in a pan, order in a restaurant or match wits with on the week-end comes in 20,000 different forms. Under that lemon butter and parsley lies a truly noble beast, the master of the seas, a creature at the pinnacle of its evolution.

There are torpedo-shaped fish, tube-shaped fish, globular fish, flat fish and fish whose shape defies description. They range from half-inch gobies to 45-foot whale sharks. There are fishes that breathe air; that fly, walk, talk and even climb trees. The oldest living vertebrates, they have, during their 450 million years of evolution, explored and become adapted to every nook and niche in the vast water world: cold, dark depths; murky, shallow waters; sunlit open seas; cavernous coral reefs; rushing streams, and stagnant pools. In fact, the evolution of fishes is a history of adjustment to new sur-roundings and modification for different modes of life.

Some bony piscians like tuna have evolved into the swiftest, most advanced fish in the sea; others like the sturgeons have remained much like their ancestors. These primitive, shark-like fish, whose eggs we eat as caviar have changed little in 350 million years. "Sturgeon" comes from a German word meaning "to rummage around." This they do with four feelers, or barbels, hanging from the lower part of their thick lips. Dragged along the sea floor, the tips of these feelers explore sediments for shrimps, crabs, clams and the sea mouse (a bristly worm named *Aphrodite*). When food is touched the small circular mouth shoots downward and sucks in the morsel. On such a diet, the toothless sturgeons attain massive sizes. The great Russian *beluga* of the Black and Caspian Seas, which furnishes most of Europe's caviar, ranges up to 20 feet in length and weighs as much as 3,000 pounds. The white sturgeon (*Acipenser transmontanus*) which ascends rivers from Monterey, California, to Alaska to give birth, reaches 12 feet in length and may weigh over 1,000 pounds. Pollution and overfishing have reduced United States sturgeon populations to the point where they are stringently protected by law. The rock sturgeon (*A. ful-vescens*), was once so plentiful in the Great Lakes that its caviar was served free at beer parlors. Now it is a luxury, smoked and sold by the quarter-pound.

Suits of Scales

Ancient sturgeons possessed skeletons of strong bone but in modern species this is being replaced by cartilage. The replacement is almost complete, most of the remaining bone being on the outside rather than the inside of their long, slender bodies. Five widely separated rows of bony bucklers run from head to tail. Sharp scutes on the upper part of the sharklike tail are used as weapons and can inflict painful cuts on those who handle sturgeons carelessly. These plates are relics of the days when all fishes wore a complete suit of bony armor made up of close-fitting, diamond-shaped scales connected by flexible joints.

As fishes came to rely more and more on speed and mobility rather than the strength of their armor, the mosaic of heavy plates gave away to thinner, lighter scales. Since about 50 million years ago, most fishes have had slim, flexible scales, overlapping like roof shingles. Imbedded in the inner layers of skin they are, despite their fragile appearance, tough enough to afford good protection.

The vast majority of fishes have scales covered with a layer of skin so thin it is almost invisible. However, some species, like swordfish and many catfish, lack scales and the outer skin of eels is so thick it covers all but the topmost parts of their scales. As opposed to the cumbersome mail that slowed the ancients down and kept them near the bottom, modern scales permit powerful, supple swimming movements and are an adaptation to a life of swift mobility in the upper waters.

Swimming speed is further increased by a layer of mucus or slime which decreases friction between the fish's body and the water, allowing it to slip through the sea more easily. Secreted by invisible glands scattered over the body, this mucus also serves as an antiseptic that prevents speed-robbing and health-endangering growths of bacteria, fungi, etc. Slime and scales combined made a resistant, waterproof covering that prevents the sea from leaking in and body fluids from leaking out.

Scales grow as the fish grows, new material continually being added as a ring around the edges. These rings are more numerous and widely separated in spring and summer when food is abundant and growth rapid. With food scarcer during cold months, growth slows markedly or stops and the rings become fewer and closely spaced. This march of seasons may also be recorded as light (summer) and dark (winter) banding in ear otoliths and certain other bones. As with a tree, each set of bands or rings represents a year's growth, and it is often possible to determine the age of a fish (or tree) by counting sets. Also because scale length is proportional to the length of the fish, the size of the animal at the end of each year can sometimes be ascertained.

In 1953 Canadian biologists counted the concentric fin-bone rings of a 215-pound sturgeon and calculated it had lived to the ripe old age of 152 years. Other long-lived fishes include a 500-pound, 60-year-old halibut and a 55-year-old eel. Large fishes and tortoises probably live longer than any other animals, aging so slowly that most of them die from accidents and illness rather than senility and declining vigor.

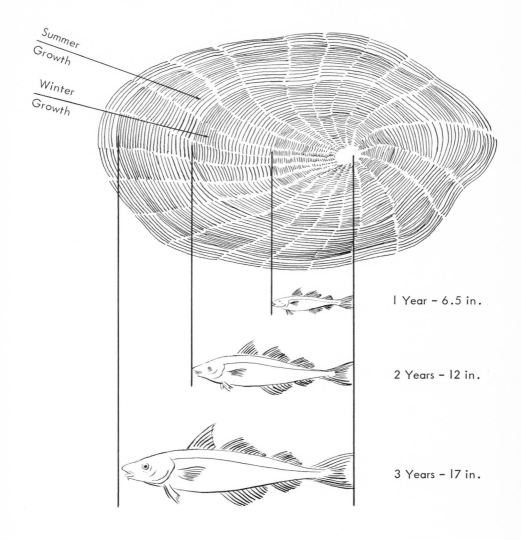

Summer
Growth

Winter
Growth

1 Year – 6.5 in.

2 Years – 12 in.

3 Years – 17 in.

A fish's age and growth history can often be determined from its scales. This 18.5 inch haddock is going on four years old.

Butterfly Brilliance

In the days of bony scales all fish must have looked monotonously alike, their shiny, tilelike scales giving them a uniform polished-ivory look. Fortunately, modern scales are transparent enough to permit the rainbows of color generated in fish skin to show through. The pale, faded bodies in a market give little idea of the beauty of living fish in their natural surroundings. As anyone who has skin dived or gazed through a glass-bottomed boat knows, fishes rival the birds and butterflies in brilliance. Whereas avian finery such as the peacock's pretentious plumage consists of lifeless feathers, piscians parade in living color originating in their body cells.

Red, orange, yellow and black pigments are contained in star-shaped cells which are different in mode of operation from the color sacs of inkfish. Nerves and hormones withdraw this pigment into the center of the cell and it becomes practically invisible, or they spread it into the arms of the star and color is manifested in varying degrees. Like squid, fishes blend their pigments into a tremendous variety of colors and patterns. Piscian ability to change livery, whether instantly or over a period of weeks, is unequalled in the animal kingdom. Most tropical groupers (*Epinephelus*) can change from black to white or scarlet to yellow in an instant, and rapidly switch on and off patterns of spots, stripes or blotches.

Changeable or not, color gives a fish certain advantages in its surroundings, making it less conspicuous for one thing. One of the common tricks of concealment involves harmonizing with the background. Bottom dwellers, particularly flounders, blend into light sand, dark mud, coarse gravel and even checkerboard backgrounds by altering the hues and texture of the marbling on their backs. Numerous plankters, fish larva and some adult fishes imitate the clearness of ocean water with transparent bodies. Near-shore creatures such as sergeant fish, ribbonfish and butterfly fish have bold arrangements of stripes and bars which, like the zigzag paint on old-time warships, breaks up their outline and camouflages their shape.

BUTTERFLY FISH has its conspicuous eyes camouflaged with a masklike band. False eyes near the tail give it the appearance of swimming backward, so when an enemy lunges for its "head" it often comes up with a mouthful of water.

Striking markings and contrasting coloration also provide instant identification. Sharks may not eat the pilotfish that live on their leavings because they recognize the little fish by its conspicuous blue stripes. Species that lead solitary lives scattered among the caves and caverns of coral reefs may recognize relatives and mates by their distinctive body insignia.

Changes in fish complexion are associated with emotion, too. They become pale and flushed much as humans do. Some Siamese fighting fish blaze with red when spoiling for a fight. The bright blue of sailfish becomes much more intense when they fight hook and line for their lives. During the excitement of breeding or to attract a mate some males take on bold and startling colors. The red underbelly of the stickleback has the same appeal to the opposite sex as the splendid plumage of the bird of paradise.

Garish livery may serve warning that the wearer's flesh is obnoxious or poisonous. The replendent hues and bizarre markings of poisonous trunkfish are a good example. The yellowish weaver or viper fish has its poisonous gill covers and dorsal fin spines colored a contrasting midnight black.

One design common to all oceangoing fish is the familiar dark back and light bottom. A silvery or white belly is difficult to see against a sunlit background when enemies and prey look up from below. Likewise, blues and greens on the back blend in with the sea and its dark bottom when viewed from above. When sunlight shines on the back a shadow is cast on the light belly, and this countershading makes a fish appear flattened and uniformly colored like the water. Sunlight turns pigments on the back and sides dark, while the underside remains pallid because it lacks pigments.

This two-toned dress is the "basic black" of the open sea. Far from coasts and the bottom there is no need for loud, flashy clothes and quick changes. Conditions are unvarying and so is the livery. The common herring (*Clupea harengus*) that roams the North Atlantic in teeming schools is always suitably attired in a bluish-greenish "jacket" and dull silver "pants."

Herring and Menhaden

A typical inhabitant of the open sea where a high percentage of all fish species live, the little herring is probably the most abundant fish in near surface waters. *C. harengus* and his Pacific Ocean brother *C. pallasi* travel in immense schools which may be several miles long and wide and contain billions of individuals. At times the sea seems to be packed solidly with their silvery, foot-long bodies.

Its abundance makes the herring family, which includes menhaden and sardines, extremely important in the economy of the sea and the economy of man. Cruising near the surface, herring selectively snap up copepods, pteropods, arrow worms and other plankters. In turn, such predators as cod, mackerel, tuna, sharks, sea birds and whisker-mouth whales eat enough herring each year to fill a freight train long enough to girdle the Earth. Humans catch an estimated 11 billion annually. Together with sardines and menhaden they are one-quarter of man's entire salt water catch.

New England fishermen land about 150 million pounds of herring every year, canning young ones (3 to 5½ inches long) as "sardines." This gentle deception dates from 1875 when Russia was at war and a shrewd Maine packer sold cases of herring to a New York importer as impossible-to-get Russian sardines.

A foot-long, large-headed herring cousin, the menhaden, supports the largest United States fishery in terms of poundage. It is the most abundant fish off the Atlantic coast from Maine to Florida, but its flesh is oily and poor tasting. Menhaden go into the manufacture of such things as fertilizer and fodder, and they are the principal source of oil used as a drying agent in paints and varnishes. This fishery is also the oldest in America, dating from colonial times when the Indians taught the settlers to place a menhaden in each hill of corn for fertilizer.

How a Fish Swims

Like other pelagic fishes (those that swim freely in the open ocean), herring and menhaden are wonderfully streamlined. Fishes are so admirably designed for speed and efficiency, that man has been copying their shape for centuries for his submarines, torpedoes and anything that must move through the water with a minimum of resistance. Since water cannot be compressed a fish must shove it aside in order to move ahead. The animal does this by parting the water with a more or less pointed head, pushing it aside with the bulky portion of its body and letting it flow smoothly along its tapering sides with a minimum of speed-stealing turbulence.

The movement of the animal is mechanically the same as a long rope that has been given a sharp sideways jerk. The

W-shaped segments of flesh you gingerly flake away from the bones of a baked fish are the muscles that do the jerking. Front muscles pull the head to one side then the other. Successive segments contract and relax passing the curve of the body backward and giving it impetus. As soon as the first wave has started back, a second is begun by a twist of the head to the opposite side. Forward thrust is imparted by pressure of the sides against the water in the space between curves. A wide, powerful sweep of the tail culminates the effort and gives an added push.

Small fish attain maximum speed from a standing start in as little as one-twentieth of a second. Such sudden spurts are more important than maintaining high speed because of the need to escape from danger quickly and get the jump on prey. Maximum speed for small fish is about ten times body length per second. In other words, a one-foot trout can swim 10 feet a second or around 6½ miles an hour. Big, muscular fish like yellowfin tuna have been clocked as fast as 45 miles an hour. The wahoo, a distant cousin of the tuna and a real feisty game fish, holds the record: 48 miles an hour.

Finny Finery

Fishes use their fins, which vary widely in placement and shape, to assist them in swimming, maneuvering and balance. The number of median or vertical fins is variable, but generally a fish has one or two back (dorsal) fins and one belly (anal) fin. In addition there are tail fins which smooth out swimming movements; a fish with an injured tail may swim like a drunk walks. The two sets of paired side fins function for balancing, braking and steering.

Species possessing thick, inflexible scales often use their fins for locomotion and their tails for steering. The incredible little sea horse, which is covered with a hard-jointed armor, swims vertically by waving its fanlike dorsal fin so fast you can hardly see it move. Brightly colored parrotfish and the boxlike trunkfish row themselves along with their pectorals. Armored trunkfish lash their tails from side to side or use dorsal and anal fins.

Less advanced piscians like herring, tarpon and salmon have their paired pelvic or ventral fins placed in a "hip" position. The more advanced mackerel, tuna and perches have them in a "shoulder" position, under or even ahead of the pectorals which are placed high on the sides. This is the best location for steering and quick maneuvering. Slower-moving fish, which use their paired fins for rowing, have paddle or spatula-shaped limbs and square cut or round tails. Swift species like tuna, which use their side fins for wheeling and rapid turns, have long, sickle-shaped fins and deeply forked tails.

Fishes such as herring and salmon have soft fins, that is folds of skin supported by pliable rays. You can pick one up without fear of a painful stab. But the stiff, needlelike fin rays of the more advanced mackerel and perch can cut to the bone. Such spines provide greater rigidity, increasing the efficiency of steering and control. They also make things

Four REMORAS hitch a ride on a big lemon shark, while jack crevalles swim below.

Marineland of Florida

unpleasant for predators and prey. An unwary glutton that gulps a triggerfish may find itself in serious difficulty if the trigger erects its first dorsal spine. The bizarre reef-dwelling lionfish *Pterois volitans* has 18 spines loaded with a venom so powerful a large dose can be lethal to a man. The belligerent scorpionfish, as poisonous as they are ugly, attained national notoriety when one of them "stung" astronaut/aquanaut Scott Carpenter as he worked in 205 feet of water off La Jolla, California.

The sea robin and some angler fish walk along the bottom on their leglike pectorals. The dorsal fin of remoras has been converted into an oval adhesive sucker on the upper side of the head. These living fish hooks attach themselves to sharks, whales, sea turtles and boats, hitching a protective ride from one feeding area to another. The fleshy, branching fins and knobby body protuberances of the golden-brown sargassum

ZEBRA FISH has long, feathery fins that imitate the coral growths among which it lives. Its spines are loaded with powerful poison.

Marineland of Florida

fish so faithfully duplicate the appearance of its seaweed habitat that the fish is almost invisible. High speed and vibrations of its peculiar tail fin launch a flying fish out of the water. It then glides (it does not fly) for as much as 1,000 feet on its winglike pectorals. Such soaring flights, on which speeds as great as 30 miles per hour may be attained, are made to outdistance fleet predators like dolphin fish and sea breams.

Buoyancy and Breathing

Salmon and trout have two dorsal fins: a soft-rayed one and behind it a small, fatty flap without support. Called an *adipose,* the latter can be used to help clear up some of the confusion surrounding the word "trout." In salt water the only *true* trout (*Salmo*) is the black-spotted *Salmo salar,* popularly known as the Atlantic salmon or "Salmo the leaper." *Sea* trout are an oceangoing group of large, tasty schooling fishes which includes the weakfish (alias squeteague), sea drum, corbina, and totuava; all lack the adipose, have spiny fins and under-the-chin ventrals.

All *true* salmon live in the North Pacific. This group, known as *Oncorhynchus* or "hook noses," includes Pacific steelhead trout, king or chinook salmon, silver or coho salmon, pink salmon, chums, and red or sockeye salmon.

All salmon and most trout that can find a clear passage to the sea are *anadromous,* meaning they are .born in fresh water, emigrate to the sea to mature then return to their birthplace to spawn. Pacific salmon spawn once and die. Most *Salmo salars* and steelhead trout also die after giving birth, but a small percentage live to spawn two, three, or in rare cases, more times.

The ability of fish like salmon to go from heavy salt water to light fresh water without sinking or being forced toward the surface is usually taken for granted. But in order to maintain their depth such fishes must swim constantly, like humans, or be equipped with gas-filled swim bladders. This bladder, which is between the stomach and backbone, is filled with a lightweight gas and works something like a balloon. When the fish swims to a lower level increased pressure squeezes the chamber, shrinking it and making the fish heavier; when it swims upward decreased pressure permits the bladder to expand and the fish becomes lighter. The animal adds or removes gas until it weighs the same as the water at the depth it wants to be. This enables a salmon, for instance, to hang motionless at the surface for hours, taking food drifting downstream with the currents. Without the gas bladder it would sink because its bones and flesh are heavier than water. As zoologist Uhl Lanham says, the swim bladder "transforms a heavy mass of flesh and bone into a weightless craft that soars in the water." Do not get the impression fishes actively raise and lower themselves by filling and dumping their bladders as a submarine would use its ballast tanks. Rather the float is a passive device which responds, over a period of days rather than seconds, to changes in pressure.

Most bottom dwellers have lost their bladders through lack of use, or need, for such an organ. Some deep swimmers carry gas at such high pressures a tank of thick steel would be needed to hold it at the surface. These creatures do not disappear in a popping explosion because the tremendous pressure of the sea at those depths squeezes inward with an equal and opposite force. If such a fish comes up or is brought up too fast, it cannot get rid of the gas as fast as the external pressure drops. This causes the bladder to swell and crush internal organs or force the creature's stomach out of its mouth. Cod, whiting and hake trawled up from only 125 feet almost always arrive at the surface dead.

Most people think of fish as swimming freely from one depth to another when in fact they may be restricted to a relatively narrow vertical range by their ability to gas up and degas. Should a piscian wander carelessly from the depth zone to which it is adapted, it may explode into oblivion, suffer the cruel fate of having its innards ruptured or "fall" belly upward to the surface.

Bladder gas is a mixture of oxygen and nitrogen, sometimes in much the same proportion as in air. This gas is

The eyes of this BLACK JEWFISH (*Garrupa nigrita*) are literally popping out of its head because it was hauled suddenly to the surface from a depth of 500 feet.

taken out of solution in the water by gills during the normal course of breathing, and is carried to the bladder by blood.

You can get a good look at a fish's gills by raising the flat, bony cover plates on either side of its "neck." You then see overlapping, fan-shaped rows of red skin folds attached to bones between the gill openings. The red color is imparted by a multitude of minuscule blood vessels covered by ultra-thin membranes. These membranes allow oxygen, but not water, to pass into the blood circulating through the gills. At the same time waste carbon dioxide, but not blood, can diffuse out into the sea. In other words, gills function in much the same way as our lungs.

Fishes pump water through their gills by alternate flattening and bulging movements of the gill covers. After giving up oxygen to the blood and picking up carbon dioxide, water flows out past the covers. It is kept from backing up by flaps of skin that act as check valves.

Sometimes smaller animals come into its mouth with the water, and the fish suffocates when these stick in the gill openings. In one case, a native pearl diver in northern Australian waters was swallowed by a giant sea bass (*Promicrops lanceolatus*). This species reaches a weight of 1,200 pounds and a length of 12 feet. Miraculously, the diver escaped by swimming out the gill openings. In a similar incident off Key West, a big bass, or jewfish, swallowed a skin diver head first down to the waist. After receiving numerous nibbling cuts, the diver got away by stabbing the jewfish with his knife.

Man has for centuries dreamed of living under the sea by breathing like a fish. In July 1964, four U.S. Navy divers on Project Sealab spent 11 days living in and working around a 40-foot-long steel chamber placed on the sea floor off Bermuda. One of them, Lt. Comdr. Robert Thompson, became so accustomed to living at the 192-foot depths he dreamed he could "breathe water." "My dreams," he said, "were so realistic that I woke up each morning thinking I was going to try it." One day, while lolling on a coral reef, he was tempted to pull off his face mask and start breathing. Fortunately, he resisted.

Later that year Thompson's dream came closer to reality when Dr. Walter L. Robb, a chemical engineer, developed an artificial gill which enabled a hamster to breathe underwater. The gill consists of an exceedingly thin (.001 inch) rubbery membrane. It was stretched over a frame to form the sides of a cage submerged in seawater. The gossamerlike membrane allowed molecules of oxygen and nitrogen in the water to seep in fast enough to keep the little rodent alive and comfortable. Without interfering with these incoming gases, exhaled carbon dioxide passed out rapidly enough to prevent suffocation. Water molecules seeped in too, but at a much, much slower rate than the gases. Salts in the water did not get across the gill because their molecules are too big, so the water was fresh. While munching his food and

riding his little exercise wheel the hamster, although completely submerged in sea water, had "air" to breathe and
fresh water to sip.

This successful experiment immediately brings to mind
fabulous and far-reaching applications. One imaginative
newspaper editorial heralded artificial gills as a solution
to the population problem and envisioned "a new suburbia
beneath the waves." But before that happens problems must
be solved. Besides the obvious ones of feeding and waste
disposal, a 170-pound man needs much more oxygen than
a 3-ounce hamster, or even a 170-pound fish. One way of
getting it to him is by way of a much larger membrane. Dr.
Robb and his colleagues are now trying to fold some 60 square
feet of ultra-thin silicone rubber into a compact portable gill
that may hasten the day when men will spend much of their
lives beneath the sea.

10.
From Talking Fish
to Living Fossils

"This is beyond me, this fish.
His God stands outside my God."—D. H. LAWRENCE

THE sea has traditionally been synonymous with silence. Novelists delight in such phrases as "the stillness of the grave," and poets love to brood over "the silent sea."

But more practical people like fishermen and sailors have long been aware that a bedlam of sound exists under the insulating roof of the ocean surface. Malayan natives dip their heads underwater to listen for fish "honks" before casting their nets. Fishermen working the Yellow and China Seas in thin-hulled boats are kept awake at night by sounds like "wind blowing through fields of bamboo." South Sea Islanders and West Africans have long listened to the sea with their ears against the handle of an oar.

During World War II navymen used sensitive electronic ears to listen for enemy submarines. They heard a pandemonium of weird and baffling noises, sounds likened to rattling chains, rumbling generators, cackling hens, and children at play. In 1942, hydrophones (underwater microphones) strung across the entrance to Chesapeake Bay picked up mysterious sounds described as similar to "jack hammers

174

tearing up a concrete sidewalk." The U.S. Navy threw up its hands in horror when it discovered underwater noises loud enough to explode acoustic mines.

After the war underwater detective work was begun to determine the sources of these baffling sounds. Obviously, animals were responsible, but which animals and why? Scientist investigators auditioned, watched and photographed hundreds of sea beasts ranging from shrimp to sea robins, puffers to porpoises. The results have convinced at least one Navy sherlock that fish "talk" to each other. Mrs. Marie Poland Fish, a super-sleuth at the University of Rhode Island who has been on the job 18 years, says each species has a characteristic "voice." With experience you can identify a fish by its sounds just as you recognize a familiar voice on the telephone.

"Tropical and subtropical species are more talkative than those living in colder waters," says the affable Mrs. Fish. "Warm inshore waters are noisiest, and all creatures are most loquacious during mating season."

Her husband, Dr. Charles Fish, and his colleagues discovered that honks and toots loud enough to set off sound mines came from male toadfish (*Opsanus tau*) calling to females during mating season. One of the most sonorous creatures in shallow waters from Maine to Cuba, male toadfish also emit a nasty, raucous growl when disturbed while guarding their nests.

The fish that caused all the confusion in Chesapeake Bay was the croaker *Micropogon undulatus*. When a single croaker calls its mate, it sounds like rapid knocking on a hollow log. But when 300 to 400 million of them come into Chesapeake Bay to spawn during May and June, they create such a din World War II sonarmen thought the enemy was jamming their submarine listening devices. There are some 150 species of croakers and their "evening choruses" can be heard in warm seas the world over.

Only a few fish indulge in what could loosely be called conversation. Most sound off when feeding, fighting or frightened, when irritated or congregating, or when trying to find their way. Like humans they exclaim involuntarily

Sailfish

Herring

Mackerel

Sturgeon

Swordfish

Bluefin Tuna

Salmon

when startled, or in times of sorrow or distress. Under duress the huge ocean sunfish *Mola mola,* which attains a weight of 2,000 pounds, gnashes its teeth and emits piglike grunts. Under attack sea robins and toadfish growl viciously, and the porcupine fish emits a grating whine that is as frightening to some enemies as its armament of sharp spines. If you capture one fish of a school, it may "shout" a warning that will cause the others to flee. Nocturnal fishes and those that live in murky waters, like marine catfish, possibly find their mates by sound.

Squirrelfish and parrotfish grind teeth in the back of their throats, and the sounds are amplified into a rasping grunt by resonating in the adjacent air bladder. Other fishes including toadfish, croakers and sea robins produce groans and growls by using their bladders like the sounding board of a bass fiddle. The "strings" they pluck are muscle fibers outside of, or embedded in, the bladder walls. Contraction and

Croaker

Sea
Catfish

Sea
Robin

Toad Fish

relaxation of the muscles sets the bladder vibrating. Several researchers report that some triggerfish have a taut, drum-like section of bladder wall exposed beneath the pectorals, and use their fins rays like drumsticks to produce a rhythmical rolling sound. The "musical voice" of the American eel, which resembles a faint mouse squeak, is produced by burping gas from the bladder.

Some fish produce sound continually and for no apparent reason. The garrulous sea robin grunts and cackles to itself when alone or in company. If you stroke a tame one gently it will cluck softly, but when handled roughly it cackles angrily like a wet hen.

A Sixth Sense

There would be no point in making sounds if they could not be heard. Fishes have neither outer "trumpets" nor eardrums, but the thick bones of their skulls are excellent sound conductors. Sound travels farther and faster in water than in air and its vibrations are conducted through these bones to the inner ears. Herring and trout have air bladder extensions intimately connected with their inner ears and this serves as a hearing aid by amplifying the vibrations.

The inner ears also maintain balance and equilibrium, in the same way as in humans. When its inner ears are removed surgically, a fish loses its sense of balance but still responds to low pitched sounds. These it hears and feels through the lateral line. The sound is felt in much the same way we would feel it by putting our hand on a guitar or piano while it is being played.

In all the animal kingdom only fishes and a few amphibians possess this highly developed sixth sense. With it both bony fishes and sharks detect the movements of enemies and prey too far away to see. A mucus-filled canal runs the length of the body on either side and branches over the head and face. Lying just below the skin these canals are sometimes visible as a dark line extending from head to tail. Short passages or pores pierce scales and connect the canals with the outside. Movements in the surrounding sea set up waves or pressure changes that impinge on the lateral line and cause motion in the mucus. This motion displaces hairs connected to the brain through nerves and clusters of sensory cells.

If fish detect vibrations generated by other animals it seems logical to assume they can pick up their own vibrations. Waves created as a fish swims along strike objects in their path and presumably are reflected back to the lateral line. If fishes sense and get information from these reflected waves, it would account for their ability to dart rapidly around obstacles in dark and murky waters and home-in unerringly on small crevices hidden among the rocks. Some scientists speculate that fishes may be able to use the sounds they make in this way, that is to estimate the distance to an object or to the sea floor by measuring the time it takes the sound to echo back to their ears or lateral line.

In addition, the lateral line gives fishes information about the speed and direction of currents, and changes in depth

Marineland of Florida

Schooling SNAPPERS.

are probably sensed as changes in pressure. Sensations along its sides may also aid an individual in keeping its position in a moving school. Some 2,000 seagoing species travel in schools, probably choosing to congregate for the same reasons people do. Most predators regard a school of fish or a community of people as a single large organism not as amenable to attack as a small individual or straggler.

Each fish remains parallel to its schoolmates with virtually equal spacing between pupils. All move ahead, turn or flee as a single coordinated unit. Millions of individuals may move as if they were a single huge creature controlled by one brain. How fish do this, science does not know. Laboratory experiments show that young fry are attracted to each other by sight, and as they grow older pairs of fry join together in increasing numbers. The visual cues they use may be color or movement or both. A number of fish have been shown to have good color vision, and piscian eye structure indicates they perceive motion easily. But sight is not the whole story because some schools stay together at night. Another sense seems required to maintain parallel alignment and fish-to-fish distance. This could very well be the lateral line.

Do Fish Sleep?

According to its eye structure a fish's view of the world must be a hazy, nearsighted one. Hazy because even the clearest water is much less transparent than air. This limits the amount of available light, and it is rarely possible to see more than 100 feet. Nearsightedness is an adjustment to this limited visibility. By contrast, humans are hopelessly farsighted under water without goggles or a face mask. With such equipment a man can see smaller objects than some tuna or skipjacks can see at the same distance.

Fish need no eyelids and they never cry. The sea, constantly bathing their orbs and keeping them free of foreign matter, serves the same purpose as lids and tears. People often ask: if fishes cannot close their eyes, do they sleep? They can sleep just as well with their eyes open as humans do with their ears open. Some snooze suspended in the water, others rest on the bottom and some even climb into the sea bed and pull a blanket of sediment over their heads.

Eyes on the side of the head give fishes the advantage of being able to see in more than one direction at once. But objects off to the side appear flat, as they would on a movie screen. A fish gets no sense of 3D or perspective except in the narrow zone ahead where both eyes view the same object together. If an interesting object is spotted off to the side, the fish whirls around to face it so distance can be judged.

Fishes cannot see very much of what goes on above the surface. In addition, bending of light rays going from air to water makes small objects like insects and lures appear to be where they are not. Despite this the small, silvery archer fish *Toxotes* can, without surfacing, spit a stream of water as much as three feet and knock flies and other tasty insects into the water.

Fishes also smell, taste and touch. Although most species can find a meal by smell alone, few have as keen a nose as sharks. It is widely believed that salmon recognize their native stream among innumerable other tributaries by its characteristic aroma.

Fishes do not have very refined tastes. Most simply bite and swallow, or gulp prey whole, without attention to gustatory niceties. One flavor they probably never savor is sweetness because there are few sweet things in the sea. However, they probably can appreciate bitter, sour and salt food. Besides using their immovable tongues, which all species do not possess, various fishes have taste buds on the lips, feelers, head, tail or scattered over the whole body.

Most fishes touch with the entire surface of their skin as we do. Free nerve endings are scattered over their bodies particularly on the head, lips and chin. But fishes also touch at a distance by means of the lateral line system.

Experiments are now being conducted to determine if humans can learn to communicate through their sense of touch. The experiments have demonstrated that people can, in a limited way, interpret sound vibrations from speech that have been transmitted as vibrations against their skin.

Through use, such an ability might be developed to the point where it would be extremely useful to the blind, deaf and mute and to astronauts, pilots and others who must see and hear many things simultaneously.

Shock and Pain

As strange as the lateral line may be to us, an even more alien sense was recently discovered in the 500 or so fishes able to generate appreciable amounts of electricity. The electric eel (*Electrophorus*) of South American waters, which really isn't an eel, puts out as much as 500 volts. This is enough "juice" to knock down a mule or light a small electric sign. Its generating organs have the same structure as those of the electric ray, but the shocking strength is much

The GREEN MORAY EEL is nonelectric and nonpoisonous, but it has a pugnacious disposition and powerful, tooth-filled jaws. Averaging 3 feet in length it ambushes fishes and crustaceans from holes in reefs. Morays have killed swimmers who torment them.

Miami Seaquarium

greater. As in the rays, such shocks repel enemies and stun prey.

But electric fishes also generate weaker currents that they use much as we do radar (radio detection and ranging). *Electrophorus* produces low energy pulses that flow outward in all directions. Anything nearby, fixed or in motion, affects the flow pattern since it conducts electricity differently from water. A fish that detects such changes may learn enough about its surroundings to avoid enemies and obstacles and find a meal. Creatures like *Electrophorus,* sea lampreys, knifefish and some freshwater species can and do detect such changes.

If fish sense such tiny variations in electric gradient, they may be able to use their galvanic powers to communicate with one another. Japanese researchers have found that some electric fishes respond to pulses from other individuals by changing the character of their own discharge. Thus, it is easy to imagine two eels signaling one another via some sort of crude, self-generated Morse code.

When the renowned German naturalist Baron Alexander von Humboldt stepped on an electric eel he complained of being "affected the rest of the day with a violent pain in the knees and in almost every joint." Do fishes feel such pain? Of course no one knows for sure, but all observations indicate they do not feel it as keenly as humans. Pain is both physical and psychological. In humans physical pain is produced in the cortex of the brain as a result of stimulation conveyed to it by sensory nerves. The fish has no cortex and no other structure comparable to it.

There is a much told story about a man who hooked a fish in the eye. When he removed the hook the eye came out too. The fellow threw the fish back in, then decided to see what kind of bait the eye would make. Almost as soon as his line hit the water there was a fish on the hook. When the fisherman examined it he found, to his amazement, that it was the same one-eyed creature he had thrown back. Evidently the fish had little psychological or emotional impression of pain and the physical pain was not great enough to prevent it from feeding.

The lower an animal is on the evolutionary scale the more stimulation is required before a pain reaction becomes obvious. This may be either because the creatures do not feel pain or they are incapable of expressing it in human terms. If every fish let out a piercing scream when hooked, fishing would be a horribly nerve-wracking experience.

"Living Meteors"

The largest, most advanced, most varied division of fishes in the sea are the spiny fins. Very likely the last of the main orders to evolve, these creatures are swift, colorful and complex, both in form and behavior. Their fins, supported by strong, needlelike spines instead of soft rays, give the group its name. Usually the forward dorsal is spiny, the after one soft. The ventrals are in the shoulder position. Often they possess advanced air bladders in which the amount of gas can be precisely regulated. But the group is so varied that any species may have only one or none of these characteristics.

The bulk of the spiny fins belong to two categories: mackerel-like fishes (tunas, jacks, bluefish, etc.) and perch-like fishes (sea bass, groupers, snappers, grunts, etc.). The former roam the open ocean, while the latter are the principal group of inshore predators. Spiny fins also include hake, whiting and cod—schooling fishes that live in deep, cold water—and flounders, halibuts and soles.

Mackerel-type fishes include the best swimmers in the World Ocean. This voracious, highly predaceous tribe consists of about 60 different kinds of mackerels and tunas together with marlins and swordfish. Many travel great distances between feeding and breeding grounds. Most present an appearance of power, streamlined swiftness and beauty. Often their flanks and bellies are silvery or iridescent and their backs are a rich blue-green. Always game for a good fight, they are the most thrilling fish in the sea to catch or watch.

Thoroughly adapted to quick and constant movement, mackerels and tunas sink or suffocate if they stop swim-

ming. Their small bladders cannot support their motionless
weight and water must continually rush over the gills to
supply them with enough oxygen for breathing. Constant
use of their muscles keeps the tunas' body temperature six
to eight degrees higher than the surrounding water.

When not hunting, tunas, which are large mackerel, swim
along just fast enough to ventilate their gills and obtain
enough lift on their pectorals to maintain a desired depth.
At the smell, sight or sound of food they quickly accelerate.
Yellowfin tuna may attain speeds of 45 miles an hour. At
such a pace the saberlike pectorals fold back into shallow
grooves to increase streamlining. The deeply forked, bone-
hard tail, shaped like a new moon, drives them through the
sea by rapid side to side strokes while the rest of the body
remains fairly rigid.

These "living meteors" are not only the swiftest creatures
in the sea, they are among the largest of the bony fish. The
bluefin variety (*Thunnus thynnus*) reaches a size of 14 feet
and 1,600 pounds. As sporting fish, bluefins are sought the
world over. Fishermen have struggled for more than 12
hours to bring one to gaff.

For many years American tuna clippers chased these tigers
of the sea from southern California to far below the equator.
Now modern purse seiners fish with immense nylon nets,
largely off Central and northern South America, scooping
up yellowfin, skipjack, albacore, bluefin and the tuna-like
bonito. United States fishermen land about 300 million
pounds annually, more than any other food fish. This catch
fills 17 million cases of canned tuna a year and its $200
million value is exceeded only by shrimp and salmon.

Tunas count among their cousins swordfish, sailfish and
marlin. The brawny swordfish (*Xiphias gladius*) have a reputation for driving their sharp, flat swords through the hulls
of boats. In November 1962, one pierced the bottom of a
39-foot Japanese tuna trawler, and the vessel sank despite
a day-long fight by 15 crewmen to keep her afloat. Whether
such attacks demonstrate ferocity or stupidity is not known,
but when one of them slashes into a school of mackerel or
menhaden there can be no doubt about its motives. Inhab-

itants of all warm seas, swordfish reach 2,200 pounds in weight and 18½ feet in length, one-third of which may be accounted for by the sword. Some authorities list them as the largest bony fish.

BABY SAILFISH, 1½ inches long, was netted by University of Miami scientists in the Sargasso Sea. They also caught the world's smallest marlin (⅛ inch) between Bermuda and the Bahamas in what is believed to be the breeding grounds of these great game fish.

Instead of having their upper jaws drawn out into broad, flat swords, marlin and sailfish have bills rounded like a spear or marlinspike. This bill is used as a billy to beat prey senseless. These two close relatives look alike except for the graceful dorsal fin that gives the sailfish its name. The purpose of this living sail remains another mystery of the marine world. It folds into a back slot when the sailfish is traveling but is fully erected during a fight. There are few sea sights more exciting than a sailfish leaping repeatedly out of the water to shake a hook from its jaws . . . unless it is a huge marlin "walking" on its tail 40 or more times during a four- or five-hour battle.

The largest fish of any kind ever taken on a rod or reel was a 14½-foot, 1,560-pound black marlin caught off Peru on August 4, 1953. Filmed scenes from the one-hour 45 minute, 49-jump battle were dubbed into the movie *The Old Man and the Sea*. Because the flesh of marlin and sails is too unpalatable to support a commercial fishery, scientists rely mostly on sportsmen for specimens and frequently time their research to coincide with fishing tournaments.

STRIPED MARLIN, found only in the Pacific, reaches a weight of over 400 pounds and a probable length of 14 feet.

Dentures and Diet

Although their appearance and diet lead you to expect otherwise, swordfish are toothless. As do most fish, they swallow their victims whole. Marlin have teeth but, like many toothed species, use them only for holding prey not for chewing.

Environment and evolution have shaped teeth, jaws and mouth so that they reflect what the fish eats and where. Some species have scalpel-like dentures for cutting and slashing. The fearsome barracuda has long canines for seizing victims and small dagger-edged teeth that slice them up as cleanly as a fishmonger's knife.

Piscians like the weird North Atlantic wolf fish have massive grinding plates in the back of their mouths for crushing armored mollusks and crustaceans. The gaily-colored parrotfish are among the few species that chew; some grind seaweed with throat teeth like a cow chewing its cud, others have dentures fused into tough beaks for snipping off the rocklike cocoons of coral polyps. Sea horses, pipefish and others have their mouths drawn out into a tube which works like a syringe, rapidly sucking in small prey.

Plankton-eating schools of Atlantic mackerel (*Scomber scombrus*), herring, anchovetas, capelin and many others

SEA HORSE'S tubelike mouth sucks in water and small animals.
Miami Seaquarium

strain food out of the sea in the same way as mammoth whale and basking sharks: comblike rakers on the inside curve of the gill arches collect the incoming plants and animals before they reach and damage the sensitive gill filaments. Muscular movements of the throat then push this food into the gullet and stomach.

Species that feed in open water or at the surface have terminal (front end) mouths, sometimes with the lower jaw longer than the upper. Those eating off the sea floor have longer upper jaws, mouths on the underside of their heads, or suckerlike craws that operate like vacuum cleaners. The swift hake, who cannibalize their younger and weaker brothers, have a diabolical set of dentures. Sharp teeth on elastic hinges bend inward to allow victims easy entrance into the mouth, then they snap back to block the exit with spearlike barbs.

Hake and cod often feed near bottom on mollusks, crustaceans and worms, but they also chase mackerel, herring and squid in upper waters. Cod roam the North Atlantic and North Pacific in vast schools that feed to depths of 1,000 feet. Atlantic cod commonly reach a maximum of 25 pounds and are abundant year around from Cape Cod to Newfoundland. They have been fished in this area by men of many nations since 1504.

New England Groundfish

The cod family includes pollack and haddock. The lustrous greenish-brown pollack or Boston blackfish *(Pollachinus virens)* is caught in November and December when it moves close to the New England shore to spawn. The pollack's cousin—the purplish-gray haddock *(Melanogrammus aeglefinus)*—roots crabs, clams, worms and starfish out of sandy and gravelly bottoms with its leathery lips. These streamlined sea hogs also gorge themselves on herring eggs deposited on the ocean floor. One of the most important food fish in the North Atlantic, haddock is the source of finnan haddie, and in northeastern United States 1½- to 2½-pounders are populárly known as "scrod."

In the New England groundfishery, haddock catches are exceeded in volume only by ocean perch and in value only by lobster. Groundfish are those which live on or near the bottom in cool water. Every year, from the 260,000 square miles of continental shelf between Long Island Sound and Newfoundland, fishermen take about 500 million pounds of haddock, ocean perch, hake, whiting, cod, pollack, porgies, cusk and flounder.

Soles and flounders, together with halibuts, flukes, dabs and turbots, make up the flatfish fraternity, which has some 600 different members. All are beautifully adapted for life on the bottom. Young flatfish swim upright and have an eye on either side of their heads like any normal fish. But soon they begin to lean to one side or the other. At the same time, the eye staring toward bottom moves across the head or through the skull until it lies beside the other orb. The fish spends more and more time on one side, its air bladder disappears, then it settles down on the bottom. The eyeless underside turns pallid, and the topside becomes pigmented to match the ground on which the fish lies. This entire transformation takes place within the first six to twelve weeks of life before the animal is more than an inch long. It repeats the sequence of changes which the ancestors of flatfish underwent during their evolution from upright predecessors, a process which took millions of years.

Most flounders have both eyes on the right side, and their teeth are more highly developed on the left or bottom side. Halibut have right-side eyes, but their uppers and lowers are equally efficient. Most active of the usually sluggish flatfishes, halibut pursue prey all the way to the surface.

These fish stand out for size and prolificacy. A record Pacific halibut (*Hippoglossus stenolepis*) attained 8 feet in length and the tremendous weight of 700 pounds. Individuals heavier than 400 pounds, however, are rare. A single female of this brown-gray species lays as many as 3½ million eggs.

However, even this staggering number is not unusual among seagoing fishes. Female cod regularly carry from 4 to 6 million eggs crowded into their ovaries. Ling, close relatives of the cod, produce between 25 and 30 million eggs.

Silver
Hake
1 lb.

Pollack
4-5 lbs.

Cod
to 25 lbs.
or more

Haddock
3-4 lbs.

Pacific
Halibut
to 400 lbs.
or more

Starry
Flounder
2-5 lbs.

Winter
Flounder
to 5 lbs.

Hog Chocker
Sole
to 6 in.

The enormous ocean sunfish lays as many as 300 million! If all these eggs became fertilized and developed into adults, the World Ocean would be packed with sunfish, cod and halibut in a few years.

But odds on survival are greater than a million to one.

Sex Life

Most common oceangoing food fishes gather at certain times and places to give birth. Females shed their heavy burden of tiny eggs into the water, and about the same time the males release milky clouds of sperm. Each sperm cell wiggles toward a naked egg, a minute tadpole endowed with only a few seconds of life to make its one and only journey. The fertilized eggs, translucent, almost invisible spheres, are deposited on the bottom or float to the surface. Hordes of hungry egg-eaters gulp them by the thousands, and thousands more succumb to unfavorable temperatures, chemistry and currents. Of five million eggs laid by a mother cod fewer than fifty thousand may survive to hatch. Then life for the virtually helpless hatchlings is equally perilous. Herein lies the reason for such prodigious quantities of sex products. It insures the survival of at least two reproducing offspring to keep the species going.

Other fishes and higher animals employ more efficient techniques such as courtship, internal fertilization and nest building. These increase the chances of sex products coming together and of survival of the young. In sharks fertilization is internal, and the eggs of most species hatch in the secure nest of the mother's womb. In addition, many sharks have an arrangement for giving the unborn more food than is supplied by the egg yolk. Only a few seagoing bony fish do this. Some shark embryos receive nourishment from the mother's blood via a placenta not unlike that of humans.

Such advanced methods of getting the young off to a good start guarantee survival of a greater percentage of them. Therefore the number of offspring can be small. Some sharks give birth to as few babies at one time as do humans. Small families become advantageous when enemies are few and survival rate is high. Large populations would soon consume all the available food.

Fishes of streams and lakes engage in nest building activities that rival those of birds. But their pelagic kin rarely exhibit such behavior since there are almost no places to rest a nest in the open ocean. Many inshore fishes utilize reef caverns, rock crevices, shallow bottoms, tin cans, sunken wrecks and other handy shelters for this purpose. Other species have evolved ingenious methods of protection for the young. Spiny catfish males incubate eggs in their mouth, doing without food until they hatch, pipefish entwine in an S-shaped embrace during which the female forces eggs into the male's abdominal pouch.

Sea horses engage in an elaborate courtship dance in which male and female swim round and round each other. At its conclusion, she deposits up to 600 brick-red eggs in his pouch, and father cares for them until they hatch. The pouch is actually a uterus, the eggs being nourished by the male's blood. At the time of birth it is father who must undergo the contractions and pains of labor.

Unmistakable pairing, preparation of nests, collaborative sex acts and care of the young show that fish exhibit instincts and emotions once thought to be confined to higher animals. Male sticklebacks build elaborate nests, change to bright colors and do a complicated zigzag courtship dance to attract females. The male dragonet tenderly supports the female with his fins and the two swim surfaceward together, discharging eggs and milt as they go. Some wrasses engage in a strange "wedding dance" in which male and female advance and retreat in a vertical position, while waving their pectorals and moving their mouths.

Sea Buddies

Most of the 450 different types of wrasse males dress up like brightly colored birds to go a-courting. Some of them also don vivid livery to advertise an important service that they perform for other fish. The late Conrad Limbaugh of Scripps Institution of Oceanography first observed this curious behavior in the 1950's while skin-diving off southern California. He spotted dense clouds of fishes gathered around a golden-brown, cigar-shaped wrasse known as a "senorita" (*Oxyjulis californica*). Upon approaching closer he was fascinated to discover the senorita nibbling copepods, isopods and other parasites from the skin and scales of the clustered fishes.

Limbaugh launched an investigation of this conduct and learned that what he had seen was not an isolated episode. On the contrary, he found that such grooming is "a constant and vital activity that occurs throughout the marine world." No less than twenty-six species of fishes, six shrimps, one worm and one crab clean parasites from "clients" that visit them. These customers benefit by increased comfort and health, and the cleaner has a readily available supply of food.

Dressed in distinctive yellow combined with green, crimson or blue, the Spanish hogfish (*Bodianus rufus*) swims fearlessly into the mouths of barracudas and forages among their dreaded teeth for its bacterial supper. Other wrasses serve as dentists to various groupers, jacks and snappers, nibbling food fragments on and between their teeth. One angelfish, known as *El Barbero* among Mexican fishermen, keeps shop in the Gulf of California and clients come from all over the neighborhood to be barbered. The ill-tempered moray eels sometimes dine on the shrimp that pick parasites out of their mouths.

Such activity is known as *cleaning symbiosis*, the word "symbiosis" meaning "living together." It is an example of one of three types of partnership engaged in by creatures of the sea, the type called *mutualism* wherein both parties benefit and neither gets hurt. Other mutual "buddies" include algae that supply corals in which they live with oxygen and receive food in return. Damselfish or clownfish bring food and victims to anemones in return for shelter among their stinging tentacles. Anemones supply crabs with food in exchange for riding to new food-gathering areas on their backs.

In another type of partnership called *commensalism* or "being at the table together," neither creature gets hurt

but only one derives any real benefit. Pilotfish eat leftovers from the tables of sharks, and remoras obtain free
transportation from them. Sharks tolerate these scroungers
without receiving any obvious advantage in return. Whiting,
haddock and man-o'-war fish shelter among the poisonous
tentacles of jellyfish. Pearlfish find refuge in the anus of sea
cucumbers, and tiny gobies under the gill covers of larger
fish.

Commensalism is a loose and casual relationship, but
over a long period of time it may evolve into *parasitism,* a
third type of togetherness in which one partner lives at the
expense of the other. Competition for food and living space
may press commensal copepods, for instance, to colonize the
surface of an animal with which they "break bread." They
then evolve from temporary pests, like mosquitoes, to permanent parasites. From here the next step is to enter body
cavities and become established in the warm, nourishing
security of the host's blood, partly digested food or internal
tissues.

Like land animals, fishes harbor protozoans, flukes, tape-
worms, roundworms and others in their gullet, gut, gall
bladder, heart, liver, stomach, kidneys, muscles, blood, spleen,
ovaries and testes. They are plagued by fish lice (copepods),
bloodsucking leeches and worms which fix themselves to
body, head, eyes, gills, skin and fins by means of various
suckers, claws and sticky substances. Nearly every fish in the
sea carries at least two or three different kinds of parasites.
Reflecting on the vast number of fishes and the fact that
whales and invertebrates have their share of unwelcome
guests, too, it is startling to realize that there exists a largely
unknown category of life. The number of creatures we see
living freely on land and in the water are far outnumbered
by the invisible legions living on them and tucked away in
their tissues.

Although a few maladjusted and evolutionary new parasites kill their hosts, the motto of the well-entrenched free-
loader is "live and let live." Destroying a host is akin to
killing the goose that lays the golden egg for the parasite
then loses its home and food. Nature works out a balance

between the two, and some of the little pests exhibit some of the most marvelous adaptations in the animal kingdom. Certainly they are creatures in their own right and should not be judged by human standards.

Out of the Past

Parasitism brings home the fact that the struggle for food and living space forces animals, with their high rates of re-production, into every possible nook and cranny that can support life. When such pressures forced the first creature to invade the body of another a giant step was taken into a new, previously unexploited environment. These same fac-tors are involved in a comparable but much more important adventure into new surroundings: the coming ashore of the first vertebrate. Neither of these giant steps was taken all at once. Rather, each consisted of a merging succession of evolutionary "baby steps" taken gradually over millions of years.

When a climatic change about 400 million years ago stagnated and dried many ponds and streams, fishes evolved means of getting to water and of surviving during dry spells. They learned to exist in shallow, stagnant pools first by utilizing the oxygen-rich layer at the surface, then by stick-ing their snouts out and gulping air. Certain fishes do this today. Goldfish may be observed doing it in a cramped or contaminated aquarium. A bubble of air is held in the mouth and its oxygen absorbed through the moist gill mem-branes. The popeyed mudskipper fills a spongy cavity near its gills with gulps of air. It then walks or skips overland on its muscular pectorals in search of food. In times of stress a mudskipper rears up on its tail and springs forward in yard-long leaps.

With the air-gulping habit established, the fishes' oxygen absorbing surface became enlarged by the development of forked outpocketings of the gullet that extended back into the body on either side of the internal organs. This was the origin of lungs.

When climatic conditions improved, a small minority of fishes retained the ability to breathe air. Some of the descendants of these creatures have survived to modern times. The Australian lungfish, which closely resembles its ancestors of 200 million years ago, rises to the surface to breathe air but cannot live out of water. It has relatives that inhabit the swamps and rivers of Africa. Should these dry up the fish burrow into the mud and breathe air through openings to the surface. The African lungfish draws a breath every hour or so and puts its tail over its lidless eyes to prevent loss of body moisture. It can survive in such hibernation for as long as three years. When water again covers the burrow, this remarkable creature "comes to life" and begins breathing through its gills. The South American lungfish hibernates in the same way, existing on a store of orange-colored fat. The gills of this fish are so poorly developed it will drown if held underwater.

Because of their landlubbing ways and air breathing habits, it is easy to imagine lungfishes evolving into the first land dwelling vertebrates. However, they are only poor cousins of the creatures to which this distinction belongs. About 375 million years ago they diverged from the group that became the ancestors of all backboned land animals—

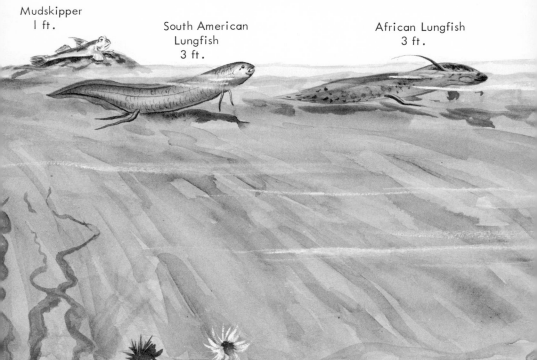

Mudskipper
1 ft.

South American
Lungfish
3 ft.

African Lungfish
3 ft.

the lobe fins or *crossopterygians.*

These were heavy, ungainly beasts with fish-shaped bodies and sharklike tails. They had paired fins consisting of toe-like and leglike bones enclosed in muscles that gave them the appearance of Ping Pong paddles. It is easy to see from this bone arrangement how such limbs could evolve into feet and legs. Formidable predators with great gaping mouths full of sharp teeth, lobe fins dominated the seas of 400 million years ago. About 350 million years before present some of them crawled onto land, venturing into an environment to which they were only partly adapted. With few enemies to plague them, they eventually solved all the problems of survival and went on to sire the ancestors of all backboned creatures from newts to men.

Other lobe fins stayed in the sea. Eventually they gave up their dominant position to sturgeonlike fishes. Later, the ray fins took over. At a point corresponding to 70 million years ago lobe fins suddenly vanish from the fossil record; no trace of them can be found in rocks younger than this. Scientists naturally concluded that lobe-finned fishes became extinct at that time.

But during the 1938 Christmas season some fishermen working off South Africa found a very strange creature among

Australian
Lungfish
4-5 ft.

Coelacanth
5-6 ft.

a net load of fish they brought up from 230 feet beneath the Indian Ocean. It was the size and weight of a small man, between 5 and 6 feet long and 127 pounds. A magnificent metallic blue in color, the fish's bulky body was covered with large, thick scales and it possessed strong paddlelike fins. When the captain bent down to take a closer look a gaping mouth full of sharp teeth snapped at his hand.

No one aboard had ever seen a beast like it. When the boat docked at the port of East London, it was taken to the local museum. Miss Courtenay Latimer, the curator, immediately recognized it as an important find and sent a sketch to the noted ichthyologist Professor J. L. B. Smith. He could hardly believe his eyes; for him the creature in that sketch existed only in museum models and textbooks.

Although only the skin and part of the skull were left by the time Smith saw the animal, he knew at once it was the most important living fish ever discovered. He identified it as a lobe fin that had survived for millions of years hidden hundreds of feet below the surface. It was a *coelacanth,* a seagoing relative of the air-breathing, fresh water lobe fin that came ashore 350 million years ago and established the vertebrate line on land. Smith named it *Latimeria* in honor of the lady curator.

Fourteen years later, in 1952, another coelacanth was brought up from the waters between Africa and Madagascar. Since then, a dozen or more of these living fossils have been found in the same area. Thus ends one of the most dramatic stories in the history of science. In the depths off East Africa man has discovered a living representative of a line long thought to be extinct, a line which includes his direct forebears and ties together the backboned animals of land and sea.

11.
Monsters
in the Deep

*"Under the whelming tide
Visit'st the bottom of the monstrous world."*
—MILTON

WITH the discovery that a living fossil had remained hidden in the sea for 70 million years, an old idea returned to grip the imagination of biologists. Do the dark depths, they wondered, shelter the seagoing equivalent of living dinosaurs and mammoths, beasts long thought to be extinct but actually still dwelling in obscurity in the deep?

This idea gained considerable momentum in the last century. In 1864 Norwegian biologists dredged up a brittle, plantlike sea lily from 1,800 feet, the likes of which had never been seen alive. But the remains of similar creatures could be chiseled and leached from rocks 150 million years old. Less than a half dozen years later a large scarlet sea urchin, of a kind known only from fossils in the 100-million-year-old "white cliffs of Dover," was dredged up from the floor of the Atlantic. Darwin had published his revolutionary theory in 1859, and scientists pictured the depths of the sea as ". . . the safest of all retreats, the secret abysses where the survivors of former geologic periods would be sure to be found."

But except for such rare finds as the coelacanth, sea urchin and sea lily, this expectation has never materialized. The British research ship HMS *Challenger* sailed around the world from 1872 to 1876 and naturalists aboard hopefully searched the deep for living clues to the past. But none were discovered, and expeditions since have found disappointingly few missing links in the depths.

Challenger's crew did, however, bring up a horde of bizarre and fascinating creatures that dispelled once and for all another erroneous theory that plagued marine biology for 20 years. In 1841 Edward Forbes, a well-known English naturalist, concluded that no life could exist below 1,800 feet. He advanced this idea after making the deepest dredgings to date, to 1,380 feet in the eastern Mediterranean. In 1818 and 1839 two rugged countrymen, Sir John Ross and his nephew James Clark Ross, had brought up worms, crustaceans and starfish from depths of 6,300 and 2,400 feet. But the Ross boys were seamen not scientists, and their findings as well as others were overlooked, or discounted on the grounds that the animals were caught by the dredges on the way up. Forbes, on the other hand, was a popular and well-known scientist hailed as a "nineteenth century Aristotle," so his theory became widely accepted.

However, in 1860 an incident occurred that could be neither ignored nor discounted. Some forty miles of cable hauled up from depths of 7,200 feet in the Mediterranean arrived at the surface with corals, squid eggs, oysters, snails and scallops fixed to it. The bases of the corals were moulded exactly to the inequalities of the cable, so they could not have been caught on the way up. Fifteen years later the *Challenger* expedition sounded the final death knell to the idea when 6,600 creatures of every kind were dredged up from depths between 3,000 and 15,000 feet.

Forbes died in 1859 at the age of 39 years, so he never suffered the humiliation of seeing his theory shattered. It may be poetic justice since the brilliant and genial Forbes, the first professional scientist to work exclusively with creatures of the sea, made many pioneering contributions to marine biology during his short life. He also inspired others to do the same. It is ironical that "the father of marine biology," as some call him, should have committed one of the most notable boners in the history of science, but it proves that scientists are people, too.

How Deep Is Life?

The tremendous pressures in the deep sea made Forbes' theory easy to believe. One noted contemporary wrote, ". . . it is almost as difficult to believe that creatures comparable with those . . . in the upper world could live at the bottom of the sea, as they could live in a vacuum or fire." *Challenger* scientists proved that creatures do live at the bottom of the oceans but the question of how far down life can survive remained unanswered for almost 100 years.

In July 1951, the Danish research vessel *Galathea* lowered a large sled trawl 33,000 feet to the bottom of a deep gash in the ocean floor east of the Philippine Islands. *Galathea's* crack crew nudged the ship slowly ahead and the trawl dragged along the bottom for a very long 110 minutes. Then it took more than seven hours to wind the miles of heavy wire back onto the truck-sized winch drum at the stern of the ship. The trawl resembled a huge monster, shapeless and dripping, as it swung over the side. Tubs and trays stood ready as anxious fingers tugged at the lashings on the bag. A mass of grayish clay plopped out, some gravel and rocks, then a rather large stone with small whitish growths on it— sea anemones! Surprise and pleasure turned to excitement as biologists picked out 25 anemones, 75 sea cucumbers, 5 clams and a bristle worm. Subsequent trawls revealed a whole community of animals—polyps, worms, echinoderms, mollusks and crustaceans—living at 33,431 feet.

This amazing discovery pushed the known limits of life 7,500 feet further into the abyss. Eight and a half years later, on January 23, 1960, the limit of life was extended to the bottom of the world. Jacques Piccard and Lt. Don Walsh spotted a solelike fish and a bright-red shrimp from the window of a bathyscaph 35,800 feet under the Pacific Ocean in the Marianas Trench. In the same trench the Russian research ship *Vitiaz* later sounded the deepest part of the World Ocean, 36,200 feet.

The deeper a creature lives the greater the weight of water pressing down on it. A one-foot cube of water weighs over 60 pounds, so man or beast does not have to go very deep to encounter crushing forces. For every 33 feet a fish or skin diver descends the pressure increases almost 15 pounds per square inch. Creatures living at 330 feet must withstand 150 pounds of pressure per square inch of body surface, at 3,300 feet this increases to 1,500 pounds. An organism living in the deepest parts of the ocean, 33,000 to 36,000 feet, has 7½ tons pressing down on every square inch of its body. How can animals survive such forces; what prevents them from being crushed to jelly?

The truth of the matter is, deep dwellers take no more notice of the overlying water than we do of the heavy ocean of air at the bottom of which we live. In both cases living tissues are permeated with fluids and gases at the same pressure as the outside surroundings. The body fluids of marine creatures push outward with the same force as the seawater pushing inward; hence the water pressure is cancelled out and the beast goes about its business unaffected.

Some creatures—certain clams, snails and sea cucumbers, for instance—tolerate enormous differences in pressure and range from shoreline to abyss. One brittle star feels equally at home 15 or 15,000 feet beneath the sea. But such animals are a minority. Most shallow water species suffer irreparable damage when placed under high pressure. Therefore it must be a limiting factor and something to which animals must adapt before they can live in the depths. That shallow and deep animals are fundamentally different has been demonstrated by bacteria dredged up from below 33,000 feet by the *Galathea* Expedition. Dr. Claude E. Zobell of Scripps Institution of Oceanography discovered that these deep-dwelling microbes reproduce more rapidly at the high pressures and low temperatures in which they live than under milder conditions near the surface.

Dr. Jean A. Gross of the Illinois Institute of Technology has conducted experiments which indicate that pressure enables deep-sea plants to live better. It either empowers them to more effectively utilize the dim light available for photosynthesis, or it forces them to "eat" organic scraps instead of making their own food. He envisions deep-sea farms of the future with three or more layers of edible algae growing simultaneously, each species being cultivated at the level it grows best. Says Gross: "A limited marine area, free from radical seasonal changes, might be cultivated in three dimensions . . . yielding great blooms of algae" for human consumption.

Cold Fish

Temperature also restricts the depths to which animals go, but it is difficult to disentangle its effects from those of light. The sun warms the ocean and failure of its rays to penetrate very deep causes temperature to drop with depth. In the open sea, temperature is fairly uniform in the 65 to 1,600-foot-thick layer above the thermocline, drops rapidly in the thermocline zone, then falls slowly to near freezing in the deepest layers. (Officers aboard the *Challenger* used mud dredged up from the Atlantic Ocean floor as a substitute for ice to chill their champagne.) A rich concentration of life exists around the thermocline. The late Dr. Anton F. Bruun, leader of the *Galathea* Expedition, believed this is because warmth-loving creatures are kept from venturing lower by the cold, and deep animals do not ascend above this layer because of higher temperatures and perhaps the stronger light.

Warm waters above the thermocline extend as deep as 1,600 feet in the tropics, just about the depth total darkness would begin for a human eye. But deep-dwelling animals,

especially fishes, probably have more sensitive eyes than we
do and may be able to see objects in what would be total
darkness to us. Photographic plates, much more sensitive
than human eyes and perhaps fish eyes, have detected some
glow as deep as 3,000 feet.

The character of this light changes with depth. Sunshine
(white light) is a combination of different colors, or wave-
lengths. These colors have varying energies, therefore all
do not penetrate to the same level. Red, least energetic, is
absorbed first, followed by orange, yellow, green, then blue.
In bathysphere dives to 2,510 feet, the American naturalist
William Beebe found that nearly all red light disappeared
at about 20 feet. At 50 feet red objects looked deep maroon or
brown, and orange became the dominant color. Continuing
down into the waters south of Bermuda, Beebe and his diving companion Otis Barton discovered that orange was gone
at 150 feet and yellow at 300 feet. Most of the green had
faded at 350 feet. Eight hundred feet down they saw "only
the deepest, blackest-blue imaginable . . . quite unlike anything . . . ever seen in the upper world . . ."

This change of lighting with depth exerts a profound
effect on the appearance of deep dwelling animals. In the
well lit upper waters, down to about 500 feet, a transparent
or two-toned livery is best to help a beast escape notice.
Between 500 and 1,600 feet, in the twilight zone, silvery
fishes predominate. Faint shadows are cast in the dim, bluish
light so counter-shading provides the same survival value as
nearer the surface. Finger-long lantern and hatchet fishes
have silvery, grayish or iridescent bellies and brownish backs.

Living in dimmer light below and coming up to prey on
these fishes are jet black, velvety brown and unshaded silvery
species. Some possess iridescent skins that gleam golden,
copper and greenish. Invertebrates cloaked in deep red,
purple and brown share this night zone below 1,600 feet.
Scarlet shrimps snap up crimson worms and reddish copepods,
bright red jellyfish float gracefully by in the blackness; while
red, violet and black squids dart nervously to and fro in
search of prey. Brown four-inch-long whale fishes with bright
red or orange jaws, and dark dagger-tooth fishes with binoc-

ularlike eyes, dine on these colorful invertebrates.

No one knows why boneless creatures, especially crustaceans, wear such blushing livery while fishes prefer somber blacks and browns. Such colorful attire seems a waste since red rays do not penetrate this far and the beasts appear gray or black to other animals. In his book *Half Mile Down,* Beebe notes that between 20 and 50 feet a large red shrimp he had brought along in a bottle was "no longer scarlet, but a deep black with an orange tone." Thus what would be a gaudy and conspicuous wardrobe in sunlit waters must have a concealing effect in the twilight. But why not just wear brown or black like the fishes?

Twilight Swimmers

Even jellyfish, so colorless or lightly shaded near the surface, don robust reds or chocolate browns in the deep. Some have flaming red stripes on the underside of their bells, others resemble purple water lilies (*Atolla*) or frilly, dark-blue jester's caps (*Periphylla*). *P. periphylla* grows to at least 12 inches across the bell and, as is the case with many deep-sea organisms, younger individuals live above the older ones. *Galathea* scientists brought up numerous jellyfish from as deep as 21,700 feet, including a beautiful brown and violet individual (*Crambionella orsini*) with a delicate paper nautilus attached.

From 12,000 feet down in the China Sea came a beast never before seen by the eyes of man. Looking like an oval pillow, one-foot long and dark violet in color, it was a swimming sea cucumber. Christened *Galatheathuria* in honor of the expedition, this creature soars through the night zone by "flapping" a pillowcaselike fringe running along either side of its body. One of its relatives, also a sea cucumber, looks like a violet octopus and swims mouth upward by means of a tentacled skirt around its lips.

Alongside jellyfish and cucumbers are the ubiquitous copepods, fluttering through the twilight waters in a succession of hopping and sinking movements like swarms of nervous insects. During this jerky dance, their assorted paired limbs twitch constantly in feeding movements. Some are translucent, others are colored yellowish or reddish by globules of oil in their bodies. Further down live red and blackish species, some with feathery arms of brilliant golden or bronze. Like nearly all deep-water plankters, copepods grow larger than their near-surface relatives—up to one-third inch.

Crustaceans are as numerous and important in the deep as in near-surface waters, blood-red shrimps being the most characteristic members of this group. Vivid scarlet giants up to a foot long pounce on small black *Cyclothone* fish like a cat on a mouse. One jumbo shrimp was found with a 2-inch fish filling·its stomach. Unlike their whisker-mouthed vegetarian kin who comb invisible plants out of sunlit waters, deep-living euphausids have teeth and powerful claws to grasp smaller shrimpers, worms, tiny adult fish and fish fry.

Some crustaceans angle for their food. Sleek, powerfully-built Sergestid shrimps have long antennae surprisingly like a rod and line. Some antennae even bristle with curved hooks. A number of biologists, including Sir Alister Hardy, think these shrimp catch prey with the hooked "lines" then pull them toward cruel clawlike spines on their feeding limbs.

For many creatures the most fearsome fishing lines of all are the rubbery arms of a squid or octopus. One group of twilight squids have their enormously long tentacles equipped with sharp, cat-claw hooks and luminescent organs. Weak swimmers, it is believed that they stay in one place and victims are attracted to the lighted tentacles like insects to a lamp. Dressed in sinister cloaks of dark red, black and purple, deep inkfish range in size from Lilliputians an inch long to the terrible giant squid. Whaler Frank Bullen saw in the latter's staring, humanlike eyes, which may be as big as beach balls, "a whole inferno of hatred for everything living." Some species have eyes of different sizes, one as much as four times larger than the other. Dr. Gilbert Voss of the University of Miami suggests the small eye is used in lighted waters while the large one functions in the dim depths.

Inkfish dwelling in the night zone are generally flabby and formless, many having watery tissues and weak muscles

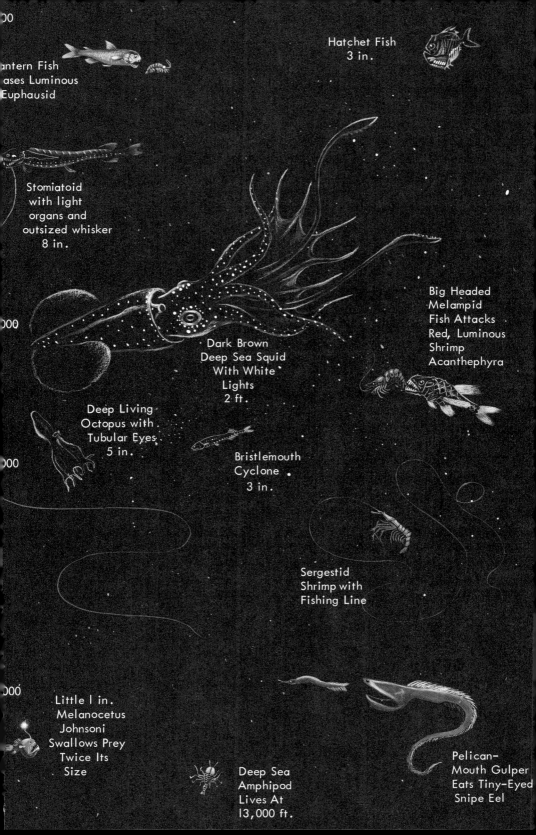

00

Lantern Fish
Chases Luminous
Euphausid

Hatchet Fish
3 in.

Stomiatoid
with light
organs and
outsized whisker
8 in.

000

Big Headed
Melampid
Fish Attacks
Red, Luminous
Shrimp
Acanthephyra

Dark Brown
Deep Sea Squid
With White
Lights
2 ft.

Deep Living
Octopus with
Tubular Eyes
5 in.

Bristlemouth
Cyclone
3 in.

000

Sergestid
Shrimp with
Fishing Line

000

Little 1 in.
Melanocetus
Johnsoni
Swallows Prey
Twice Its
Size

Deep Sea
Amphipod
Lives At
13,000 ft.

Pelican-
Mouth Gulper
Eats Tiny-Eyed
Snipe Eel

invaded by jellylike material. One looks like a dirty floor mop, others resemble jellyfish. Such construction increases buoyancy, allowing the beasts to float at a given level with a minimum of effort. Operating strong muscles and carrying around firm flesh require too much energy with food so scarce in the depths. Sometimes octopuses abandon their dark cloaks for a translucent shift and swim head downward by means of a thin web connecting their flabby arms. This membrane pulses in and out in graceful, fluid motion like a jellyfish bell. It is as if part of the sea had condensed into a pulpy, oozing mass endowed with the spirit of life.

Where darkness is eternal, ink would not hide or confuse, so the ink sacs of deep cephalopods are small or absent. One squid ejects a slimy secretion that turns into a luminous blue cloud when it contacts water. In the blackness this sudden burst of brilliant light has the same effect as a cloud of dark ink in sunlit waters.

Squids have been brought up from at least 11,500 feet. The octopus *Grimpoteuthis* lives 9,000 feet down on the icy bottom of Antarctica's Weddell Sea, the coldest part of the World Ocean. Here in grave-like darkness it slithers over the siliceous "headstones" of billions of diatoms.

In warmer waters from about 3,000 down to 10,000 feet lives a creature described by William Beebe as "a very small but very terrible octopus, black as night, with ivory white jaws and blood red eyes . . . its cupped arms all joined together by an ebony web." Scientists have given it a name as terrible as its appearance—*Vampyroteuthis infernalis*. Neither octopus nor squid, this rare beast is a ten-armed survivor of a once-large band of cephalopods, most of whom disappeared millions of years ago. Two of its arms are long, wormlike feelers which coil up and fit into special pockets. Although this "vampire squid" spends all its life in darkness or the faintest of green light, it has large keen eyes. Perhaps these are used to spot the living lights of other night creatures, such as the small lantern organs scattered over the bodies of many of its inkfish kin.

Roaming the same levels as *V. infernalis* is another antique cephalopod called *Spirula spirula*. In keeping with its tamer name this little squid appears much less ferocious. It has a jarlike body three inches long, including a fringe of short thick arms that dangle straight downward. *Spirula* swims in a head down position and is found along the steep continental slopes of warm ocean basins. Its white and rust body contains a spiral, internal shell divided into chambers filled with gas. *Spirula* probably regulates its depth by varying the amount of gas in the largest chamber. This marine balloonist is the only living member of a tribe that flourished 125 million years ago. One individual was the prize catch of the *Challenger* Expedition, whose scientists anxiously searched every net for a ghost of the past. But, alas, even the best naturalists of that day did not recognize *Spirula's* ancient ancestry.

Great Gulpers

Although "the stuff of which legends are made," vampire squid and other deep cephalopods do not measure up to such gigantic monsters as the two-ton rubber squid that required 24 men to manipulate in the movie *20,000 Leagues Under the Sea.* No vampire squid found was longer than 8½ inches. Giant squid do not spend all their time in the night zone, and those inkfish that do rarely grow longer than two feet.

Although some crustaceans reach, for them, gargantuan size, few deep dwelling fish get very big. This led Prof. C. P. Idyll to comment in his book *Abyss:* "If a group of surrealist artists had engaged in a contest to see which could create the most grotesque and improbable monstrosities, surely they could not have approached the astonishing shapes exhibited by the fishes of the deep ocean. . . . And then having had the audacity to invent such creatures, which of our competing surrealists would have had the imaginativeness to reduce the monsters to diminutive size, making them objects not of awe but of absurdity?"

But small size does not mean small appetite. Equipped with huge mouths and expandable stomachs, somber *gulpers* and *swallowers* living in the gloom below 5,000 feet can devour meals as big or even bigger than themselves. Their jawbones form a system of hinged levers which permit the mouth to gape open like a living cave. The stalactites and stalagmites of these caves are daggerlike teeth, which sometimes bend inward to permit easy entrance of prey. A rubbery stomach at the end of the cavern stretches to several times normal size if necessary. One captured big mouth had a codlike fish in its stomach nine inches long, although its own body was only six inches in length.

Gulpers sometimes attain the comparatively enormous size of six feet but most of this usually consists of ropelike tail. One species wears a red light on its tail which may be used to attract victims. Whether or not it ever happens, it is easy to imagine a creature who comes too close to the light being swiftly lassoed by the tail and passed into the enormous mouth. Another member of this improbable group *Eurypharynx pelecanoides* or "pelican mouth," is a two-foot long, flabby bag of mouth and tail found in all warm oceans. Lacking strong bones and muscles it sinks long, curved teeth into a victim then draws itself over the body like a snake.

The swallowers take even greedier mouthfuls. Toothy, black *Chiasmodus niger* never grows longer than six inches but it gulps fish eight or ten inches in length. One fingerlength individual was found with an eye staring through its grotesquely distended stomach; the eye belonged to a member of its own species that was twice as long as the swallower.

Such eating equipment comes in handy in the depths where meals are few and far between. The diner must accommodate itself to whatever food comes along and the bigger the mouthful the longer hunger pains stay away. Unlike snakes and humans, gulpers do not become sluggish after a big meal. As one zoologist puts it, "quiescence is impossible in the depths," so the search for food must begin again at once.

The eel-like *stomiatoids* form another piscian group characterized by trap-door mouths, runt size and "rubber" stomachs. They include quick-tempered, saber-tooth viper fish, with canines so large they must have difficulty closing their

A grotesque DRAGON FISH (stomiatoid) known as *Chauliodus sloani* pounces on a group of big-headed Melamphid fish. The foot-long dragon can flick the elongated first ray of its dorsal fin forward and use it for angling.

mouths. Black, brown or silvery, and slim of body, stomiatoids are best known for their fleshy whiskers or barbels. These range from cigarette-sized stubs to tapering, whiplike threads as much as ten times longer than the body. Some barbels take the form of a single strand ending in a simple swelling; others branch and rebranch like a miniature tree or bunch of grapes. Any slight stirring of water near these chin feelers will cause the fish to snap viciously and repeatedly. Sometimes barbels end in a lure such as a bright

red tip that resembles a tasty copepod. The sea is full of such
traps for the unwary.

One stomiatoid is probably the most common fish in the
sea, possibly exceeding even the multitudinous herrings,
sardines and menhaden in numbers. Called *Cyclothone
elongata* or "bristlemouth," the minnow-sized fish lives at
mid-depths and is seldom seen by anyone except scientists.
This rapacious creature looks like a "normal" fish except
for its big head and a trap-door mouth full of bristlelike
teeth. If economical deep-water fishing gear could be developed, bristlemouths might be caught and canned like
anchovies. They also might serve as the base of a fish protein
concentrate (fish flour) which would help to alleviate the
cruel grip hunger holds on half the world.

Second place in the deep-fish population poll goes to lantern fish, small, big-eyed piscians that look much like familiar
shallow water species. Most of them live between 300 and
1,600 feet, but many journey to the surface at night to feed.
Here we sometimes get a dramatic idea of their abundance.
One night a British weather ship in the North Atlantic
sailed through a sea of twinkling, leaping lantern fish for
five hours. It must have been a fabulous sight for these fish
take their name from rows of buttonlike lights along their
silvery undersides and on their flanks, head and tail. Some
of the tail lights are so bright you can read by them, others
on the body sparkle like green gems occasionally tinged
yellow or red. Although it may take hundreds to make a
pound, each has as many as 100 lights on its body. Everyone
of the 170 or so species has a distinct arrangement of lights
and Beebe claimed that ". . . I could tell at a glance what
and how many of each species were represented in a new
catch, solely from their luminous hieroglyphics."

Often the daytime colors of lantern fish are as striking as
their night lights. Some species have iridescent copper backs
touched with deep blue, or silvery bellies and flanks tinged
with shimmering pinks or greens. Gloomy-looking hatchet
fish share the twilight depths from 500 to 1,600 feet with
lantern fish and wear much the same attire. Short handlelike
tails, compressed bodies and straight, bladelike bellies give

DEEP SEA ANGLERS (to scale). These bizarre-looking, believe-it-or-not beasts actually catch their prey with line and lure. The large (20 in.) lantern mouth at lower right is *Galatheathaum axeli*. A 3-in. *Linophryne argyresca* (above center) has swallowed a victim larger than itself and carries a degenerate male attached to its stomach.

them the appearance of miniature hatchets. When brought up in a net, these creatures look like shiny silver coins scattered among the black and red fish and shrimp of darker depths. They are about the size of a half-dollar or half-crown and smaller than lantern fish. Hatchets have big mouths with sharply down-turned corners that give them a perennially sullen expression. Some have binocularlike eyes that always look upward, giving them the appearance of wistfully watching the sunlit zone for the coming of a meal. All have oval blue or, more rarely, bright red light organs that shine downward into the darkness.

Fish That Fish

In dim depths a hatchet fish may lunge for what looks like a juicy copepod or luminous shrimp and suddenly find itself drawn helplessly into a dark, menacing cavern. The little fish may attempt to whirl and swim for its life, but sharp, curved teeth spring up to block the way or impale the doomed victim. Then smaller dentures stoke the prey into an expandable stomach. The angler fish has bagged another meal.

At once ludicrous and ferocious-looking, these little believe-it-or-not beasts actually catch their food by fishing for it much like a human angler. Weak swimmers, the solitary, pear-shaped anglers float motionless or lie in wait on the ocean floor between 3,000 and 12,000 feet. The first ray of their spiny dorsal fin has separated from the others, lengthened into a fishing pole and moved forward to the front of the head. Some possess short, stubby poles, others use a rod several times longer than the body. One species has an extendible spine that slides along its back and inches the bait closer and closer to its enormous mouth.

Through the trial and error of evolution anglers have selected a variety of exotic lures from nature's tacklebox. Sometimes they use only a fleshy swelling on the end of the fishing line, but often it is branched to resemble a tasty worm or shrimp. So the victim can spot it easily, the bait of all but two of the 80-odd species of deep anglers is

SHALLOW ANGLER *(Antennarius ocellatus).* This small tropical frogfish lies among the Atlantic seaweed and sargassum, luring victims to its capacious craw by means of a wormlike "bait."

equipped with a light. One has luminous teeth. *Galathea's* scientific fishermen brought up a new species with a forked light organ dangling from the roof of its mouth. Dr. Bruun called the black 20-inch-long, broad-headed beast "unquestionably the strangest catch of the Expedition . . ." It was given a name as formidable as its appearance—*Galathea-thauma axeli* in honor of the ship and Prince Axel of Denmark.

Muscles cast the angler's line and twitch the bait so that it mimics a moving morsel. When the victim moves in close enough, the floor of the angler's cavernous mouth drops like a trap door, its jaws turn outward and the gill covers suddenly expand. This creates a strong current and the victim is sucked into the yawning craw with the inrush of water.

Most of them are no bigger than a man's fist, but anglers can engulf prey as big as themselves. One species, the ugly, black *Melanocetus johnsoni,* can swallow prey twice its own length. A 3½-inch individual was captured with a lantern fish considerably larger than itself coiled up in his bulging stomach.

Concentrated between 5,000 and 6,500 feet, deep anglers probably descended from shallow-water species like the familiar monkfish (*Lophias piscatorius*). Such anglers are abundant among the rocks and seaweed along tropical and semitropical shores where they fish with a forked flap of skin on a retractable rod. Shallow-water males carry good angling equipment but most of the deep species let females do the fishing. When old enough to reproduce, most of the abyssal males sink their curious buck teeth into the belly, flanks, face or other part of a female. Gradually his lips and mouth fuse with her skin and all his organs, except those concerned with reproduction, degenerate. Their two blood streams become one and the male receives all his nourishment from the female's blood. In turn he fertilizes her eggs. Reduced to little more than an external sex organ, the male continues to grow but never reaches more than a fraction of the size of the female. The smaller the male the better, since less food will be required to keep them both alive.

Living Light

This unusual brand of sex life is an adaptation to life in the sparsely populated darkness where eligible mates are hard to find. For their size male anglers have one of the keenest noses in the animal kingdom to help them smell out females. They probably also employ sight, perhaps squinting into the dark with their large, tubular eyes to pick up flashes of light from a prospective mate's luminous organs. Creatures in the depths of the sea may flirt by flickering lights just as fireflies wink at each other across darkened meadows at mating time. After a full moon, in fact, female fire worms (*Odontosyllis enopla*) wiggle out of their burrows in the bottom of the sea and glow bright green until a male responds with the proper loving flashes.

The pattern and color of lights could serve to advertise the wearer's sex just as male and female birds can be distinguished by differences in feathers. Male lantern fish carry large, powerful lights atop their tails, while females have dimmer lamps on the underside of the tail. Perhaps lantern fish recognize a member of their own species by the arrangement of lights on its belly and determine whether it is male or female by tail lights.

Living light could conceivably take over all the functions that color performs in sunlit waters. Take schooling, for instance. Recognizing the lights of relatives might stimulate some species to form schools, or at least enable the pupils of a school to keep together. Brilliantly lighted shrimps and prawns often travel in populous schools and some carry green torches which one biologist estimates can be seen as far as 330 feet.

Euphausids are well-known both for swimming in large schools and for the intensity and profusion of bluish-white lights on their bodies. More powerful lamps on their heads follow the movement of the eyes and spotlight whatever the shrimpers look at. Perhaps euphausids use these head lamps in the same way as some stomiatoids use light organs near their eyes. While working in Antarctic waters Dr. E. R. Gunter, an English biologist, saw a foot-long stomiatoid shine a beam of strong blue light upward from a depth of about five feet. A cloud of euphausids was caught in this spotlight and the eel-like fish snapped them up like a trout taking flies. Beebe watched "good-sized copepods and other organisms" swim into the sheet of light cast downward from the belly lights of a lantern fish. "Whereupon the fish twisted around and seized several of the small beings."

One would think that a creature with rows of lights on its belly and flanks would be as conspicuous as an ocean liner on a dark moonless sea, hence an easy mark for predators. But if that were true the lights would gradually be eliminated through natural selection instead of being carried by a majority of deep sea fishes, crustaceans and squids. No, they must provide some kind of an advantage and Dr. William D. Clarke thinks he knows what it is. He says nearsighted enemies prowling beneath do not see lines of separate lamps when they look up, rather the luminous organs merge into a diffuse blur of pale light. Seen against the dim blue ceiling of the twilight zone, the torch carrying animal is practically invisible. Without the lights the same creature would appear as a dark and edible silhouette.

If you wake up in a dark room and switch on the light you become momentarily blinded. A hungry gulper that has the glaring tail light of a lantern fish turned on in its face may experience the same sensation. As Beebe says, "a better method of defense and escape would be difficult to imagine." In addition to squid that exudes a flaming ink cloud, some shrimp (*Acanthephyra*) seem to "explode" into a hundred glittering sparks when in danger. Certain angler fishes, too, discharge a blazing yellow-white mucus to avoid becoming a meal.

No matter what it is used for the light is produced in one of two ways. Either it comes from luminous cells that are part of the creature itself or from luminous bacteria. Remarkably, the latter always cluster in the same place on a host, generation after generation. In both cases, the light is "made" by a complex chemical reaction. A substance known appropriately as "luciferin" combines with oxygen and a catalyst to yield *oxyluciferin,* water and energy in the form of light. Some living torches switch their lights on and off by nervous impulses that start and stop the chemical reaction. Bacteria leave their lights burning all the time, so hosts turn them off by rotating the organ out of sight or closing a curtain of skin over them.

The size and structure of light organs, known as *photophores,* is as diverse as the numbers and arrangement from species to species. They may be equipped with reflectors, transparent windows, focusing lenses, muscle-powered diaphragms to control the amount of light or color filters. Bacteria, sponges, jellyfishes, worms and snails prefer blue or yellow; fish, squid and crustaceans favor blue-green, red or white lights.

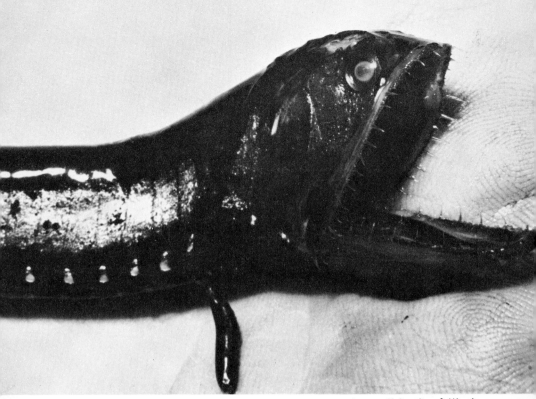

University of Miami

This monster in miniature, a STOMIATOID only a few inches long, was brought up from depths of 4,000 feet in the Sargasso Sea. Light organs are spaced along its underside and a sausagelike parasite has attached behind its tooth-filled head.

This living light is cold. You cannot comfortably grab a light bulb that has been burning for a few minutes because over half the electricity supplied to it is turned into heat. But you can hold luminous creatures in the palm of your hand without discomfort. Japanese officers did this during World War II, reading messages by the ghostly blue light of ostracods when too close to American lines to risk a flashlight. Less than one percent of the chemical energy involved in luminescence is wasted as heat. If man could learn how sea beasts produce energy so efficiently, he could light his cities and highways much more cheaply and effectively.

By no means do all deep dwellers carry torches. Those that do are concentrated between 1,000 and 8,000 feet. Ultrasensitive light meters lowered into the Atlantic several hundred miles southeast of New York City detected a maximum number of flashes at 3,000 feet, both during the day and night. When nets replace light meters they bring up maximum numbers of fish, shrimps, worms, salps and jellyfish from the same general depth, around 2,600 feet. This area may be so popular because here the last vestiges of sunlight fade into unending darkness and animals can easily hide from predators. Aquanauts making inner space voyages in bathyscaphs report that abundant plankton near the surface taper off to a zone of minimum life at about 1,000 feet. Between 1,300 and 2,600 feet plankton again become rich and abundant. Below this, life decreases as depth increases.

12.
Life in the World's Basement

"The dark and backward abysm of time."
—SHAKESPEARE

WHEN the sun begins to set and the diffuse zone between light and dark creeps upward, many animals follow it toward the surface. It is as if some irresistible biological urge simultaneously mobilizes armies of deep dwellers all over the World Ocean and compels them to move upward. From the early days of tow-netting, naturalists knew they got much larger catches near the surface at night than during daylight hours. But these creatures begin to disappear as the first rays of the rising sun knife into the silver-gray water, and soon the vast migrations have reversed direction.

Schools of fishes and squids; swarms of shrimp, winged snails and worms; hordes of feeble-swimming copepods, jellyfish and protozoans all engage in these mysterious vertical journeys. The distances covered and speeds of travel are remarkable considering some of the animals involved. Copepods as small as a grain of rice climb from 350 feet to the surface at astonishing rates of 50 to 100 feet an hour. Then they make a seven-hour downward trip to get "home" in the morning. Frail, insectlike mysids and amphipods take strenuous 1,300-foot journeys twice a day. Euphausids and

223

shrimps move from depths of 2,700 to 700 feet and back down again.

During such treks a creature may face terrific pressure changes (40-50 atmospheres) and experience differences in temperature equivalent to going from Iceland to the equator. Why do so many different animals undertake such arduous journeys twice daily? The migrations are so universal they must have profound biological significance, but what could it be?

The most obvious answer is that small creatures come up to feed on the luxuriant vegetation near the surface, and larger animals come up to feed on the smaller ones. But why don't these beasts live in the shallow forests of the sea all the time, why expend so much energy commuting every day? Again, the most obvious answer is that they retreat into the dim "caves" of the deep, like nocturnal feeders in the forest, to avoid becoming a meal themselves.

But by no means all biologists believe these are the right answers. Professor Alister Hardy proposes that weak swimmers migrate from slow-moving deep waters to take advantage of faster, near surface currents for transport to new feeding grounds and the widest possible distribution. Stronger swimmers like fish and squid would merely move up and down to follow their food.

Most biologists will say only that light is the principal factor governing vertical movements with perhaps age, physical condition, temperature and pressure limiting the extent. It may be that different creatures simply prefer to live in certain intensities of light, hence follow them up and down as the sun rises and falls. Certainly the beasts are very sensitive to small changes in illumination. Even moonlight will drive them lower in the sea and they will come up higher on cloudy days.

Whatever the reason for these ups and downs they are tied in with another mysterious phenomenon in the sea: deep scattering layers or DSL's. During World War II, physicists working on ways to detect submarines with sound waves kept getting records showing "bottom" at 900 feet when they knew the water was much deeper. Also, shallow water was reported by ship captains where no shallows existed, and over the years nautical charts came to display hundreds of shoals marked "ED"—existence doubtful. Evidently the sound waves were bouncing off something between the surface and sea floor. But these "somethings" did not stay in one place. They rose toward the surface at sundown then disappeared, reforming again with the first light and descending to their normal depth. In other words, the layers showed the same pattern as migrating animals. Martin W. Johnson, an American zoologist, surmised that the sound must be scattered and echoed by marine creatures on their mysterious daily expeditions.

Later studies revealed DSL's to be almost continuous and worldwide in occurrence. During the day, three—sometimes five—layers 150 to 300 feet thick hang like decks of stratus clouds between 700 and 2,400 feet. Each night the ghostly scatterers rise to the surface and disperse or merge into a broad band extending down to 500 feet.

For years, scientists, fishermen and kibitzers speculated on what kind of animals make up these roving layers. Nearly every group of creatures had its turn in the spotlight. Schools of squid were among the first suspects, then fishermen became unduly excited about the prospect of vast schools of commercially valuable fish.

Lowering nets and cameras into DSL's; bouncing sound waves off various beasts in the laboratory and spotting creatures from bathyscaphs, scientists have finally concluded that the principal scatterers are small fish, shrimps and siphonophores. All occur worldwide, seem to swim in well defined layers and are capable of moving over the ranges of DSL's. The shells of shrimps and euphausids effectively scatter sound and could easily cause the appearance of "phantom bottoms." Gas in the floats of siphonophores and the bladders of fishes would do the same.

On bathyscaph dives off San Diego, Dr. Eric G. Barham spotted concentrations of siphonophores lying motionless between 850 and 1,450 feet, their long tentacles stretched out in all directions like "a living net." He has repeatedly seen concentrations of four to six inch fish between 650 and

1,000 feet, and on one dive spotted so many shrimp between
1,200 and 1,500 feet he could not count them. In the next
200 feet were a large number of lantern fish. Then between
2,150 and 2,300 feet, Barham encountered the greatest concentration of fish he saw on any dive.

The famous aquanaut and aqua-lung pioneer Jacques-
Yves Cousteau always keeps a sharp lookout when descending through DSL depths, but, unlike Barham, he has never
viewed any exceptional increase in life. He did, however,
dive through submarine "snowfalls" that became thicker as he
went deeper. Five other bathynauts, including Beebe, have
observed this "snow." Cousteau has suggested the snowflakes
are living animals, but Professor Hardy says they probably
consist mostly of dead material such as the slowly sinking
shells of molting crustaceans and armored plankters. Per-
plexed by the mystery, Cousteau stated "there must be
somewhere an unsuspected link in the cycle of marine life
yet to be discovered." Indeed, the answer to the problem
seems to be the discovery that dissolved organic material
comes out of solution by sticking to air bubbles. Dr. Gordon
Riley, one of the biologists who found that these organic
clumps grow into visible particles of food, believes they are
the mysterious snowflakes seen by Cousteau and other bathynauts.

This remarkable uncovering of a new link in the food
chain of the sea also solves the vexing problem of how
deep-living zooplankters survive. Scientists long doubted
that the slow rain of dead and dying organisms escaping
through the many waiting mouths above was enough to sustain deeper creatures. About nine-tenths of the slowly sinking plants are devoured in the upper 600 feet or so. And as
Dr. Anton Bruun pointed out, "dead organisms are as rare
a sight in the sea as they are on land. Sick or weak animals
fall prey to stronger enemies and are devoured; at most, a
large whale or giant shark might sink to the bottom without
being completely eaten."

To perpetually hungry animals living in the cold, dark
depths organic snowflakes must look like manna from heaven.
Riley says bubble food decreases with depth for the first
1,500 feet, then a steady level is maintained by new organic

matter being created at all depths. This particle food must support many of the creatures of deep scattering layers who in turn provide meals for bigger beasts, including fishes that reach our tables. Edible species in DSL's are too deep, fast and sparsely scattered to provide a direct source of human nourishment.

There are other food supplies for ravenous maws in the depths. Many deep-dwelling adults spend their early youth in the richly endowed surface waters. These inexperienced youths attempting to descend to their parental homes blunder into hordes of hungry mouths. Also, daily commuters returning home with their lunch-bucket bellies full of "goodies" from the upper layers become food for creatures at lower levels, and so on down to the deepest corner of the abyss.

Everything ends at the bottom in the cold ooze. Numbers of bacteria increase from relatively few cells scattered in the water to millions, even billions, in a few ounces of bottom mud. The remains of any creatures which fall to the deep floor, the corpses of crawlers and creepers, leaves and other material washed down from the land, all are broken down by bacteria and incorporated into the ooze. As in shallow waters, worms, sea cucumbers and sea urchins gorge themselves on this mud to get the organic nourishment mixed with it, and in turn become food for larger more active animals. Worms and tunicates seem able to survive indefinitely on bacteria alone, so the microbes may well be an important food source for many bottom dwellers.

As distances from land and the surface increase, life becomes scarcer and changes in character. The deep floors of the central ocean basins, particularly the wide South Pacific, are among the most barren areas on Earth. They reflect the desertlike aspect of the blue waters above, and demonstrate that the supply of food from the surface is important in determining the distribution of deep life.

Rat-tails and Brotulids

The commonest fishes of the deep ocean floor are rat-tails (Macrouridae) and brotulids (Brotulidae). The former outnumber the latter and both might become important food fish when economic deep-fishing methods are developed. Before they would be acceptable to housewives, however, something would have to be done about their appearance. Although not related, they resemble each other and the resemblance is quite unappetizing. Both have large, heavy-looking heads and short bodies that taper to long, compressed tails. As in the case of ratfish, these pointed extremities, which often end in a thin filament, give rat-tails their name. In both groups dorsal, anal and tail fins merge to form a continuous fringe around the teardrop shaped bodies. Other fishes living on the deep ocean bottom take this same odd, teardrop shape. Therefore, it must provide some advantage in the harsh surroundings, but scientists do not yet know what this is.

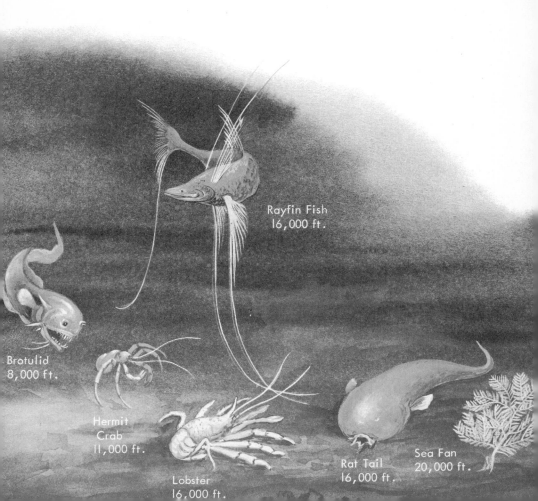

Rayfin Fish
16,000 ft.

Brotulid
8,000 ft.

Hermit
Crab
11,000 ft.

Lobster
16,000 ft.

Rat Tail
16,000 ft.

Sea Fan
20,000 ft.

Rat-tails are closely related to codfish; nearest shallow water kin of brotulids are the blennies. Rat-tails grow larger than brotulids and both range in size from a few inches to about three feet. Many individuals in the two families have armored heads and snouts, fleshy chin "whiskers" and shovel-like mouths for digging prey out of the bottom. Members of both groups also wiggle up into the overlying waters to feed on crustaceans, lantern fish and others.

Almost all rat-tails have well-developed eyes that grow larger as the fish gets older and swims deeper. Brotulid eyes, on the other hand, generally are smaller and weaker the further down a species lives. Below 3,000 feet they can just see the living lights of other night creatures. Blind, colorless brotulids living at 10,000 feet and below look much the

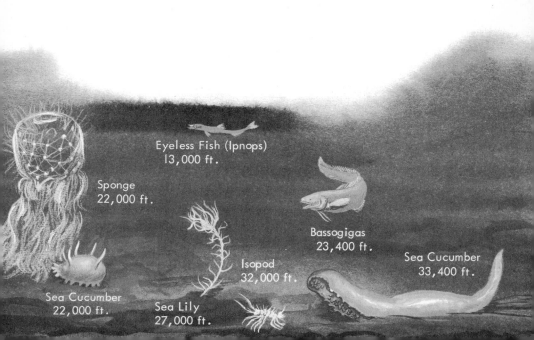

Eyeless Fish (Ipnops)
13,000 ft.

Sponge
22,000 ft.

Bassogigas
23,400 ft.

Isopod
32,000 ft.

Sea Cucumber
33,400 ft.

Sea Cucumber
22,000 ft.

Sea Lily
27,000 ft.

same as their sightless relatives that inhabit dark caves on land. Dr. Bruun called this resemblance "nature's reply to the conditions of life in perpetual darkness, where other senses than sight are important, and where in the struggle for existence colors are quite useless."

Brotulids with poor eyes must come to rely heavily on the lateral line. As their sight dims they gain increased ability to detect slight water movements made by animals feeding, moving or breathing nearby. Blind invertebrates, too, develop other senses to enable them to keep up with keen-eyed competitors. If one crawls, wiggles, hops or swims along the ocean floor far enough it is bound to smell, touch, taste or bump into something edible. Most of these sightless deep dwellers descended from sharp-eyed ancestors that lived in shallow waters hundreds of millions of years ago. Apparently, as the animals moved deeper and deeper they had less use for sight so their eyes gradually degenerated.

A number of deep crabs and lobsters cannot see, but blind or otherwise, crabs, lobsters and shrimp have never been found below 16,500 feet. Some of their cousins—amphipods and isopods—hop, skip and jump all the way down to 32,000 feet. Many of these crustaceans are equipped with extremely long, spindly legs, adapted for walking on the soft, powdery ooze without sinking in. Like shallow water species, heavily-armored deep lobsters, buoyed up by the sea, trod so light-footedly they can scamper across the backs of dozing flatfish without disturbing them.

Rayfin fishes, many of which are blind, or small-eyed, have enormously elongated fin rays. These may be used to finger the ooze for worms and other food, or the fish may walk on them like stilts. A photo taken from the bathyscaph *Trieste* at 23,000 feet shows a fish called *Bathypterois* standing on its sticklike ray fins as though supported by a tripod. It is said that this fish can use its fin limbs to spring across the bottom like a cricket.

The eyeless, legless echinoderms are among the most numerous of the deep bottom dwellers. Photos show tangled masses of brittle stars, as many as 500 in a square yard, forming a living carpet on the abyssal floor. Since prey must outnumber predators in order to survive, there must be vast numbers of snails, clams and worms on which the voracious stars live. In the largest haul ever made at depths of 23,400 feet *Galathea*'s crew brought up over 3,144 sea cucumbers from the Sunda Trench in the Indian Ocean. This and other samplings reveal an astonishing wealth of life down to 25,000 feet, suggesting that food problems in the abyss are not as serious as scientists have always thought.

A Watery Hades

The deepest parts of the ocean, the very basement of the world, are the *trenches*. These narrow, crescentric ditches gouge out about five percent of the Earth's surface and extend from 20,000 feet down to the greatest depths measured—36,200 feet. If you have ever looked over the rim of the Grand Canyon you can get some idea of the enormity of trenches by realizing that they are two to three times deeper. Most of these oceanic gorges curve along the seaward side of islands in the western Pacific, but there are two in the eastern Pacific, two in the Atlantic and one in the Indian Ocean. Trench depths have been christened "hadal," since the eternal darkness, near freezing cold (34° to 39° F.) and crushing pressure qualify them as a kind of Hades.

No sharp dividing line or differences separate animals of the continental slopes from those of the deep ocean floor, one fauna grades into the other. Nor does any striking change occur down to 20,000 feet. But down in watery Hades the breeds of beasts are different from any other on Earth.

All major groups of invertebrates have members that live in trenches, but inability to adjust to pressure causes the number of species to diminish rapidly with increasing depth. Only one-third as many species live between 33,000 and 35,000 feet as live between 20,000 and 23,000 feet. No starfish have been found beyond 25,000 feet, and bryozoans, barnacles, tunicates and fishes are rare in the trenches.

Until recently the deepest fish ever caught was a 6½-inch brotulid (*Bassogigas profundissimus*) dredged up from 23,400

feet in the Sunda Trench (south of Java) by the *Galathea*
Expedition. One of only three species known to live in the
trenches, *Bassogigas* held the record until Soviet scientists
snagged one at 24,900 feet in the northwest Pacific. A flatfish
of unknown species was spotted from the bathyscaph *Trieste*
35,800 feet down in the Marianas Trench.

Hadal creatures are grayish or white and the majority
are completely blind. Many of the crustaceans have extremely
long legs and often reach a gigantic size compared with their
relatives from lesser depths. One trench-dwelling isopod
grows to more than twice the average size of its group (1.8
inches as opposed to 0.7 inches). Trench-dwelling mysid
shrimp and amphipods are the largest of their breed. Dr.
Torben Wolff, a Danish authority on hadal life thinks the
tremendous pressure plays a major role in causing gigantism.
It probably speeds up metabolism and growth. Therefore
animals either grow bigger than usual before reaching sexual
maturity or reach larger sizes because they live longer.

Trench sponges, which live as deep as 23,000 feet, have
skeletons of complexly interlaced siliceous spicules that give
them the appearance of sunken birds' nests and the horrible
feel of a jumble of glass splinters. Like other sedentary bottom dwellers, these glass sponges sit atop stalks or stems so
their feeding parts do not become clogged with sediment
when large mud-eating cucumbers and urchins plough past.

According to the latest figures, the total number of species
inhabiting trenches is around 300, including sponges, jellyfish and sea spiders. Of these, about 100 live nowhere else
and some have been found in only one ditch. Each trench
in fact seems to have its own separate assortment of animals.
Isolated in these enormous canyons at the bottom of the
world they have evolved into new species especially adapted
to their surroundings.

The number of creatures also varies considerably from one
hadal gorge to another, according to how far it is from land
and the amount of food at the surface. Those that dominate
numerically are sea anemones, bristle worms, amphipods,
isopods, snails, clams and sea cucumbers. The largest variety
of species is found among isopods, sea cucumbers, little

"Beard Bearer" or Pogonophora.

green echiuroid worms and strange, threadlike beasts only recently "discovered" by science.

In the 1920's British scientists shoveled these "gubbins," as they were called, overboard by the ton, some of the best biologists of the day failing to recognize their status. Years later the Russian research ship *Vitiaz* dredged up almost 2,000 specimens from 29,500 feet in the Kurile Trench of the northwest Pacific. It was Soviet scientists who recognized that these wormy, insignificant-looking individuals represent an entirely new phylum of the animal kingdom, a division on a par with chordates, mollusks and arthropods. Biologists, certain that they knew all the major groups of animals on Earth, were left aghast. Dr. Libbie Hyman, the distinguished American zoologist, remarked: "The finding of an entirely new phylum of animals in the twentieth century is certainly astounding."

The phylum was named Pogonophora or "beard bearers," and once biologists started looking for such beasts instead of throwing them overboard they found over 80 different species. These inhabit all oceans from the shallows to 33,000 feet, but the majority live below 6,500 feet. Anchored to the bottom and enclosed in a vertical tube of their own making, these remarkable animals are as thin as a piece of string and as long as five feet. The "beard" is a plume of hairy tentacles which the bearer retracts into its chitinous tube when in danger, or pushes out the top when feeding.

What puts them in a phylum by themselves is the fact that they have no guts. A simple brain, nervous system, sex, a heart and red blood—yes; but stomach, intestines, anus or mouth—no. Vibration of tiny hairs drives water into the hollow tentacles and both oxygen and plankton are extracted from it. In a primitive way the arrangement of organs in beard bearers is similar to that in chordates, and the anatomy of these stringy creatures indicates they are related to echino-

derms, acorn worms and *Amphioxus*. Since they fit into
the unknown area between invertebrates and vertebrates,
zoologists believe an intense study of pogonophores will
solve some of the most perplexing mysteries of evolution.

The Living Dead

The deep sea keeps yielding additional clues to these
mysteries. Near the end of their cruise *Galathea* fishermen
found ten live specimens of a remarkable limpetlike mollusk.
They were imbedded in dark, muddy clay dredged up from
11,878 feet off the Pacific coast of Costa Rica. Each individual lives in a fragile, spoon-shaped shell 1½ inches long
and ½ inch high. Pale yellowish in color, the oval shell resembles a flat night cap with a low peak at the front end.
The animal inside probably eats mud and slides along the
bottom on its large blue and pink foot. The foot is surrounded by five pairs of primitive gills.

Despite careful examination scientists could not classify
Neopilina galatheae, as it came to be called. The beast resembles no modern mollusk. Its closest match is a make-
believe creature put together by paleontologists, their idea
of the animal from which evolved today's snail, clam and
squid groups. Scientists thought such a creature became
extinct 350 million years ago, but so close is the similarity to
Neopilina the latter could have been used as a model for
constructing the museum piece. This so startled the two
biologists entrusted with publishing the animal's description
they waited from 1952 to 1957 before announcing the discovery.

Neopilina turned out to be a missing link in the chain of
evolution, tying together worms and mollusks. Its gill regions
has segments similar to those of annelid worms, dispelling
any doubt that it descended from ancients much like the
familiar earthworm. At the same time, *Neopilina's* lopsided
shell and horny rasping "teeth" prove it is a descendant of
the creature that gave rise to the earliest snails and became
the ancestor of all mollusks.

As with the coelacanth, one catch was soon followed by others. In 1958 Dr. Robert Menzies found four specimens at a depth of 19,150 feet in a trench off northern Peru. In

Seagoing scientists found this six-inch VIPER FISH living 3,000 feet down in the Caribbean.

Miami Seaquarium

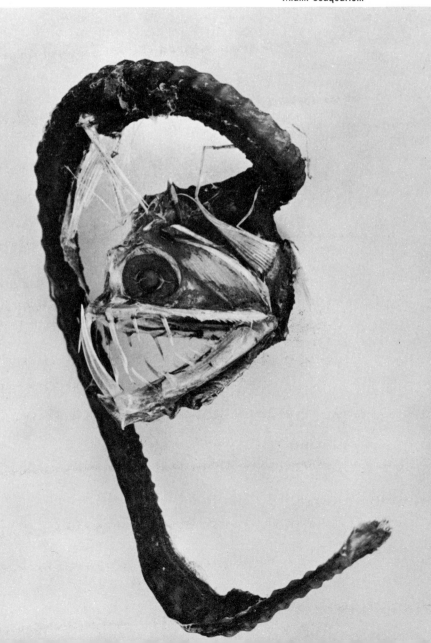

December 1960, he recovered 14 more *Neopilinas* from the sloping sides of the Cedros Trench off Lower California. Such catches are the exception rather than the rule and no serious scientists believe they justify the conclusion that the night zone is full of living fossils.

Probably during every geologic age some creatures withdrew from the populous shallows into the dark depths to escape powerful predators and those with whom they could not compete for food. After gradually adapting to increased pressures such individuals would change very little because of the stable or very slowly changing conditions. With little opportunity or necessity to change, the slow hand of evolution would be all but stilled. A few such living fossils undoubtedly exist at all depths (*Latimeria* was found at 230 feet, *Neopilina* at 19,000). Whether there are more in the shallows or the abyss is something scientists still argue about, sometimes heatedly. The debate will only be settled as the watery Hades, dark abyss and twilight zone yield their secrets to net, camera and hydrospace ships. Marine biologists are ever on the alert for more beard bearers and *Neopilinas*. Always there is great excitement and quickened pulses when the nets come up from the hidden corners of the world's basement. For who knows what new creatures the sea will give up for the first time to delight the eye and stimulate the intellect of man?

13.
Sea Snakes and Global Travelers

"Behold a strange monster our wonder engages."
—BLACKIE

ABOUT 350 million years ago, an air-breathing relative of the coelacanth *Latimeria* hobbled out of the water on clumsy lobe-finned feet and became the first backboned creature to take up life on land. Plants and invertebrates had already spread from the sea up rivers to fresh water and on to the land, so the vertebrates were greeted by luxuriant primitive forests swarming with scorpions, spiders and ancient insects. With a warm, stable climate and plenty to eat the lobe fins soon evolved into the first amphibians, creatures that live part of their lives on land and part in the water. These sluggish beasts then gave rise to all the wonderful variety of backboned land animals and all the reptiles, birds, and mammals of the sea.

The vertebrate conquest of land, begun by the amphibians, was completed by reptiles, which first appeared about 300 million years ago. Amphibians never completely broke their ties with the water, and even modern-day frogs, toads and salamanders must return to it to lay their eggs. Reptiles had a tremendous advantage over their predecessors in that they developed a shelled egg that could be laid on land. This made it possible for them to breed without returning to water. The

237

yoke provided an abundant supply of food and the tough shell safely screened the embryo from the hostile outside world. Reptiles also evolved a body frame (skeleton) that is better suited for a terrestrial existence. For about 200 million years, the reptiles enjoyed a period of tremendous development and soon came to dominate the entire earth—land, sea and air.

Amphibians never succeeded in re-invading the sea from fresh water, and today there are no marine amphibians. But the reptiles began returning to the sea 200 million years ago, and they have been there ever since. Possibly dangerous enemies and severe competition on land forced them to retreat into the water. But more probably they returned because the sea provided a new, relatively untapped source of food. All the adaptations that made them efficient, independent land-dwelling animals had to be modified. The problems of breathing air, supporting themselves against gravity and finding a way to move across a solid surface were traded for those of staying afloat, moving through the much denser water and bearing young away from land. Marine reptiles retained lungs in place of the gills their ancestors had lost. Their legs and feet were transformed into paddles or flippers, and new types of tails were evolved for efficient propulsion. All in all they adapted quite well, and by 100 million years ago the seas abounded with large reptiles—porpoiselike ichthyosaurs, dragonlike plesiosaurs, gigantic sea lizards (mosasaurs) and swift crocodilians (geosaurs).

Sixty million years ago these magnificent saurians of the sea, the spectacular dinosaurs that ruled the land and the fabulous flying reptiles mysteriously disappeared. What brought about these mass extinctions no one knows. Evidently a series of changes in climate, land elevations and food supplies occurred. Most species could not adapt to these changes so they died out one by one. Modern reptiles—snakes, lizards, crocodilians and turtles—are all that remain of the glorious past. But these fascinating creatures must not be passed over lightly. They represent highly successful animals that have adapted to many changes, outwitted their enemies, and survived for over 100 million years.

Sea Snakes

Snakes have survived by becoming secretive creatures, living in dense foliage and among rocks, burrowing underground and retreating into the water. Also, about 25 million years ago some species evolved the characteristic that makes them one of the most dreaded of animals: the ability to inflict violent death by poison. There are some 50 different species of snakes that make their homes in the sea and all are poisonous. Occasionally they grow as long as ten feet, but on the average sea snakes do not exceed three or four feet in length. Like other reptiles, they live only in the tropics and subtropics and all but one or two species stay fairly close to land.

Sea snakes have tails flattened from side to side like an oar blade. This special adaptation enables them to swim with greater ease. They wag their tails from side to side in a sinuous or sculling motion which propels them forward or backward with equal speed. Their scales do not overlap as they do in land snakes, but butt together to give the creatures a smoother, more streamlined form, another adaptation to water life.

Marine snakes thrive in abundance along the coast of Asia from the Persian Gulf to Japan, south to Australia and east to the Samoan Islands. Fishermen in the Philippines may bring in as many as 100 with one net haul. In the waters around Malaya, natives sometimes average one snake for each drag of the seine. One frequently sees a Ceylonese fisherman put his bare hand into a net, pull out a writhing snake and casually toss it back into the water.

These creatures sometimes congregate on the surface in enormous masses. In 1932, a tangle of snakes 10 feet wide and 60 **miles** long was sighted in the Straits of Malacca, between Malaya and Sumatra. An estimated one million snakes made up the twisted, wiggling mass. The reason for such tremendous congregations is unknown, but the best guess is that it is for mating purposes.

For certain animals sea snake venom is ten times as virulent as that of the cobra. Fish, their main food, are particularly susceptible to the poison. Some humans bitten by them have died in 2½ hours, while others have only felt dizzy or faint for an hour or two.

Sea snakes generally do not bite when out of water, and they rarely molest people in the water unless excessively provoked. Fishermen get bitten most often, and this is usually the result of accidental and violent contact such as stepping on one. There is hardly a fisher-family living in the Gulf of Siam, which literally teems with snakes, that cannot tell you of a snake-bite fatality. Death usually comes within 24 hours as a result of heart failure, or suffocation due to failure of the respiratory system. For those who do not expire recovery may take from a few weeks to six months, but the victim may be left with permanent kidney damage.

Sea snake dispositions range from mild and inoffensive to downright mean. All species are more volatile during the breeding season, and there is evidence that changes in water salinity may have something to do with the way they feel.

All species have nostrils on top of their heads, allowing them to breathe by exposing only a small portion of themselves. When submerged the nasal passages are closed by skin valves that keep air in and water out. Experiments show that some sea snakes can "hold their breath" for as long as eight hours. Most species hunt food beneath the surface during daylight hours. They lie quietly in wait on the sea floor and capture prey by sudden and rapid attack, exactly like terrestrial snakes. Victims, including fish twice their own diameter, are swallowed head first.

Sea snakes in turn fall prey to sharks, and sea birds. While traveling in Malaya, Malcolm Smith, a British herpetologist, wrote: "I have seen a large buoy covered with the remains of sea snakes, the birds having brought their meal to this spot and left the bodies after devouring the internal organs." Like other snakes, they sometimes eat each other. Often two individuals will start to consume the same prey at opposite ends. They keep right on eating when they meet, the smaller snake disappearing into the larger.

But the sea snake's worst enemy is man. Around Southeast Asia, Malaysia and Japan they provide an important source of food. Scales and skin are removed, the animal is deviscerated and the meat around the ribs and back cooked and eaten. Malcolm Smith writes that he saw sea snakes on sale at a market on Hainan Island, off the South China coast. Here he says "they are chopped up and made into sausage meat."

Marine snakes are excellent and graceful swimmers, completely at home in the water. Most species have been able to sever all ties with the land. They bear their young alive in the open sea and never need to come ashore. The newly born are quite large, nearly half as long as the parents in some cases. Far from being helpless, these infants swim and forage for themselves from the moment they leave the womb. A placenta forms around each egg in the mother's body. This supplements the small amount of food supplied by the yolk, allowing the embryo to grow to a large size and reach an advanced stage of development before birth.

The coloration and markings of many sea snakes are rich and striking. The yellow-belly, *Pelamis platurus,* is a splendid-looking reptile that often has a gleaming blue-black back and a bright yellow or brownish yellow belly. A maximum of four feet long, *Pelamis* is one of only two species that have succeeded in penetrating far east and west of the waters around Southeast Asia and the Malay Archipelago. *Enhydrina schistosa*—a sea snake grayish in color and aggressive in personality—and the yellow belly have wandered to the east coast of Africa and are now found as far south as Madagascar. *Pelamis,* the best adapted of all snakes for life in the open sea, has managed to go on as far as Cape of Good Hope at Africa's southern tip. Experts believe this venturesome creature has been prevented from reaching the Atlantic by the cold water of the Benguela Current, which is encountered immediately after rounding the southern tip of Africa.

Pelamis, who feeds on small fishes at the ocean surface instead of diving for food, is also the only snake that has crossed the Pacific. It has established residence along the west coast of South and Central America from Ecuador to the Gulf of California. In 1961, a live specimen was found on a beach only 300 miles south of San Diego.

Yellow bellies are frequently seen around the Pearl Islands, which lie about 50 miles west of the Pacific entrance to the Panama Canal. Thus the colorful, adventurous *Pelamis* stands at the front and back door of the Atlantic. It might be possible for individuals to slip through the Panama Canal or to survive in the cold Benguela Current long enough to be swept into warm water. Some herpetologists believe it is only a matter of time before the Atlantic has a sea snake population.

The Great Sea Serpent

From time to time, reports of gigantic serpentlike creatures turn up to whet the curiosity of scientists, frighten mariners and delight journalists. Descriptions of a Great Sea Serpent can be found in many languages, and references to such beasts go back two thousand years.

Many accounts of the Great Unknown of the Seas, as it is also known, can be dismissed as seamen's yarns aided by strange tricks of memory, the power of suggestion or the effects of alcohol. Other stories might be explained as dolphins or porpoises swimming in line, their arched backs resembling the sinuous coils of a prodigious snake. The giant squid with its 35-foot tentacles is a good candidate for the Great Sea Serpent, as is the oar fish which grows to a length of 20 feet and swims with undulatory movements at the surface.

However, a small body of knowledge and a few reliable reports exist which cannot be dismissed in this way. One of the most authentic accounts comes from the British ship *Daedalus.* While cruising off the west coast of Africa on August 6, 1848 her crew sighted a serpentlike creature about 100 feet long swimming a short distance away. In sight for 20 minutes, the monster slithered along at a speed of about 15 miles an hour. A sketch made by one of the ship's officers portrays a beast with a head about as big around as a moderate-sized tree trunk, and one report states that it had large, jagged teeth.

Another well-documented incident occurred off the coast of Brazil on December 7, 1905. Two trained, sober zoologists spotted a four-foot-long, blackish dorsal fin sticking out of the water. "Suddenly," they wrote, "an eel-like neck about six feet long and of the thickness of a man's thigh, having a head shaped like that of a turtle, appeared in front of the fin." The beast disappeared below the surface before the zoologists could identify it.

No other trained observers have clearly seen a Great Sea Serpent so scientists do not agree that such creatures live, nor do they completely deny their existence. Accordingly, the view that there is some unknown animal behind these reports persists. There have been many guesses as to what this creature may be, but the mystery still remains.

Virtually everyone agrees, however, that the Great Sea Serpent is not a true snake. Even the soberest and most responsible observers always describe the monster as at least 20 feet long. No sea snake longer than ten feet has ever been found, and the majority do not exceed four feet. Most sea serpent stories come from the Atlantic, but sea snakes have never been seen in this ocean. Finally, the major number of serpent sightings have occurred far from land, while marine snakes, except for *Pelamis* stay close to shore.

Interest in the sea serpent gained new impetus in 1959, when Dr. Anton Bruun described a six-foot larval eel captured off the coast of Africa at a depth of 1,000 feet. Zoologists believe a baby that size would grow into an adult 60 to 70 feet long. Thus far no adults have been found, but such creatures looping their way across the surface could rightly be called "Great Sea Serpents." In 1960 a 3-foot baby eel of a different species was found off New Zealand. This infant had a snakelike head, large sharp teeth and its adult length would be about 30 feet. Perhaps, then, the Great Sea Serpent is a gigantic, deep-living eel that only visits the surface on rare occasions.

A party of tourists may have photographed one of these giant eels in 1965. In eight feet of clear water on the Great Barrier Reef, they spotted a 70 to 80-foot beast with a highly domed head that tapered back to a long, whiplike tail. Two men in the group approached within 20 feet of the black and brown "thing," and they could see small green eyes on the 4-foot-wide head. The beast gaped at them "like a moray eel," then sluggishly slithered away. Dr. F. H. Talbot of the Australian Museum examined phototgraphs the men took and he thinks the creature was some variety of enormous eel.

Dr. Robert J. Menzies of Duke University has actually fished for the Great Sea Serpent. "I know that some of the stories told about sea monsters and sea serpents sound weird," he says. "But it would be ridiculous to pooh-pooh them completely and not even look for the monsters. . . . I literally 'fished' for them with a giant hook nearly two feet long which was baited with a squid that would have been a mouthful even for a monster. I got the hook back, badly bent, large and strong as it was."

Modern Dinosaurs

No lizards or crocodilians venture as far from land as their cousins the snakes. Some crocodiles lumber into salt water to catch food, but these play an insignificant role in the living world of the sea. The only lizard that regularly enters the ocean is the iguana *Amblyrhynchus cristatus*—the black lizard of the Galapagos. (A group of equatorial islands about 600 miles west of Ecuador.) These gentle beasts have tails flattened from side to side for easy swimming, and they dive off the rocky shores of their island homes in search of tasty seaweeds.

Various turtles have become well adapted to life in the sea. Descended from the same ancestors as dinosaurs, turtles have changed little in the past 200 million years. Their remarkable preservation is due for the most part to the heavy, armored shell, which makes them almost invulnerable to attack. Turtle ribs have grown outward in such a way that they support the *carapace,* or upper part of the shell. A bony covering, called the *plastron,* protects the bottom surface. Securely ensconced in these impregnable fortresses, turtles probably live longer than any other animal. Sea turtles may possibly live as long as the venerable land tortoises which may reach the age of 150 years.

Of the giant Galapagos turtles Herman Melville wrote: "They seemed hardly of the seed of earth . . . heavy as chests of plate, with vast shells . . . dented and blistered like shields that have breasted a battle. . . . These mystic creatures . . . seemed newly crawled forth from beneath the foundations of the world. . . . The great feeling they inspired was that of age: Dateless, indefinite endurance. . . . Consider that impregnable armor of their living mail. What other bodily being possesses such a citadel wherein to resist the assaults of Time?"

Two hundred million years ago turtles had teeth, but these were gradually lost during evolution and their jaws became covered with a horny beak. Capable of strong shearing action, this beak is equally effective for eating animals or plants. Like their ancient ancestors, modern sea turtles cannot draw head, legs and tail into the shell.

The plastron of seagoing turtles has a longitudinal hinge, which allows the chest to expand so large quantities of air can be inhaled for long periods of submergence. The heavy

GREEN TURTLE "flying" through the water.
Marineland of Florida

limbs have become modified into large paddlelike flippers. The manner of using these in swimming is different from that of fresh-water species, from which they probably descended. Fresh-water types "row" or push themselves through the water. Sea turtles work their big flippers up and down much like a bird flapping its wings. They literally "fly," through the water at speeds of three miles an hour or more.

Marine turtles cannot reproduce in the open sea, and must come ashore every one to three years to lay their eggs. Although some species breed year around, this journey usually takes place in the late spring or summer. Since their flippers are not suited for moving around on land and they are quite helpless out of the water, egg-laying is carried out under the cover of darkness.

On the night of May 19, 1962, a dozen female loggerhead turtles (*Caretta caretta*) laboriously dragged themselves onto a sandy beach near Cape Canaveral, Florida. Heavy with eggs and weighing about 200 pounds each, they worked themselves up the beach with convulsive movements of their flippers. Nearby, hundreds of scientists, engineers and technicians were getting ready to send Lt. Comdr. M. Scott Carpenter into orbit around Earth aboard a marvelously complex rocket at the incredible speed of 17,500 miles an hour. Oblivious to the space age, these ancient reptiles, answering an instinctive urge that is as old as life, struggled with all their strength to move a few yards to the soft sand above the high water mark. Here, they used their hind flippers to dig holes about 18 inches deep. Straddling the hole for almost an hour, each mother laid 75 to 200 eggs the size of golf balls. When finished the mothers carefully covered the eggs, and, with their foreflippers, disturbed the sand over a wide area so that the exact location of the nest would be obscured. Then, completely exhausted, they ponderously worked their way back to the sea, leaving the young to their fate.

All sea turtles nest this way. Their eggs incubate in the sun-warmed sand and near summer's end the hatchlings dig their way out. About an inch in length, they head immediately for the water. For many the journey ends abruptly in the claws of a crab, the beak of a bird or the teeth of such land animals as dogs or raccoons. The survivors climb dunes, skirt debris and work their way through tangles of brush to reach the sea. These infants seem to know exactly where the ocean is in spite of the fact they have never seen it before.

According to Professor Archie Carr, who has devoted much of his life to studying turtles, the babies find their way by an inborn instinct which causes them to move toward the more brightly illuminated sky above the sea or toward an uncluttered horizon. Such an instinct is easy to imagine. If you step off a train or bus some distance from the shore, it is easy to tell the direction of the beach by the paler, clearer sky above the sea. When a baby turtle sees such a sky it suddenly increases its pace. A wave breaking white in the moonlight or a fiery display of luminescence produces the same response.

At their first feel of water the hatchlings become very excited. They break into a flying swimming stroke as the farthest part of a spent wave slides under their flippers. After some awkward flapping and stumbling in the sheet flow, they quickly learn to swim smoothly, and they dive under breakers that threaten to toss them back onto the beach. Once clear of the surf, the turtles disappear and often are not seen again until years later when they return to the same beach as adults to mate and nest.

Brotherhood of the Green Turtle

Almost nothing is known about where sea turtles go and what they do during their early years. Baby green turtles *Chelonia mydas,* the most succulent species, probably wander from place to place looking for invertebrates to eat. A herd of young greens, weighing from 10 to 90 pounds, shows up to browse on turtle grass in the shallows between the Suwannee River and Tarpon Springs, Florida, every year. By the time they have reached this size the greens have stopped eating meat. Like hard-shelled cattle they stay in one place all day and graze leisurely on rich pastures of turtle and eel grass that spread continuously over great areas and know no seasons in the underwater climate. On such fare they may reach an adult bulk of 500 pounds, although 150 to 300 pounds is the most common weight range.

Greens are mild of disposition and comprise 20 percent of all turtles found throughout the warm seas of the world. They were once much more numerous. Since they are too big and hard for most predators and too fast and wary for the rest their numbers were limited only by the available feeding space. When white men first came to the Caribbean they found green turtles in countless numbers, turning the grass at the bottom of the sea into good savory meat. For 300 years these vast herds were a prime factor in the growth of the Caribbean, feeding hungry sailors and settlers of half a dozen nations. "All early activity in the New World tropics," writes Carr, "exploration, buccaneering and even the maneuverings of naval squadrons, was in some way or degree dependent on turtle."

Under this pressure the abundant herds were destroyed one by one, disappearing from the shores of Bermuda, the Greater Antilles, the Bahamas, the east coast of Florida and the Cayman Islands. People who know no other life have followed the declining herds from one place to another right up to the present time. In a warm and eloquent book *The Windward Road* Carr pleaded with man to stop the slaughter of a creature so important to his well-being. This book sparked the formation of the Brotherhood of the Green Turtle, an organization that expresses itself lightheartedly but has the earnest purpose of restoring the green turtle to its former abundance.

The Brotherhood formed the Caribbean Conservation Corporation in 1959 to "save the green turtle from destruction, to redistribute it to all those beaches where it was once common and to increase the food supply of undernourished Latin American countries." To this end a hatchery was established on the black sand beaches of Tortuguero, Costa Rica, the only important nesting center remaining in the western Caribbean. Slaughter of pregnant females on this important beach has virtually ceased. Eggs from one 2-mile section are moved to the safety of a wire enclosure where they hatch in artificial nests. Many of these hatchlings are then flown to and released in parts of the Caribbean that no longer have turtle populations. The CCC hopes the hatchlings will return to these beaches as adults to nest, thus establishing new turtle colonies and sources of food.

In October 1961 the U.S. Navy entered the picture. As part of Operation Green Turtle, a seaplane began airlifting thousands of turtle babies to sites in Colombia, Mexico, Florida, various Caribbean islands and to a new turtle farm in the Bahamas. At the latter location a shallow area of sea grass has been fenced off and the CCC hopes green turtles can be raised here like aquatic cattle.

Greens take about five years to reach sexual maturity, then they nest only every two or three years. Therefore, a long wait is required before it can be determined if the airlift experiment has been successful. So far no definite evidence exists that the displaced reptiles are nesting at the new grounds, but CCC has high hopes. Carr reports, "there is growing indication that a part of the introduced stock is taking up residence in waters adjacent to some sites of release."

However, the plight of *Chelonia* and other Caribbean sea turtles continues to worsen. An increasing market for turtle calipee and shell, and new processing facilities being built, tend to undo the work of nature and the Brotherhood of the Green Turtle. These animals are being threatened with extinction before we can find the answers to some fascinating questions about them.

Master Mariners

The Navy is airlifting turtles because it is particularly interested in one of these questions: how turtles can navigate so well. A lowly green turtle flippers its way across 1,400 miles of open ocean and makes a landfall on an island no wider than seven miles. The Navy has officers who can't do that with the help of sextants, chronometers and nautical almanacs.

It was Archie Carr who first brought this ability to light. He put on a scientific foundation what the Cayman Island turtle catchers believed for years—that greens migrate long distances between feeding and nesting grounds. The old bronzed fishermen told Carr of turtle voyages across more than 800 miles of open water. Captured greens transported from Nicaraguan waters to Florida and Cayman escaped from storm-flooded crawls and reef-wrecked schooners to make their way back to the very same rock where they were first caught. To check this scientifically Carr clipped metal identification tags to more than 3,200 turtles nesting at Tortuguero. These tagged turtles were found feeding up to 1,500 miles away in Florida, Cuba, Mexico and Venezuela.

What really puzzled Professor Carr, though, were the herds grazing on lush submarine prairies off Brazil. Although he and his students at the University of Florida searched up and down the east coast of South America they could not discover where these turtles nested. The beasts disappear from Brazilian feeding grounds some months before large numbers of greens appear to lay eggs on the lonely beaches of Ascension Island, 1,400 miles away in the middle of the Atlantic. This nesting and mating begins in February. No pastures of turtle grass grow around the isolated 6 by 7-mile volcanic island so the turtles depart again by June, just before the return of increased numbers of turtle herds to Brazilian waters. Is it possible, Carr asked himself, that primitive reptiles somehow navigate across more than a thousand miles of shifting, unmarked ocean and land on a small, rocky spire lost in the vastness of the South Atlantic?

He and his colleagues began tagging turtles on Ascension Island in 1960. By 1965 nine of these tagged greens had been hauled out of the Atlantic by fishermen working off the coast of Brazil. In 1963 and 1964 five marked turtles showed up back on Ascension. After one or two round trips to Brazil, these individuals had returned to nest almost at the same spots where they were tagged. The difficulties facing such journeys, notes Carr, would seem insurmountable were it not clear beyond reasonable doubt that the turtles are surmounting them.

How do they do it? Carr believes Ascension may have been originally colonized by egg-bearing greens accidentally carried from Africa by the westward-flowing South Equatorial Current. Babies born on the island could have been carried west to Brazil by the same current and could have information imprinted in their "memories" which would allow them to retrace their steps. After reaching sexual maturity, young greens might make their way along the Brazilian coast until they see, taste or smell the vicinity of their first landfall. This would put them at or close to the latitude of Ascension. They would then have to set off on a proper course and struggle eastward against a three to four knot current for some two months.

Turtles making the crossing touch not a morsel in all this time but live on stored-up fat. They must not sleep much either, for as soon as they stop beating their powerful flippers the current would carry them backward. After 60 or more days of tireless paddling, avoiding the crushing jaws of sharks and holding a course without error, the turtle receives some clue that it has reached the vicinity of Ascension. Perhaps the island has a distinct smell or taste that is washed down to them on the current. Or they may "remember" the sight of 5,000-foot-high Green Mountain with its crown of clouds and circling birds.

Males either travel with the females or make a precisely timed rendezvous in the surf off the natal beaches. Both have enough strength left for the strenuous business of courting, mating and, sometimes, fighting. These encounters serve to fertilize eggs to be laid two or three years hence, not during the current landing. Only the females go ashore and they have been seen pushing their snouts into the sand as if trying to find the home beach by smell.

Studying this journey, one reaches the inescapable conclusion that turtles possess an inborn compass sense which enables them to determine direction by sun and stars. Many different kinds of creatures, including primitive invertebrates, can do this. Honeybees fly a beeline to a source of nectar by taking bearings on the sun and they relay the correct course to their hive mates by means of a complex

LOGGERHEAD TURTLES mating.

dance. Such animals must possess a time sense for the sun moves across the sky during the day and to hold a fixed heading they must be able to take this movement into account. Starlings, pigeons, night-flying warblers and other birds have this time sense, so it is not stretching reason to attribute the same abilities to turtles.

But even if seagoing creatures steer a straight course in the open ocean by biological compass and clock, even a slight sideways drift could displace them hundreds of miles from their destination. A turtle might swim on a constant heading corresponding to the direction from Brazil to Ascension, but currents would probably push him far off a direct path between these two places. Evidently turtles, and migrating fish, are able to compensate for such drift by making repeated course changes.

Carr thinks it conceivable that turtles do this by determining the sun's height above the horizon at noon. This is what a ship's officer does when he sights through a sextant at midday. He measures the vertical angle of the sun above the horizon, and this is equal to his latitude. If turtles can "measure" the same angle, and this would be a truly amazing accomplishment, they could reach a destination by keeping to a constant latitude instead of a constant direction.

The reptilian mariner might sail up or down the coast of Brazil until his sights reveal he is on the same parallel as Ascension. He would then turn eastward. By "eyeballing" the sun each noon he would know if he had drifted to, say, 7° 45′ south latitude when he should be at 7° 55′ south latitude. He could then set a more southerly course by his compass sense and hold it until noon sights tell him he is at the correct latitude to pick up whatever beacon turtles use to home-in on Ascension.

This may be too complicated an explanation or it may be too simplified. Scientists just do not know yet how animals find their way across long stretches of open water. However, more and more evidence points to the theory that they navigate by sun and stars. Dr. Arthur D. Hasler of the University of Wisconsin took white bass from their spawning grounds at the edge of Lake Mendota, Wisconsin, and released them out of sight of land. On days when the sun was visible the displaced bass set a course straight for their spawning grounds. But on cloudy days they swam around in a random, disoriented fashion. Hasler and helpers kept track of the fishes' movements by hooking balloonlike plastic floats to their backs, which the piscians obligingly but unwillingly towed along the surface.

By similar experiments, Hasler demonstrated that silver salmon have a compass and clock sense, and he feels certain that they and other salmon use these senses to navigate from feeding areas to the mouths of rivers where they spawn. Some silver salmon travel 1,500 miles from feeding grounds in the Gulf of Alaska to home rivers in northwestern United States. Their cousins, chum, pink and sockeye salmon from Washington, British Columbia, Alaska, Japan and Siberia, make round trips of as much as 3,500 miles to feed in the central Aleutians. King salmon tagged off Adak Island swam

2,500 miles to spawn in the Columbia River system as far inland as the Salmon River in Idaho.

Some of these salmon slow down or stop entirely when darkness falls. Others have been observed to hold a straight course at night and it is reasonable to assume that they use the stars to accomplish this. Like turtles, salmon must have some way to compensate for currents that push them this way and that. Hasler thinks the height of the sun, and perhaps water temperature, play a role in this ability.

Follow Your Nose

There is also the question of how salmon find the stream of their birth after successfully negotiating hundreds of miles of open water. Generation after generation return to the same stream so consistently that fish in tributaries only a few miles apart evolve into separate races. This is because the differing physical surroundings bring out different hereditary characteristics.

Some salmon exert enormous efforts to get home, swimming hundreds, even thousands, of miles against strong currents. During such treks they travel day and night without rest or food, but some species like steelhead trout and Atlantic salmon will snap at a fly. Yukon River salmon swim 2,000 miles upstream between spring melting and fall freezing to lay their eggs. Rhine River salmon may go a year without eating. Frequently the migrants must make their way past man-made dams and locks and over rapids and waterfalls. Contrary to a popular belief, they do not jump over the falls. The leap takes them over turbulent water at the base, then they gain the top by a hard swim up the falling sheet of water. If a salmon fails to get over a fall on the first pass, it will keep trying until successful or until it falls back into the stream exhausted.

Fisheries biologists at California's Prairie Creek Hatchery got a demonstration of salmon resourcefulness and determination in 1964. A 14-inch, 2-year-old silver salmon swam up Redwood and Prairie Creeks, made its way through several drainage ditches, climbed a narrow vertical pipe, negotiated a 90-degree turn in it, knocked out a wire screen cover, cleared a nearly impassable net and plopped wearily into its old spawning tank. Amazed hatchery employees christened the fish "Indomitable."

How does a salmon like Indomitable distinguish one stream from another and find its way home? Dr. Hasler believes each tributary has its characteristic smell and a salmon sniffs its way home like a bloodhound following a scent. According to his theory a young salmon becomes "imprinted" or conditioned to the odor of its parent stream before it first goes to sea. After two to seven years in the ocean it returns with the aid of celestial navigation, then swims upstream, rejecting all odors, until it smells the tributary of its birth.

To test this theory, Hasler trained salmon fingerlings to discriminate between the waters of two different Wisconsin creeks. The trained fish picked the correct creeks every time, until the olfactory organs of half of them were cut out. Afterwards the noseless ones were unable to choose between streams while the unchanged half found their way "home" as usual. The experimenters then took sexually ripe coho salmon from two branches of a Washington State river. The fish were moved downstream, half had their nostrils plugged and all were turned loose below the fork to make their run again. All those whose nostrils had not been plugged got home while very few of the fish that could not smell made it.

Experiments with eels show that they, too, use odors as a guide to find a home stream. However, instead of spawning in fresh water and spending most of their lives at sea, eels spend most of their time in fresh or brackish water and migrate to the ocean to spawn. Scientists believe salmon originally evolved in fresh water and have never been able to sever ties with their birthplace. Today's migrations to sea are a result of venturing farther and farther away from their ancestral home in search of food. The reverse must be true of eels. Their ancestors probably lived in the sea and they must return to it to give birth.

Like Pacific salmon, eels die after spawning. Their young

are carried back towards the land by currents and rely
on smell to get them into brackish and fresh water. In the
laboratory, elvers show no preference for tap water over seawater. But when natural fresh water full of the earthy odors
of dead vegetation, humus and animal excretions is used,
the little eels wiggle right to it.

Young eels swimming in from the ocean feel the tug of
the tide. Then they drift passively until they smell inland
water. It does not take much, only one or two invisible
molecules in its nasal sacs will turn an elver from the sea.
Slender, glasslike miniatures of their parents the youths
swim actively on the incoming tide, then hug bottom as the
tide ebbs in order to avoid being swept back to sea. Males
settle down in brackish estuaries, while hordes of females
squirm upstream to the farthest creeks and headwaters.

For 2,000 years Europeans savored eel flesh, and Americans watched their slithering antics in backland ponds with
a mixture of wonder and disgust. But no one ever saw ripe
eels, or eel eggs or eels mating. People once believed baby
eels sprang spontaneously out of mud, or were transformed
from horsehairs or came into existence when adults rubbed
off pieces of skin against rocks. When autumn rains swelled
the creeks and rivers mature females could be seen heading
downstream to meet the males. Then they disappeared out
to sea together, out of sight and knowledge. The following
spring, transparent elvers shorter than a man's finger swarmed
in from the sea to take their place.

Finding some of the frail fry in the sea off the Faeroe
Islands, Danish biologist Johannes Schmidt became intrigued
with the eel mystery and decided to search the ocean for
their birthplace. From 1904 to 1922 he towed nets from the
English Channel to Chesapeake Bay and from Greenland to
Puerto Rico. As Schmidt hunted farther and farther west
and south from European rivers, the eel babies he caught
grew progressively smaller and less like the adults. Finally
about 1,500 miles east of Florida, 600 southeast of Bermuda,
Schmidt found clouds of newly hatched larvae far below the
surface of the sea. Their bodies, as colorless as crystal,
blended in with the ocean and made them difficult for

predators to see. They resembled tiny willow leaves with black pinpricks for eyes, so unlike the adults that the first man ever to find one thought it was a different species.

All eels wiggling in the streams of North America and Europe are born in this dark corner of the Atlantic, some 1,200 feet below the surface. Here the long, unknown journey of the adults ends. They release their sex products into the warm water, then disappear forever into deeper blackness. The fertilized eggs hatch in late winter or early fall and the newborn float up to merge with the Gulf Stream.

In the classic pattern of aquatic movement, the weak young drift downstream with the currents. (Adults, who are better equipped, must work their way upstream or against the currents to spawn.) Schmidt theorized that American and European eels drift together but grow at different rates. By the end of about a year, when they are off the United States coast, the Americans (*Anguilla rostrata*) have grown twice as large as their European cousins (*A. anguilla*). The former feel the urge to move inland and they head for streams from Maryland to Maine. The Europeans keep drifting. Not for almost two more years are they ready to metamorphose into the tubular form of the adults, and by this time currents have carried them to the mouths of European rivers and bays.

Do these youths find and settle down in the same streams as their parents? Prof. Alister Hardy thinks it unlikely. Baby eels drift thousands of miles from their spawning grounds with the currents, so he believes "their distribution must surely depend on chance." It seems too much to suppose that larvae from the eggs of, say, Spanish or Maryland eels should by chance of ocean drift be carried to the mouths of the same streams on the coasts of Spain or Maryland.

It has been discovered that European eels spawn in an area to the east of, but overlapping, the area used by American eels. This fits in perfectly with Schmidt's ideas: eels from the western part of the spawning grounds could drift northwestward to the American coast, the others could move northeastward and eventually take up residence in Europe

This would be a beautiful natural arrangement in which an eel's larval life is perfectly adapted to the Gulf Stream's speed and the distance from the spawning grounds.

But a minority of scientists do not believe European eels ever make it to the spawning grounds. Investigations by Dr. D. W. Tucker lead him to conclude that they are too degenerate and sapped of vitality at the beginning of the journey to swim all the way to the edge of the Sargasso Sea. He theorizes that only American eels make it to the spawning grounds. Eels entering European streams get there as a consequence of being accidentally carried over by currents. However, recent research on the blood serum of the two eel stocks suggests that they are completely separate and favors Schmidt's version over Tucker's.

Whoever is right, eels starting from hundreds, maybe thousands, of different river mouths find their way to the same remote spot in the deep Atlantic. What routes they follow and how they navigate remains a mystery. Do the adults swim near surface and use the sun and stars like turtles and salmon; do they hug bottom and follow submarine valleys and mountain peaks or do they use some yet unknown methods to navigate in mid-water?

Tagging Tuna

Like eels and salmon, tuna make long migrations in the open sea, but they shun fresh water. These fleet fish cross both Atlantic and Pacific, but surprisingly little is known about where they come from or where they go. Each May and June the eastern edge of the Gulf Stream, between Florida and the Bahamas, comes alive with schools of tuna moving north. Many of these bluefins (*Thunnus thynnus*) are in the giant class, 300 pounds or more, and a few may weigh over a 1,000 pounds. No scientist, fisherman or sportsman knows where these schools come from. Captured individuals have little food in their stomachs, and the condition of their roes indicates they are actively breeding or just finished.

These bluefins probably spawn somewhere east of the Bahamas, in the Caribbean, in the Gulf of Mexico, or in all three places. When seen off the Bahamas they are bound for waters between Long Island and Newfoundland, which teem with vast schools of herring and mackerel in summer. They fatten on this fare until about mid-October then disappear again until the following May.

In spring bluefins that spawn in the Mediterranean, off North Africa and near the Azores also migrate north, traveling as far as arctic waters off Norway. Until recently scientists believed these stocks never intermingled with those of the western Atlantic. But five bluefins tagged by sportsmen off Cat Cay, Bahamas have showed up in Norwegian waters. In 1961 two of the muscular migrants made the crossing in less than four months. The following year, another giant bluefin made the 5,000-mile journey in 50 days, a long distance swimming record. Two smaller bluefins tagged off Massachusetts in 1954 were recaptured five years later off France in the Bay of Biscay. This leads Frank J. Mather III of Woods Hole Oceanographic Institution to believe that many of the bluefins passing Bahama in spring travel all the way to European waters to feed. The next thing he wants to find out is where they go from here. Do they complete a circumnavigation of the Atlantic, wintering off sunny Spain or east of Bahama, or do they come back via New York?

Fishing Japanese long-line style, with hundreds of hooks on a miles-long line, Mather found large concentrations of bluefins 6,000 feet down off New York and New Jersey. This was in November and December, and he says, "it seems probable that they were schooling in preparation to moving south to their wintering grounds." There may be no witnesses to this journey because the tuna stay far out to sea, east of the Gulf Stream, and feed in deep water. However, no giants were taken in this deep fall fishing off New York. Therefore two separate stocks may exist—giant bluefins that travel to Europe to feed and smaller tuna which move up and down the western side of the Atlantic.

Many more individuals need to be tagged and recaptured before biologists learn the tuna's secrets. With the help of

Prof. Archie Carr (right) and student measure and tag a green turtle on the beach
Tortuguero. Another turtle waits its turn in the background.

more than 1,200 sport fishermen, Mather and his WHOI
colleagues have tagged thousands of tuna, marlin, sailfish,
swordfish and amberjacks since 1954. Such programs, also
carried out by State and Government agencies, are the best
means of obtaining knowledge about the migratory habits of
marine creatures.

Tagging dates back to the seventeenth century when Izaak
Walton tied ribbons on the tails of fish to find out where
they went. In the 1920's Italian zoologist Marsino Sella made
migration studies by means of hooks and harpoon heads of

different nations which were found in captured fish. He took a hook made in Akron, Ohio, out of a bluefin caught off Sardinia, and this was the first suggestion that tuna from both sides of the Atlantic mixed.

It took many years to develop tags which did not harm the animals and would stay on fast swimmers as they grew larger. Tags today range from simple plastic tubing and disks attached to the back muscles of fish to sophisticated sound and radio wave transmitters. Dr. Hasler and his colleagues have developed a sonic tag smaller than the tip of a pencil which is inserted into a fish's stomach. It emits a high frequency chirp that enables a boat with underwater receiving equipment to track the fish's every move. Some of the tiny batteries in such transmitters have a life of 100 hours.

Fishermen off Florida have been startled to see turtles towing rafts with brightly colored balloons attached or wearing small radio transmitters that broadcast signals when they surface for air. Archie Carr hopes to track Ascension-bound greens by such means. His future plans call for a tracking antenna atop Green Mountain to pick up signals from turtle-back radios. Carr has also suggested that "tracking the Ascension migrants by satellite could easily prove to be the most efficient method of learning the route they follow." Signals from turtle transmitters would be picked up by a satellite whizzing hundreds of miles overhead and rebroadcast to control stations where the reptiles' plodding paths would be precisely plotted.

Carr does not believe turtles and other migrants have a goal in mind when they travel. A salmon does not say to itself: "In a few weeks I'll be leaving for the old spawning grounds; gee, it'll be good to see the home stream again." Rather, changes in temperature or the increasing length of day stimulate glands to secrete hormones, and the animal feels an instinctive, irresistible urge to be off. Some creatures move only a few miles offshore or along the coast, others cross oceans or wander from the tropics to polar waters. On the way, they react to cues from their surroundings and unconsciously follow guideposts that have led generation after generation of their species to their destination.

The use migrants make of cues from the sky is strenuously disputed, but use them they must. "It is unthinkable that the struggling races of Earth should have missed the chance for survival in the stars," says Carr. He supposes that animals use the whole sky and every part of it that changes regularly with time or place. On a clear night a turtle, whale, bird or fish might sense he is in the wrong place because the whole sky has a strange, unexpected look. Perhaps in one direction there are familiar constellations, so he heads that way. He may just keep traveling in directions that make him feel more comfortable. This way he could gradually improve his position until the sky overhead matches the sky imprinted in his memory.

Marine animals use the information they get from the sky in combination with cues from land and sea. Each current and water mass has a distinct temperature range and salt content, so fish can probably tell when they leave one and enter another. Minnows can smell the difference between Sargasso Sea and Georges Bank water. Eels may recognize their oceanic spawning site by odor. During any journey an animal may switch from one guidepost to another.

"Different kinds of animals," writes Carr, "probably get out of their environment different kinds of travel information, just as they get different kinds of food." This information is acquired through highly developed senses, senses so keen and versatile they pick up signals that humans may never suspect exist. By responding to these signals the animals get to places where food is plentiful or where conditions are ideal for the development of the young. In other words, migrations increase their chances for survival. Over millions of generations creatures that follow nature's signposts survive, the others do not. Thus, the ability to navigate is an adaptation to the surroundings which is reinforced by natural selection. One of the most striking aspects of animal behavior, it is the product of evolution operating at its peak, of natural selection in an environment that extends out to the stars.

14.
Whales, Dolphins and Porpoises

"Suddenly a mighty mass emerged from the water, and shot up perpendicularly into the air. It was the whale."—MIRIAM COFFIN

WHALES are great wanderers. When the sun no longer lingers in the sky and autumn blows its icy breath across the ocean, many grow restless. As ice creeps over their pastures of krill, antarctic and arctic leviathans migrate to the tropics in search of food and warmth, to mate and to give birth. In Indonesian and West African waters; off Hawaii, the Galapagos and the Azores; in the Caribbean and Arabian Seas, hardy polar species like the blue, finback and humpback whales feed beside semitropical sperms, seis (sighs) and huge schools of dolphins. When spring returns, they move back to the ends of the Earth in time for the new-born to be weaned on armies of krill that feed on blossoming diatoms.

Americans can see one of these great migrations for themselves. Between March and May thousands of gray whales travel along the United States coast from shallow, sheltered waters around Baja California to their summer homes in the cold, lush waters of the Bering Sea. But the best months for whale watching are from late December to March when the barnacled grays move in the other direction, southward

263

close along the Oregon and California coasts on the 6,000-mile-trek to their Mexican breeding grounds. The best spots for whale watching include Marineland of the Pacific, Point Loma where the National Park Service runs a Public Whale Watch, Laguna Beach Cliffs and Point La Jolla—all in the Los Angeles-San Diego area. Sluggish swimmers, grays grow to 45 feet. They get their name from the grayish appearance caused by blotches of white barnacles on their black hides. Off California whale watchers see a procession of curved, knobby backs; low, voluminous spouts, and the toss of tail flukes (like huge butterflies) as the grays slide beneath the sea.

Spouting is part of the whales' heritage for they descended from land animals and must surface periodically to get a breath of air like you or me. Thor Hyerdahl wrote of encountering a whale while drifting across the Pacific on the raft Kon-Tiki: "It was so unusual to hear real breathing out at sea . . . that we really had a warm family feeling for our old distant cousin the whale, who like us had strayed so far out to sea."

Like us, whales are warm-blooded, large-brained mammals (not fish). They have lungs, a four-chambered heart and whale mothers suckle their young. The common ancestors of whales and men descended from reptiles. In fact, the evolution was so smooth and gradual, it is an academic question where reptiles leave off and mammals begin.

Reptiles also gave rise to birds about the same time, that is some 150 million years ago. Today, the only birds completely adapted to life in the sea are the flightless penguins. These jolly, and captivating birds "fly" underwater by gracefully flapping their long, flipperlike wings. They move with rapid, darting motions, breaking the surface together for a breath, like a school of tiny, tuxedo-clad porpoises.

By the best paleontological estimate, land mammals began returning to the sea about 100 million years ago and were well established there by 60,000,000 years B.P. (Before Present). They may have been forced to seek their living in the water by harsh conditions on land or competition for food and space. But, more likely, these highly adaptable creatures just naturally began to exploit the abundance of food in the sea, as some reptiles did 50 million years before them and many mammals are doing today.

From polar bears to whales we see mammals in all stages of transition from a land to a seagoing life. Scarcity of food on the barren arctic ice pack causes polar bears to spend considerable time in the more bountiful water. As a result, they have evolved narrow, streamlined heads and elongated bodies, partially webbed toes and slender legs so jointed they can swing through an exceptionally wide arc. Using their forefeet for locomotion and their rear legs for steering, polar bears turn and dive with great agility and swim long distances at speeds of three to six miles an hour.

Because the charming, fun-loving sea otters spend more of their lives in water than polar bears they are better adapted to it. Short hind legs with webbed toes make for easy paddling, and they swim as fast as 10 mph. Sea otters spend weeks away from land and dive to depths of 30 to 300 feet to capture crabs, abalones, urchins and other benthic morsels. There are few more appealing sights in nature than an otter indolently floating on its back, dexterously cracking open shellfish against a rock balanced on its chest. Sometimes females doze peacefully in this position with a nursing pup clasped to their bosom. You seldom see such delightful sights anymore for the otter wears the world's most valuable pelt, and man's greed has made it a rare and wary animal.

Homely, mild-mannered sea cows represent another step into the sea. To improve their ponderous streamlining, natural selection—nature's handmaid—has taken away hind legs and outer ears. These eight-foot beasts weigh up to a ton and come in two varieties, the manatee of warm Atlantic waters and the dugong of the tropical Indo-Pacific. Both use their fore flippers for swimming and to push seaweed into their mouths. Manatees have tails shaped like a large table-tennis paddle; dugongs possess horizontal forked tails bearing close resemblance to whale flukes.

These sluggish vegetarians have prominent bosoms situated in the normal human position and, supposedly, distant glimpses of them gave rise to sailors' tales of mermaids. But

MANATEE. Is this bosomed, blubbery-faced beast responsible for the mermaid legends?

such glimpses must have been blurred by imagination, grog and long, womanless days at sea. A close look reveals a bald, hare-lipped, blubbery beast with the head of a walrus, the flippers of a seal and the skin of an elephant.

Just as daffy-looking but larger in size and louder in voice are the bellowing, blob-faced sea elephants or elephant seals. Like other true seals, they have short fore flippers and rear limbs that extend backward and are turned palm to palm. Seals and sea elephants swim in a fishlike manner by moving these rear flippers alternately from side to side.

Walruses possess the same type of foot-tail. They cruise at about 2 mph by using both front and rear flippers, but employ their "feet" more than their "arms." Walrus movements are considerably more awkward and less precise than those of true seals. On land, they flip their foot-tail forward under the body and use it as a pair of clumsy land legs.

Sea lions and fur seals do the same with their rear legs and move fairly rapidly on land by using all four limbs in a peculiar loping run. This maneuverability, coupled with a natural playfulness and gregariousness is responsible for their employment as barking, ball-balancing circus "seals." In water, the long, pointed fore flippers are used like penguin wings. The beasts soar through the sea with powerful but leisurely strokes like a bird in slow-motion flight.

Sea lions and fur seals differ from true or hair seals by having small external ears or *pinnae*. Also, true seals are less doglike and unable to swing the rear flippers under their bodies. They move on land by hunching, inchworm movements or by repeatedly rolling over sideways. On ice they flop on their bellies and employ claws on the small fore flippers to propel themselves along. In water they move as fast as 8 to 12 miles an hour by gracefully stroking their fish-like foot-tail from side to side. They are not as fast as sea lions, who can probably sprint 15 mph, but they are much swifter than the blubbery, earless walruses.

Some true seals are well on their way to becoming permanent residents of the sea. They stay away from land indefi-

Miami Seaquarium

HARBOR SEAL. Friendly and engaging, these mammals make excellent pets if you can afford ten pounds of fish or shrimp a day. Note small clawed fore flippers and absence of ears.

nitely and remain submerged as long as 28 minutes. In exceptional cases, they bear young in the water. Someday seals may follow their cousins the whales and break all ties with the land.

Whale Genealogy

The whale's past is extremely obscure. All we know is that sometime after 100,000,000 B.P. some smallish, four-footed land animals began a series of extraordinarily rapid evolutionary changes. In the geologically short span of 50 million years they learned to swim instead of walk, and to reproduce offspring able to swim from the moment they left the womb. By 20,000,000 B.P., these beasts lost their ears and hind legs, evolved a torpedo-shaped body and a horizontal fishlike tail, got rid of a covering of hair, and their nostrils moved to the top of their heads. The fact that whales wound up shaped like fish serves as an example of convergent evolution—two groups of unrelated animals developing the same form in the course of adapting to the same environment.

Whale embryos repeat this evolution in the womb. By the time an embryo is an inch and a half long all external traces of its hind legs have disappeared. The front legs start out like the arms of a human embryo. The equivalent of our upper arm and fore arm bones then become much shortened and flattened but the digits or fingers are retained. Some species like the sperm whale have five fingers, others like the blue and finback lack a thumb. All fingers of a whale's huge "hand" are enclosed in a muscular envelope which forms a short, flat, streamlined fin. These fins serve the same purpose as a fish's pectorals: balancing and steering. "Engine" power comes from the mighty tail where, wrote Herman Melville in *Moby Dick,* "the confluent measureless force of the whole whale seems concentrated."

Herein, too, lies the most striking external difference between fish and whale. Whereas fish tails are vertical, whale tails are horizontal. Whereas fishes propel themselves by flexing their whole bodies and moving their tails from side to side, whales fan their flukes up and down to get ahead. As the tail stem moves vertically the broad, flat flukes change their tilt, or angle of attack, and exert the backward thrust against the water that moves the whale forward. The "flexions" of this tail, wrote Melville, "are invariably marked by exceeding grace."

An immense 70-foot finback beats its "tail wings" once or twice a second to achieve a cruising speed of about 12 mph. Dolphins need wave their flukes only 3 or 4 times a second to keep up with a ship moving 16 knots (18 mph). This seems to be about maximum speed for dolphins and porpoises, although these small toothed whales appear to move more rapidly when they gleefully swim alongside and ride the bow waves of ships.

On the basis of such observations scientists and sailors long thought that dolphins and porpoises swim faster than their muscles would theoretically allow. The amount of work a single muscle fiber can perform is about the same for all healthy animals—man, tiger or whale. Therefore it is possible to compute the power an animal can develop by measuring its total musculature. When scientists put this figure, along with others, into their formulas, they calculated that a dolphin cannot travel faster than 12 to 16 knots. Four kinds of speed tests made by University of California scientists show that this is indeed their maximum speed. The tests also proved that dolphins have the same power output per unit of body weight as athletes, and that their swimming efficiency is 85 percent.

A whale's smooth surface and perfect curves are partially due to thick layers of oil-rich blubber and fat which underlie the skin and serve as an "overcoat." The outer part of the skin contains a spongy, waterlogged material which makes the entire body surface flexible. To explain what they thought were super-speeds, scientists theorized that this surface undulated in waves that matched waves in the water flowing past the dolphin. The animal's body supposedly changed shape to coincide with pressure variations in the sea around it.

Man hoped to apply what has been learned from the dolphin to the construction of ships, torpedoes and submarines. Dr. Max Kramer, German-born pioneer in whale hydrodynamics, suggested coating submarines with an undulating rubber-plastic skin to increase speed. The U.S. Rubber Company experimented with a rubber coating called *Lamiflo* for high speed outboards.

Having Their Spoutings Out

The U.S. Navy and other government and civilian agencies lavish money and brains on whale studies because in their 100 million years of evolution whales have solved problems that still remain beyond the grasp of man. For instance, how can whales hold their breath so long, dive so deep and come up so fast? Porpoises and dolphins usually dive for 1½ to 7 minutes, and at least one species reaches depths greater than 400 feet. Weddell seals plunge to 1,500 feet and are gone for 28 minutes searching for a fish dinner in icy antarctic waters. Sperm whales (Moby Dick was one) dive to 3,700 feet and stay down as long as 90 minutes looking for squid. The 30-foot-long bottlenose whales may stay submerged for two hours.

Whales can stay under so long because of what Dr. Per Scholander calls the Master Switch of Life. Blood, which contains vital life-sustaining oxygen, is shut off from those parts that can survive without it for a time and switched to organs that need it most. As soon as a whale or seal submerges, its heart beat slows markedly. Blood vessels leading to the flippers, tail muscles and other tissues constrict, shutting the flow down to practically nothing. The precious oxygen is shunted to the brain and heart, the areas which can least endure without it.

This is fine for staying down, but what about coming up? If a diver or sandhog ascends as fast as a whale he doubles over in pain with the bends or diver's palsy. Nitrogen and other gases which dissolved in his blood under pressure come bubbling out of solution when the pressure is relieved. The same thing happens when a bottle of soda water is opened. Bubbles form in the blood, heart and body tissues, causing the excruciating and sometimes fatal diver's palsy. But whales are not plagued with this problem because they do not continually breathe compressed air as divers and caisson workers do. Such air means a constant fresh supply of nitrogen and at the increased pressures more will leak into the blood. Whales take down only a limited quantity of air at surface pressure, hence only a small amount of nitrogen. In addition, some zoologists believe a foamy, fatty substance in the whale's windpipe absorbs nitrogen and prevents it from going into the blood, but this has yet to be proved.

Deprived of a fresh supply of air, the diving whale switches to a metabolic process by which energy to power its muscles is derived without oxygen. By doing this the body incurs an oxygen debt that must be liquidated when the animal surfaces. After a long dive, a whale "pants" like an athlete following strenuous exercise. This rapid breathing is known to whalers as "having its spoutings out."

These spoutings emanate from nostrils at the top of the whale's head, but they do not, as people used to believe, consist of a fountain of water. The spout is the whale's condensed breath, smelling strongly of fish and sprinkled with a small quantity of water from the top of the blowhole. The warm breath condenses when it hits the cooler air. Just as your own breath is visible on a cold day, so the spout is more distinct in polar waters. It can be seen in the tropics, too, probably because it escapes under pressure and expands suddenly. Such expansion is accompanied by cooling.

A herd of whales often surfaces and blows as one, a welcome sight after many days at sea and one guaranteed to bring all hands to the rail. If it is not too windy, whales can be identified by their spouts. Right whales have a double, V-shaped spout; blues and finbacks blow high, straight and single. A sperm whale's spout tips forward at an angle.

Sperm and right whales, along with grays and humpbacks, have a habit of tossing their enormous tails into the air

before they dive or "sound." Greenland rights wave their
flukes to and fro for a moment in a kind of salutation. This
may be necessary because thick blubber makes them so light
they have a little difficulty shoving themselves into the deep.
Melville wrote: "this peaking of the whale's flukes is perhaps the grandest sight to be seen in all animated nature.
Out of the bottomless profoundities [*sic*] the gigantic tail
seems spasmodically snatching at the highest heaven."

Sperms and Mustache Mouths

Whales are also known as *cetaceans,* from the scientific
name of their order, Cetacea. Sperms and rights represent
two basically different types or suborders. The sperm, or
cachalot as the French call him, is the largest of the toothed
whales (Odontoceti), a group that includes dolphins, porpoises and killer whales. Their teeth serve only to grasp and
hold prey, which are swallowed whole without chewing. The
right whale is a Mysticeti or mustache-mouth and shares this
classification with blue, finback, humpback, sei and gray
whales. Instead of teeth, two rows of horny plates or *baleen*
grow down from the roof of their mouths, one row on either
side of the tongue. It is as if they have a huge drooping
mustache hanging inside their mouths.

Consisting of the same material as our nails and the hoofs
of cattle, these baleen plates are the "whalebone" once so
widely used in ladies' corsets, umbrella ribs, buggy whips
and other items requiring both stiffness and flexibility. The
200 to 300 thin plates on either side of the mouth are separated by less than a half inch, and have fibrous inner edges
that intertwine to form a kind of plankton net. Mustache
mouths feed much like basking and whale sharks. Right
whales swim through watery acres of krill with their enormous arched mouths constantly agape. Water streams through
the openings between the baleen and passes out either side
of the mouth, leaving krill and other plankters on the
hairy fringes. When the mouth snaps shut briefly, the enor-

mous tongue licks food off the mustache and pushes it toward the throat.

Rights are sluggish whales with a venerable appearance, prodigious heads and a ponderous girth. Unlike other mat mouths, they carry no dorsal fin on their black backs and their bellies are not grooved. Rights reach a length of between 45 and 60 feet and travel alone, in pairs or in small family groups. They rarely swim faster than five knots and usually cruise at about two knots, slow enough to be approached and harpooned by men rowing an open boat. This is how they got their name; they were the right whales to hunt.

In the seventeenth and eighteenth centuries, mighty Dutch and English whaling fleets chased rights on a grand scale in the arctic. In England, the right was declared a "royal fish" and the King an Honorary Harpooner entitled to the head of all whales. In the eighteenth century, American whalers extended the hunt into the South Atlantic, Pacific and Indian Oceans. Steadily the "royal fish" was fished out of one area after another, until today rights are rare beasts stringently protected by international agreement.

Woods Hole Oceanographic Institution

BALEEN of a small whale. Part of lower jaw and tongue have been cut away.

With an increase in demand for lamp oil and candles in the eighteenth century, attention turned to the anvil-headed sperm. About 1815, this whale began to be hunted more than any other. In the following years, United States, British, French and Portuguese ships combed the oceans from 40° North to 40° South, searching for the cachalot. From 1830 to 1880 was the heyday of American sperm whaling—the era of Moby Dick (1851).

Melville lauded the sperm as "the most majestic of all whales in aspect. . . ." Surely no animal on Earth has such a distinctive and immense head. It is a solid, mostly boneless, buttresslike oblong, embracing one-third the length of the body. The front is a noseless, eyeless wall as tough as if it were paved with horses' hooves. To the bottom is hinged a surprisingly narrow, boomlike lower jaw bearing from 36 to 60 peglike teeth. These fit into sockets in the upper jaw when the mouth closes.

Sperms are said to reach 85 feet in length but whalers cruise their grounds for many a season before meeting one over 60 feet. Males average about 50 feet and 35 tons in weight. Females are much daintier, averaging about 37 feet and a mere 26,000 pounds. The sperm, or *Physter catodon* as zoologists call him, is usually dark bluish gray with a humplike fin and a series of smaller knobs running along the rear of his back. On a short sprint, these whales may reach 20 knots, but they prefer to cruise leisurely along the surface at half that speed.

Squid is *P. catodon*'s bread, and completely intact individuals ranging from 3 to 34½ feet have been taken from sperm stomachs. Since a sperm can swallow a giant squid he could easily accommodate Jonah, but he is the only whale with a big enough gullet to do so. There are many stories of sailors being swallowed by whales, but James Bartley, crewman of *The Star of the East*, is supposedly the only one ever to survive the experience. Bartley reportedly spent several hours inside a sperm whale in 1891, but the story is not generally accepted by scientists.

The name "sperm" comes from *spermaceti*, an oily substance found only in this whale's head. Melville says it was once thought to be that "quickening humor" which the first syllable expresses. He himself believed this lightweight oil buoyed up the front of the head, causing it to break surface first. In the cranium, spermaceti is a fragrant, limpid liquid, but when exposed to air it becomes a glistening wax-like substance. In Melville's day it went into the manufacture of superior candles; today spermaceti goes into face creams, salves and ointments.

P. catodon is the sole source of another exotic substance: ambergris. It comes from the intestines of some but not all individuals. Melville describes it as resembling "rich mottled old cheese, very unctuous and savory . . . highly fragrant and spicy." Now as then, it is used as an ingredient in perfumes. In mid-nineteenth century it was worth "a gold guinea an ounce," today it brings about $100 a pound. A 920-pound lump cast up on an Australian beach in 1953 sold for $120,000. Ambergris was long thought to be produced by sickness; it is now believed to originate as hardened whale dung which collects around the indigestible beaks and cuttle bones of squid. (Think of that, madam, next time you dab some exotic essence behind your ear.) One of Melville's shipmates imagined the hard squid parts were sailor's trouser buttons.

The Vanishing Leviathans

Melville called the sperm a leviathan, considered him the colossus of the seas. But *P. catodon* is a runt compared to *Balaenoptera musculus*—the blue or sulphur bottom whale. Here is a cetacean of superlatives—the king of whales—the largest creature that has ever inhabited Earth. A full grown adult may reach 100 feet long and weigh 136 tons, as much as three of the biggest dinosaurs, 30 Indian elephants, 200 cows or 1,600 men. The heaviest whale ever weighed was an exceptionally fat, 90-foot-long blue cow that tipped the scales at 136.4 tons (272,800 pounds). These are maximums, but even an average blue attains a length of 80 feet and weighs close to 100 tons.

Gray Whale

Fin Whale

Humpback Whale

Sei Whale

ght Whale

Sperm Whale

Blue Whale

Melville described *B. musculus* as a "retiring gentleman, with a brimstone belly, doubtless got by scraping along the Tartarian tiles in some of his profounder divings." But, alas, his "sulphur" bottom has a much more mundane origin; it is due to a yellowish film of diatoms that covers his belly and flanks after about six weeks of feeding in polar waters. Also, the blue (he gets that name from his bluish back) does not engage in "profound divings." He and the other big whisker mouths rarely go below 300 feet, except when harpooned or frightened.

Blues, finbacks, humpies and seis, known collectively as *rorquals,* have their bellies wrinkled or pleated like an accordion from chin to navel. This allows the cavernous craw to open like some Brobdingnagian bag and take in hogsheads of shrimp-laden water with each gulp. They feed somewhat differently from the pleatless right whales, closing their tremendous mouths more frequently. As they do this, the accordion belly contracts and the gigantic tongue, which may weigh as much as a full-grown elephant, moves up into the baleen like a piston. No one has been able to determine exactly how the tongue operates, but it somehow wipes or squeezes the shrimp out of the baleen and pushes them towards the gullet.

Blue whales usually travel leisurely at 10 knots, surfacing to blow every 15 minutes or so. When in a hurry, they reportedly can sprint up to 20 knots for about 15 minutes. Finbacks, na ied for their prominent dorsal fin, cruise at 10 to 12 knots. They may reach 85 feet in length and supposedly can swim underwater at speeds up to 30 mph for a very short time. But the sei whale is the sprinter *par excellence.* Slimmer than other rorquals and growing to 50 or 60 feet, this warm-water whale is said to move as fast as 35 mph at the surface.

For centuries such speeds saved these whales from hunters in oar-powered boats. However, the advent of fast, steam-powered catcher boats made pursuit of the rorquals both possible and desirable. In the 1860's Svend Foyn, a Norwegian, developed a practical harpoon gun and later armed it with a shell that explodes inside the whale. This led to a vast expansion of land whaling stations and to extensive expeditions to polar seas in pursuit of blues, finbacks and humpies. In the first half of this century, 25 million tons of blue whales were taken in Antarctica.

Today whales are harpooned by small fleets of 6 to 18 catcher boats. They are towed to ocean-liner-sized mother ships, which take the entire whale aboard via a stern ramp and process it with the efficiency of a factory. Now the ship swallows the whale and Jonah is avenged a thousandfold.

Meat and blubber are cut from the body, and about 25 tons of fatty oil is extracted from the blubber of each blue whale by boiling. No longer needed to light the lamps of the world, rorqual oil now goes into the manufacture of soaps, margarine, and, to a lesser extent, paint dryers. Bones are cut up by power saws, ground and sold for making glue and gelatin. Blood and bowels become fertilizer. The liver which may weigh over 2,000 pounds supplies vitamin A, and glands like the pituitary yield hormones. Nothing need go to waste and very little does.

Norway and Japan are the only two countries where whale meat is eaten regularly. I have dined on whale steak and found it on a par with grass-fed beef, having only the slightest suggestion of fish flavor. Blubber is consumed in Japan and Iceland, but this is something you really have to acquire a taste for. The Soviets make an edible protein-rich meal from whale meat.

In 1946, an International Whaling Commission was formed and 17 member nations agreed to refrain from capturing species in danger of extinction, to observe closed seasons and areas, and to spare small whales and cows accompanied by calves. An overall limit was placed on the number of whales that could be taken by factory ships every season in antarctic waters, the last of the great whaling grounds. But all this was too late to save the blue whale; they declined from 76 percent of the catch in the peak season of 1930-31 to less than 6 percent in the 1950's. As blues became less abundant whalers turned on the finbacks, which yield only about half as much oil, then on the seis which yield about a sixth.

Antarctic factory ships failed to catch their limit in 1962-63 and 63-64, a sure sign that the whales are disappearing. In July 1964 scientists advised whalers that the total number of whales caught between 1964 and 1967 should be drastically and progressively reduced. They recommended that the quota for antarctic factory ships be decreased to the equivalent of 4,000 blue whales in 1964-65. This means either 8,000 finbacks, 10,000 humpies, 24,000 seis or any combination thereof. But Norway, Russia and Japan felt this was not high enough for their profit requirements and privately agreed on a quota of 8,000 blue whale units. Although this was the lowest limit in history, 15 factory ships working from December to April failed to reach it by 1,019 units. The

RIGHT WHALE blows in the Atlantic. In 1965 whaling nations agreed to limit their catch in Antarctic waters in order to allow the whales to replenish their depleted numbers. They also agreed to establish whale sanctuaries.

Marineland of Florida

catch consisted mostly of seis, and proved the scientists' contention that in the past more blues and finbacks were caught each season than the whales could replace by new births.

Many observers feel that the end of the illustrious history of whaling will soon be written; indeed, some think it already has. Norway sold the last of its open ocean whaling ships to Japan in 1965. Japan and Russia now do virtually all of the pelagic whaling and they have agreed to limit their catch of the diminishing antarctic species enough to allow the whales to replenish their numbers. If they do this, the oceans could sustain an annual harvest of about 5,000 blues and 20,000 finbacks. If they do not do it, the Earth's greatest living animals will become as extinct as dinosaurs. When one looks at man's record of greed and ignorance in the exploitation of sea creatures, he can see little hope for the whales.

Sex and Salvation

Whales cannot keep up with man's depredations because of their slow rate of reproduction. Mamma whale usually has only one calf at a time with more than a year between births. Female whales have twins about as often as humans (once in 80 to 87 births) and bear between 6 and 15 young in a lifetime of 15 to 30 years.

Cetacean mothers carry their young about a year and the newborn are enormous. Baby blues average 23 feet long and weigh around 5,000 pounds. The newborn comes into the world tail first, and must be able to swim to the surface for its first breath. It then begins to hunt for its mother's nipples, which are protruded from slits on either side of the womb back near the tail. By contracting huge muscles, mamma shoots as much as 130 gallons of fat-rich milk into her baby's mouth every day. Young blue calves may gain as much as 200 pounds a day on this nourishing fluid, which tastes like an oily mixture of fish, liver and milk of magnesia. At weaning, some six months after birth, the blue's baleen has grown long enough to filter krill, and the youngster himself may be 50 feet in length, the size of an adult humpie or sei.

PILOT WHALE hurls its 35-foot bulk out of the water at Marineland of Florida.

Adult blue whales are said to leap completely out of the water. If true, this would be the most remarkable display of agility in all the animal kingdom. Sei whales often jump clear of the surface as do the 30-foot killer whales. Why they do this no one knows. Nor is it known why some males and females clasp each other with their fins and shoot vertically out of the water together. Humpbacks, the most gamesome of the whales, turn series of somersaults above and below water. Like huge, barnacled kittens, these knobby cetaceans roll on the surface and slap the water with their flukes or long, winglike pectorals. When whales slap the surface with their flukes—whalers call it "lob-tailing"—or come back down from a leap in the air the resounding splash can be heard for miles.

Along with right and gray whales, humpbacks have been known to support a wounded comrade until they themselves fell victim to whalers. Humpies come to the assistance of pregnant females and young, as do dolphins. In April 1956, a small group of Mediterranean fishermen who caught a female dolphin were attacked by a delphinian rescue party ten strong and almost lost their lives. When in labor pregnant bottlenose dolphins are always accompanied by a female companion to ensure that mother and baby are not left behind or attacked by sharks. If a newborn dolphin has trouble taking its first breath, the mother or this "aunt" pushes it to the surface. They do the same to a stillborn calf. Dolphins at Marineland of Florida took turns caring for a dead baby for two days.

Stories of dolphins and porpoises pushing drowning people to safety go back to ancient Greece. One of the most recent cases occurred off a Florida beach in 1949. A woman wading waist deep was suddenly pulled down by an undertow. "As I gradually lost consciousness," she wrote later, "someone gave me a terrific shove, and I landed on the beach, face down. . . ." When she caught her breath and turned over no one was near, but "in the water about 18 feet out a porpoise was leaping around. A man who had been standing on the other side of the fence said that the porpoise had shoved me ashore."

BIRTH OF A BOTTLE-NOSE DOLPHIN. Mothers carry their young for nearly twelve months before giving birth, tail first. The baby nurses (above) for as long as 18 months. An "aunt" stands by in all photos.   Marineland of Florida

Despite a record of good deeds going back 2,500 years, scientists do not credit porpoises and dolphins with consciously realizing another species is in danger and deliberately trying to save a life. Rather, floating objects seem to arouse some sort of "lifting" behavior or deep-seated desire to push things. During World War II, a dolphin tried to push four downed American airmen in a rubber raft toward the nearest island. But the flyers had to drive the helpful mammal off because the island was enemy held. They may push as many distressed people away from shore as they do toward it, but the former never survive to tell the story. Dolphins have been observed pushing dead turtles, pieces of tin and wood and even a waterlogged mattress. Perhaps this behavior is a form of sport or amusement related to their natural playfulness.

Playboys of the Sea

The names "dolphin" and "porpoise" are used interchangeably in the United States, but because there are also a couple of feisty game fish called dolphins, and because of habit of usage, "porpoise" is gaining in acceptance among scientists. For a long time zoologists referred only to the beasts with the built-in grins as dolphins. Those they called porpoises lack the grin and a "beaked" snout.

The word "porpoise" means "pig fish" or "fish hog." This may be a reference to their portly girth; usually dolphins are more streamlined. The common harbor porpoise *Phocaena phocaena,* seen off the United States Pacific Coast, has a rounded snout and a dark gray and white body. It grows to about 6 feet and 120 pounds.

The 50 or so species of dolphins range from 4 to 30 feet in length. *Delphinus delphis,* the common dolphin, has a beaked snout, a black back, and yellow and white markings on its sides. *Delphis* prefers the open sea and is the "porpoise" frequently seen gamboling about the bows of ships. It is also the Mediterranean species that was held sacred in ancient times and the hero of the many Greek and Roman dolphin stories. Flipper, Carolina Snowball and the lesser

Killer Whales

Common Porpoise

Bottle Nose Dolphin

Common Dolphin

known dolphins cavorting in the Marinelands and other seaquariums are known as bottlenoses for obvious reasons. Members of this group (*Tursiops*) average 8 feet long and about 350 pounds. They prefer warmer coastal waters. *Tursiops gilli* lives off the southern part of the United States Pacific coast. *T. truncatus* inhabits the waters off the Atlantic and Gulf coasts. In all probability the porpoise that rescued the woman on the Florida beach in 1949 was an Atlantic bottlenose.

In their wild, untrained state bottlenoses leap into the air, frolic around ships, toss dead fish and other objects into the air and try to catch them. Aquaria dolphins tease fish by pulling their tails, ride turtles and others on their noses, fling unwanted fish out of the tank and throw objects at spectators with their mouths. They have retrieved things that tourists accidentally dropped in the water. When rewarded with fish, bottlenoses can be trained to jump through hoops, leap as high as 20 feet, play basketball, dance on their tails and "sing" squeakily.

But these small whales are not all play. Like bigger cetaceans they adhere to a strict pecking order, lashing out with their tails, butting others with their snouts and adopting a threatening attitude to assert social superiority. Dolphins sometimes inflict terrible gashes and broken bones on each other in social disputes or battles over females. In 1948 males at Marineland of Florida butted to death a pilot whale in the same way dolphins kill sharks, ramming it in the gills and underparts with their tough snouts. They attack humans when handled roughly or antagonized. A number of scientists and trainers have been butted and bitten during experiments and training.

One of the most curious and fascinating aspects of dolphin behavior involves riding people on their backs. This is the kind of stuff that sea stories are made of and dolphin-back tales date from ancient Greek and Roman literature. Pliny the Elder (A.D. 23-79) started it off with several accounts. One related the adventures of a boy named Hermias who rode a dolphin across the Bay of Naples to school and back for several years. When a sudden storm caused the boy to lose his life on one trip the dolphin pushed his body to shore then, as Pliny tells it, stranded itself on the beach in remorse.

Hundreds of people witnessed dolphin rides in 1955-56 near the small town of Opononi on the northwest coast of New Zealand. An 8-foot female dolphin, named "Opo" after the town, began her acquaintance with humans by following fishing boats and having her back scratched with an oar or mop. After overcoming some initial reluctance, Opo began to spend hours a day cavorting with bathers, particularly the gentler children. She learned to toss and catch a beach ball, whack it with her tail, and balance a beer bottle on her nose. Opo had a favorite human, 13-year-old Jill Baker. "On several occasions," the girl wrote, "when I was standing in the water with my legs apart she would go between them, pick me up and carry me a short distance before dropping me again. . . . She would also let me put little children on her back for a moment or two." Opo stranded and died on March 8, 1956, the very day Opononi passed a law to protect her from harm.

All such dolphin rides have been short and most were made by children. Many straddled their sea mount in front of the dorsal fin rather than behind. All rides of which there are detailed and accurate accounts took place after repeated meetings between animal and human and some practice attempts. In sum, such excursions seem to be rare and special events, restricted to exceptional animals. By no means are they part of the usual behavior of wild or even captive dolphins. Rare or not, such events exemplify the dolphin's unusual interest in and genuine fondness for an alien species, at least when there are no other dolphins around.

Opo formed definite social ties with people. The same may be true of the dolphin Keiki (Hawaiian for "child"). This young male bottlenose was used by University of California scientists for speed research. "Keiki," according to Dr. Kenneth Norris, head of the project, "solicited bodily contact of various sorts" from swimmers who spent an hour a day with him to keep him from getting lonely. The men often responded to these solicitations by stroking and patting him.

NAVY EMPLOYEE. The U. S. Navy trained a 7-foot, 270-pound dolphin named Tuffy to take lines to lost divers, carry packages between divers and the surface and retrieve objects. Ten-year-old Tuffy was then assigned to Project Sealab where he served as general assistant and shark guard for 20 scientists and divers, working 205 feet down off the California coast.

When Keiki was taken out in the open sea and released as part of the research, he made no attempt to escape at first. Norris was pleased when the dolphin returned to an underwater wire cage each night at the sound of a whistle. He thought Keiki had developed social ties with man and depended on him for food. But one day when he was released for a run in the open sea Keiki swam away and never returned.

The Killers

Dolphins have a cousin with the reputation of being as cruel and bloodthirsty as they are warm-hearted, fun-loving and affectionate. Man has always considered *Orcinus orca,* the killer whale, the most hateful and dangerous beast in the sea.

Killer whales roam over the World Ocean in packs ranging from 2 or 3 up to 40 individuals. Because of their intelligence, speed, size and power they go unchallenged and unopposed. Primarily fish eaters, they have even competed with man for food. In 1956, killers caused losses of $250,000 in the Icelandic fisheries. They also enjoy warm-blooded prey, making gluttonous feasts out of seals, sea lions, young walruses, penguins, porpoises and dolphins. One captured 20-foot specimen had three pregnant porpoises in its stomach, fully-formed and obviously swallowed whole. Another 24-footer had the remains of 13 porpoises and 14 seals in its stomach, together with a fifteenth seal in its throat.

Killers feed like dolphins, first encircling their prey then drawing the ring tighter and tighter. They sometimes display a cruel sense of humor, bumping seals and sea lions into the air and playing with them before the kill. Off California's Santa Barbara Island one was seen to flip a helpless sea lion into the air repeatedly for some 20 minutes.

Male killers grow to 30 feet and have a sharp, triangular dorsal fin as high as 6 feet. Females seldom exceed 15 feet and their dorsals are smaller. The upper part of the body in both sexes is midnight black, while belly and throat are livid white. The white extends up the flanks and sometimes is splashed behind the eyes and dorsal fin. Killers can maintain speeds somewhat in excess of 23 mph, and they cooperate in attacks on large baleen whales. A wolf pack goes after the bigger whale's tongue, sometimes eating it out of his head then leaving him to die.

Orcas also work as a team to break ice from under seals and penguins. They slam into it with their backs, one after another, until the prey topples into the sea. A photographer on one antarctic expedition was almost knocked into the water in this way. The killers might have mistaken him for a seal, or were after sled dogs on the ice with him. No clear-cut case exists of a deliberate attack on man, although quite a few swimmers have been caught in the water with them.

However, killers must be considered dangerous until proven otherwise, and one can easily understand the caution of scientists in dealing with a two-year-old, 2,300 pound male captured off Vancouver, Canada. Harpooned at sea, the killer was nursed back to health in a flooded dry dock and astounded everyone by turning out to be as playful and love-able as a puppy, and almost as friendly. Moby Doll (his captors thought he was a she at first) remained in captivity for 3 months before dying. In that time he learned to eat fish served by hand, talked to his captors in a beepy, squeaky voice and would roll over and allow his stomach to be scratched. After eating its fill of salmon, Namu—a 24-foot, 10,000 pound killer at the Seattle, Washington, Public Aquarium—allows trainer Ted Griffin to ride on its back. Maybe man has assigned *Orcinus orca* the wrong personality after all.

Senses and Sonar

Unlike the keen-nosed fishes, killers cannot smell a thing. They and other toothed whales have no "nose," and the sense of smell is almost to the vanishing point in their cousins, the mat mouths. Melville waxed philosophical about this: ". . . The Sperm whale has no olfactories. But what does he want of them? No roses, no violets, no Cologne-water in the sea."

Although whales swallow their food whole, they apparently have a taste sense. And their sense of touch is well developed, particularly in the lips, tail and flukes. Melville wrote of a whale's tail: "there is a delicacy in it equalled only by the daintiness of the elephant's trunk. . . ." Dolphins love to rub against rough surfaces, to have hoses played on them like children, and to be stroked and patted by people and other dolphins.

Because of light conditions at sea, whales probably cannot see much farther than 75 feet. In other words, a big finback or blue rarely sees its own tail. In air, where there is more light, dolphins can spot a hoop or the movement of a trainer's hand 50-100 feet away.

Whales often swim fast enough to "outdrive their headlights" and would get into all kinds of difficulties if their hearing were not so keen. They possess no outside "trumpet" and the ear hole of the biggest species is so small you can barely slide a ball point pen into it. Nevertheless, cetaceans hear sounds that are faint to sensitive electronic equipment and so high in pitch as to be inaudible to human ears. Helping hearing is the fact that sound travels more than four times faster in water than in air, or at a speed of nearly a mile a second.

But acute hearing cannot keep them from running into things in the dark, and many whales hunt food at night. In the late 1940's Arthur McBride, an oceanarium curator, found that dolphins could dodge nets set in water so murky that visibility was practically nil. When some of these bottlenoses were captured and examined in the laboratory, researchers discovered they would respond to sound energy as high in frequency as that used in sonar. Such pulses, inaudible to human ears, are sent out ahead of submarines and bounce off objects in their path. Ships with equipment to receive these returning echoes are able to detect objects that human eyes and ears and radar cannot.* The fact that dolphins could pick up such ultrasonic pulses lead scientists

---

* Radar waves do not travel far enough underwater to be of use for detection or communication.

to wonder if they could use them in the same way as man. Researchers began conducting experiments to find out if the animals possessed a natural sonar.

Dr. Winthrop Kellogg of Florida State University discovered that bottlenose dolphins can successfully maneuver through a field of closely-spaced vertical poles without collision. They can do this in extremely muddy water or on a moonless night. Kellogg put real fish and plastic fish in the dolphins' tank when visibility was zero. They quickly learned to distinguish which was which and seldom missed a meal. Confronted with a clear passage and one blocked by plate glass, or fish out in the open and behind a glass screen, the grinning bottlenoses made the correct choice every time. This was definite proof of their abilities; the next question was how do they do it?

Day or night, when anything splashed into their muddy pen, underwater microphones picked up a series of sharp clicks that merged into a sound like the creaking of rusty

Chow Time.

Marineland of Florida

hinges. Kellogg's dolphins headed straight for the object and the clicking became more rapid the closer they got. Even the soft plink of a $\frac{3}{16}$ inch BB shot or the gentle plop of a teaspoon of water dropped into the tank would trigger the clicking and bring the dolphins over for a look.

These clicking creaks, it was learned, are pulses of dolphin sonar. Traveling outward in the form of high frequency sound waves, they bounce off objects in their path and echo back to the animal's "receiver." As the target is closed the time between echoes becomes shorter. Thus a dolphin can determine distance in terms of the rate of return of its clicking sounds.

Even when resting quietly in the pen, Kellogg's dolphins would constantly "glance" around by spontaneously emitting short bursts of clicks every 20 seconds or so. If a fish were noiselessly slipped into a corner of the darkened pool, the dolphins would usually find it by this means. Kellogg and colleagues tried the old wartime trick of jamming the sonar by broadcasting hi-fidelity recordings of dolphin clicks into the water. But the uncanny whales were able to sort out the confusing signals from their own echoes and continue maneuvering through the pole maze without mishap.

Since dolphins have no vocal cords, how do they produce these clicking sounds? Dr. Kenneth Norris thinks they do it by forcing air past small, tonguelike flaps located in two horn-shaped sacs on either side of the forehead. The flaps are extensions of the valves sealing off the nasal passages during submergence, and they may emit clicks as the air rushes past them.

Dolphins concentrate their clicks into two narrow, cone-shaped beams emerging parallel to the jaws and extending slightly above the head. The animal points its high forehead in the general direction of the target, then swings it from side to side in a scanning motion in order to accurately home in. Norris thinks returning echoes are picked up by the ears and by two narrow channels in the lower jaw which connect with the inner ear. If he is correct the personable dolphins "talk" off the top of their heads, "listen" with their jaws and "look" through their ears. They must also possess the equivalent of a computer in their fatty heads to separate echoes coming from the target from those bouncing off other objects and being reflected then re-reflected from the surface and sea bottom.

According to Dr. Sidney Galler of the Office of Naval Research, the dolphin's "echo-location system and navigation capability is far superior to the most sophisticated system we have in our most modern submarines." The best electronics the Navy can put together take up a great deal more weight and space than dolphin sonar and, no matter how sophisticated, cannot even distinguish between a whale and an enemy submarine. But Alicia, a typical 7-foot, 300-pound fun-loving bottlenose at the University of California, can tell the difference between 2½ and 2¼-inch ball bearing from as far away as 10 feet, while blindfolded.

Alicia and her tankmates, combining this ability with brainpower, almost outwitted scientists testing them. When the dolphins could no longer detect any difference in the size of balls, they would make a choice anyway in the hope of picking the right one and getting a fish reward. Said one scientist: "We had to check on them all along the way by throwing in identical balls to see if they were cheating."

Dolphins are not the only sea-going mammals that emit clicking sounds, so in all probability they are not the only ones equipped with sonar. Other toothed whales, including sperms and killers, as well as sea lions and seals have been heard clicking away. Because man would like to find his way in the underwater world as swiftly and unerringly as mammals, and do it with such "miniaturized" equipment, United States, Russian, Italian, and Japanese scientists and navymen spend considerable sums of money studying these creatures. Because of size, amiability, intelligence, adaptability to captivity and a fairly long history of observation, bottlenose dolphins continue to get most of this attention.

Dolphin Dialogues

When researchers lower hydrophones into the water with bottlenoses they hear, in addition to trains of sputtering

Two "talking" dolphins check out an underwater microphone.

clicks, a noisy assortment of whistles, squawks, quacks and blats. A lone animal remains silent most of the time. When meeting another dolphin the two whistle and buzz at each other. Groups of bottlenoses engaged in play, courtship or intercourse emit whistles, clicks, squawks, quacks and blats. Whistling sounds are heard most frequently and scientists are convinced these are used for communication. Researchers have isolated a vocabulary of 32 different whistle patterns including a distress signal and possibly a greeting and "come hither" call.

When bottlenoses experience trouble breathing, are in pain, or when an infant is separated from its mother, they emit a short, sharp, high-pitched whistle that rises then falls in volume. A distressed dolphin will keep up this whistling until it is rescued or sinks from exhaustion. If lucky, the SOS will bring other animals who will push their heads under the chin or pectorals of the sufferer and quickly lift it to the surface for air. Then the animals carry on a complex whistle exchange. In one such situation a sick female in captivity kept falling over on her left side. Her whistles summoned two healthy companions who took turns supporting her against the tank wall or holding her between them. This treatment, together with some squeaky "conversation," continued day and night for four days, then intermittently for two weeks until the ailing animal recovered.

Similar vocal exchanges were recorded in the wild by scientists studying sea noises in a Baja California lagoon. A gang of Pacific bottlenoses found their way blocked by a line of buoys floating with 12 feet of their length underwater. When they detected the obstacles by sonar the animals immediately turned into shallow water and gathered in a tight group. After a complex whistling conversation, overheard on sea bottom hydrophones, one dolphin broke away and made a run along the barrier. When the scout returned there was another whistle exchange, then a second scout swam out to examine the buoys. After he made a whistling report, the group moved off and passed cautiously under the barrier.

Of the 32 whistle patterns so far identified, at least five are used by both the Atlantic and Pacific bottlenoses, common dolphins in the Mediterranean and pilot whales. In some cases these different animals use the same groups of whistle patterns when engaged in similar activities. Since these creatures cooperate in the sea, there might be a common, international or interspecies "language" by which a variety of toothed whales communicate with each other.

Each of the 32 different whistles may represent a complete expression, in which case dolphins would be limited to voicing 32 needs or emotions. But if each represents a syllable or word, they could be combined into innumerable expressions, into a language, provided the animals have the intelligence to use a language. In other words, delphinese could be like the chirping of birds or the barking of dogs, or it could be like the human whistle languages used in some parts of the world. The Mazateco language of Mexico consists of whistles. For a thousand years the natives of the Canary Islands have communicated over distances as great as five miles by a whistle language based on the spoken word. In the mountain village of Kuskoy, Turkey children learn a whistle language in school.

The amount of information dolphins can put into their communications, then, depends on their intelligence. A number of scientists believe they are brighter than dogs, and some think they are smarter than chimpanzees. The grinning cetaceans do possess big, complex brains with about as many cells in a given area as our own. But whether this gray matter is used for thought or for separating and processing all the complex sound information they receive is unknown. However, a small minority of scientist-types are so impressed with the dolphin brain they think this mammal is as smart as people. A few will even go as far as saying dolphins may be more intelligent than humans. Dr. John Lilly, controversial director of the Communications Research Institute at Miami, thinks dolphins may be the first nonhuman species with which man will hold intelligent conversations. He says: "It is my firm conviction that within the next decade or two human beings will establish communication with another species: non-human, alien, possibly extraterrestrial, more probably marine."

Efforts are now being made to translate delphinese into English by matching recordings of their sounds with movies of their actions, and by employing a computerlike device that memorizes dolphin whistles and buzzes. But Lilly is going about it the other way; he is trying to teach dolphins to speak English. His prize pupil is Elvar—a frolicsome 7-foot, 350-pound male bottlenose. By rewarding him with fish and sending pain or pleasure evoking jolts of electricity into his brain, Lilly and helpers have trained Elvar to vocalize in air. The dolphin reportedly can match in number and duration a series of as many as 12 nonsense syllables shouted by a human. This is far more than parrots and mynah birds can handle. According to Lilly, Elvar can mimic such phrases as "More, Elvar" complete with southern or New England accent.

When the gamesome whale squirted water in pretty blonde Alice Miller's direction, the lady physiologist admonished, "Stop it, Elvar!"

"Stop it!" Elvar mimicked.

When the frisky dolphin is tired of waiting for class to begin, Lilly says he sounds off with something like, "All right, let's go."

But scientists who have heard records of Elvar's voice are dubious. One comments, "They didn't sound like human words to me." He thinks desire may play a role in Lilly's research and says, "If you want to hear those words badly enough, you will."

Yale University zoologist Dr. R. J. Andrew is not impressed with the dolphin's ability to mimic human sounds. ". . . Mimicking can be evolved in the absence of very high intelligence . . . ," he says and cites as an example birds that mimic.

Although Lilly's many critics consider the award inexcusable, the National Aeronautics and Space Administration was interested enough in his work to give him $80,700 for a year of study. NASA wants to know what Lilly can learn about communicating with other species. They feel there is a good probability that life exists elsewhere in the universe, and if intelligent creatures on one of these alien worlds tries to get in touch with us these techniques will come in handy. Says Dr. Dale W. Jenkins of NASA: "This work may help us toward an understanding of the communications of other organisms, some of which may have communications techniques far more effective than ours."

Bull sessions with dolphins have staggering philosophical and practical consequences. Skipping philosophical conjecture until more is known about bottlenose brain power, it is easy to envision dolphins working as scientists, saboteurs and blue-collar workers. Lilly and others visualize them as cowboys on undersea ranches herding schools of fish into nets or suction pipes as they now herd fish into a tight circle before making a meal of them. Dolphins would make great underwater demolition men, or finny spies and scouts to locate enemy mines, plant explosives or detectors, etc., etc.

Even without conversation an obliging dolphin could be trained to carry oceanographic instruments any place in the top layers of the World Ocean, or to place and retrieve equipment on the continental shelves. Take Keiki, for example. Without trying to talk to him Dr. Norris trained that dolphin to wear an instrument harness, swim at high speed on command, and return to him when a certain sound signal was played. Says Norris: "The development of a trained porpoise that can be manipulated in the open sea opens the way to a variety of experimental possibilities. Several captive porpoises have been broken to harnesses, which allow the attachment of a variety of instruments. Such animals could be used to perform a variety of human-directed tasks in the sea."

Tuffy, a scrappy 10-year-old, 270-pound bottlenose did just this on the U.S. Navy's Sealab II project. Equipped with a harness to which could be clipped tools, messages and lifelines, Tuffy acted as mail carrier, messenger and lifeguard for a team of divers living 205 feet down on the sea floor off La Jolla, California. Those who planned the project reasoned that the dolphin would also protect divers from sharks, but none showed up to bother the aquanauts. Tuffy, in fact, got his name from scars of shark battles on his body and from the fact that he butted and bit several trainers. One pretty college girl, who helped train him to retrieve objects blindfolded and home in on buzzing and clicking sounds, suffered a broken rib and was bitten several times on the hands.

In September 1965, Tuffy worked with the Sealab aquanauts for five days. Three groups of divers each stayed down for 15 days, during which time they lived in and worked around the vicinity of a 57-foot-long, 12-foot-diameter capsule placed on the sea floor. Astronaut Scott Carpenter worked two consecutive shifts, remaining down a total of 30 days; Tuffy put his time in on the second shift. On his first day at work, Tuffy became confused and frightened by the noises, lights and unnatural objects on the bottom. In answer to an SOS buzzer he came within a few inches of a diver supposedly lost in the murky water 150 feet from the undersea station. But before the diver could take the lifeline Tuffy shot abruptly up to the surface. He returned minutes later but failed to get close enough for aquanauts to remove pliers and screwdrivers attached to his harness.

After the first tough day, Tuffy got used to his surroundings and on the following four days he delivered about 25 letters and carried 10 packages between divers on the bottom and between the surface and Sealab. Tuffy made as many as 20 round trips a day, diving to 205-foot depths in 45 seconds. He rescued "lost" divers three times, taking lifelines to them which they could follow back to their tank car-sized base. When one diver failed to award him with a fish for this work, Tuffy gave him a sharp slap on the head with his flukes. Dr. Samuel Ridgeway, research veterinarian on the project, said the experiments with Tuffy "didn't work out as well as we hoped. However, we have learned a lot and demonstrated the feasibility of using dolphins to expand the capabilities of divers living and working on the ocean floor."

Tuffy will work with divers again as will other dolphins. Eventually man may integrate these animals and other marine mammals into undersea operations just as dogs and horses have been put to work on land. Dr. George Bond, head of the Sealab program, says experiments with Tuffy were preparation for the day when men and the dolphins will cooperate to explore and exploit the ocean and its resources. The scientific and evolutionary results of such cooperation will be more fascinating than any fiction. Perhaps dolphins and kin will help us return to the sea as they did.

15.
Food From
the Sea

". . . The sea is a green pasture where our children's grandchildren will go for bread."
—A NANTUCKETER, 1690

WHISKER-MOUTH whales grow to be the largest, strongest creatures on Earth on a diet of small reddish shrimps, so why don't we scoop this krill out of the ocean and use it for human food?

A baby blue whale puts on an average of 80 pounds a day and grows to be a strapping lad of 65 feet by his second birthday. Therefore raw krill soup must be nourishing enough. According to Dr. Willis E. Pequegnant, a zoologist at Texas A&M University, these crustaceans are rich in protein and fats and contain about as many calories as other shellfish. How about taste? I sampled the little beasts on an expedition to Antarctica and, although one batch gave me a terrific stomachache, on the whole they tasted like salty shrimp.

Dr. Pequegnant figures there is an average of about a thousand pounds of krill per acre of Antarctic feeding grounds. He compares this to rich pasture land which yields about 700 pounds of cattle and sheep per acre per year. Since big whales have been hunted nearly to the point of commercial extinction Pequegnant suggests that antarctic whaling fleets might turn their attention to whale food. "My own calculations," he says, "indicate that krill trawling might be more profitable than whaling."

Professor Alister Hardy envisions artificial steam, diesel or atomic-powered "whales" gulping krill by the shipload and reguritating it into the larders of the world. "By 1984," he says "krill may be making the greatest addition to man's food supply of the century. . . ." According to the U.N., one-half of the world's population, one and a half billion people, do not get enough to eat. And each day the number of children that must be fed increases by a staggering 158,800. Hardy asks: "Can we not save the starving children of the world with krill?" He answers: "I am sure we shall."

Krill are members of the plankton and plankters are the most abundant creatures in the sea. Most of them live over the continental shelves. Cannot undernourished nations reap the floating protein at their doorsteps and feed it to their hungry people?

The crew of Kon-Tiki sampled various plankton dishes as the raft drifted 4,800 miles from Peru to Polynesia. Thor Hyerdahl, expedition leader, reports that jellyfish and their near relatives were "bitter and had to be thrown away. Otherwise everything could be eaten, either as it was or cooked in fresh water. . . ." Two of the six raftsmen could not stomach the "bad smell" and "nasty" appearance of plankton, but the others agreed that hauls dominated by copepods reminded them of shrimp paste, lobster or crab. Meals dominated by fish eggs "tasted like caviar and sometimes like oyster." Dr. Alan Bombard, another adventurous raftsman who crossed the Atlantic via currents, said his plankton dinners "tasted like lobster, at times like shrimp and at times like some vegetable." Hardy writes: "Boiled in sea water, strained and then fried in butter and served on toast, *Euchaeta* (a group of copepods) is a delicacy which one day might support a small luxury market."

But a tremendous gap exists between a small luxury market or satisfying the appetites of men adrift and a profit-making fishery. Beside a wide disparity in quality (some plankters are poisonous) quantity varies unpredictably from place to place, season to season and even day to day. Plankton herds are so widely dispersed in the sea that even in ant-arctic waters krill concentrations can be difficult to find in spring. Guesstimates of effort vs. yield run something like this: In ordinary temperate coastal waters a plankter-man would have to strain enough water to fill 15 one-story houses in order to get the nutritional equivalent of a pound of beans. In rich areas like the Gulf of Maine or North Sea 5,000 tons of water would have to be strained to get 10 pounds of plankton.

To make such an operation profitable an extremely inex-pensive energy source is necessary. Hardy once suggested that the motion of tides might do the trick. He proposed stretching nets across the mouths of narrow lochs on the coast of Scotland where plankton supports armies of herring and battalions of basking sharks. Each net could filter 22,000 tons of water an hour in the two knot tides that prevail 12 hours a day. One thousand such nets, Hardy estimated, would collect enough plankton every day to feed 37,500 people, if they would eat it. These people would not have to live on plankton alone, but it might make a nutritious supplement to their diets. It could also be converted into the flesh of chickens and cows via a protein-rich meal.

Hardy sums up the results of his experiments: "For two years we made a survey but failed to get plankton in large enough quantities to make the venture worthwhile. The plankton is too uneven in its distribution and an enormous quantity of water has to be filtered to give sufficient yield in even a very rich area." Experiments along these lines in the United States lead to the same conclusion. However, where Americans and British have failed the Japanese have succeeded. Faced with a shortage of land on which to grow food for their multiplying millions they managed to establish a flourishing fishery for two planktonic shrimp (Sergestids), one of which seldom grows larger than a half-inch.

This is a step toward filtering the sea with the efficiency of a blue whale. A healthy adult blue needs about a million calories a day to keep going and gets them by gulping between 2,000 and 6,000 pounds of shrimps daily. As Thor Hyerdahl mused from his raft: "Our own method of capture . . . seemed to us sadly primitive when we . . . saw a passing whale send up cascades of water as it simply filtered plankton through its celluloid beard." Our ineptness at straining the sea means a plankton meal would cost about $3.00 a pound more than steak. As one biologist put it, "We'll have a long wait for the first twenty-five cent planktonburger."

Someday the problems of filtering and uneven quality and quantity may be solved by raising desirable species in large tanks or ponds. This is already being done on a small scale with one-celled, fresh water plants of the genus *Chlorella* (green algae). Such algae crops can be harvested every three days, and in a year an acre of pond yields 30 tons as opposed to a one-ton yield of wheat per acre of fertile land. With the grass taste bleached out, algae can be artificially flavored to taste like meat and vegetables. The National Aeronautics and Space Administration is considering raising algae in space ships to feed astronauts on long, interplanetary missions.

Food Pyramid

Until planktonburgers are produced in commercial quantities at competitive prices all man can do is to rely on the efficient filters of such creatures as anchovies and herring. They catch the plankton, then we catch and eat them.

By waiting for plenteous creatures of convenient size to concentrate the plankters we make things easier for ourselves, but 80 to 90 percent of the food value gets lost in the process. This is because only about ten percent of what an animal eats goes into building its own body. The rest is burned on the altar of metabolism to maintain the creature's bulk and to keep him going. On Georges Bank, a rich feeding ground off Cape Cod, it takes an estimated 1,000 pounds of such plants as diatoms to support 100 pounds of copepods and other zooplankters. In turn these animals feed only ten pounds of fish. If a man eats ten pounds of herring, only one pound can be built into his fat and muscle. If he waits for a tuna to eat the herring and then eats the tuna, his share of the herring diminishes to one-tenth of a pound.

You can think of the hierarchy of seagoing predators as forming a sharply narrowing pyramid. Countless billions of invisible plant cells compose the foundation of the pyramid; they literally support the entire animal kingdom. These tiny bits of life become transformed into bigger but fewer bundles of living material at each tier or level. At the pyramid apex stand the great predators like man and the killer whale. Plants must outnumber the animals that feed on them; herring must outnumber tuna. The lower down on the pyramid an animal feeds the more food is available. Said another way, the largest population can be supported on the shortest food chain. If we could eat diatoms we would be eating as efficiently as possible from the sea. The same holds true on land. Man can support the largest number of his species by becoming a vegetarian.

Baleen whales and the biggest sharks eat only one link down from the sun itself, avoiding the rapid loss of energy as it passes from one level to another.

Davy Jones' Larder

Granting that the food chain from sea to man's dinner table consists of at least three links, how much food can we get from the ocean? Strangely enough, in an age when we talk of giant atom smashers and journeys to the moon, scientists cannot answer this basic question because most of the ocean is unexplored from a biological point of view.

The best estimate comes from a study by the Committee on Natural Resources of the U.S. National Academy of Sciences. Based on admittedly inadequate information, they calculated that 19 billion tons of lifeless carbon is photosynthesized into living matter every year by ocean plants. After passing through the food chain, this represents from 180 to 1,400 million tons of new fish flesh produced in the sea annually. There is some evidence that these figures also approximate the weight of fish in the World Ocean at any

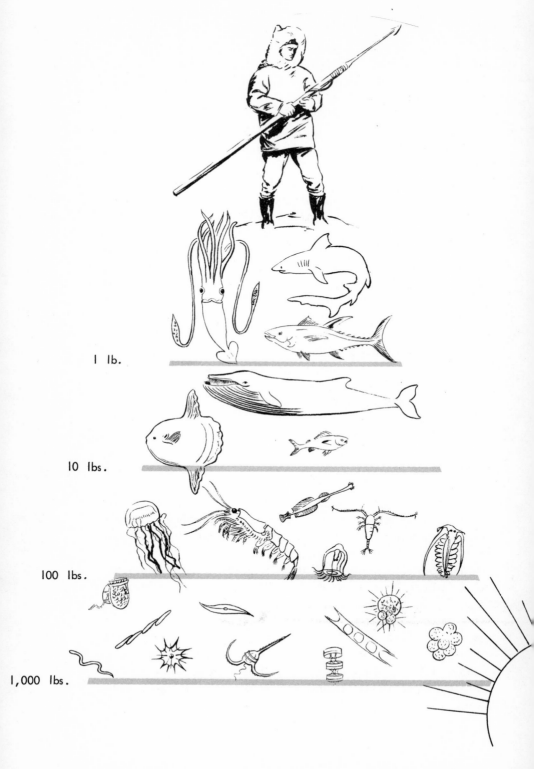

1 lb.

10 lbs.

100 lbs.

1,000 lbs.

FOOD PYRAMID. The lower down on the pyramid an animal feeds the more food is available.

one time. Taking the liberty of averaging the extremes, we come up with 790 million tons of fish in the sea.

According to U.N. statistics, five million commercial fishermen in the world netted, hooked and trapped some 50 million tons of seafood in 1963. About 45 million tons were fish.* Hence if everybody's calculations are correct, only between 3 and 25 percent of the available fish are being caught. (Yet some species have been depleted by overfishing.)

A billion and a half people need some of the fish that got away. In Africa and Latin America millions of mothers listen to their undernourished babies cry themselves to sleep at night. In Asia a billion people suffer from malnutrition. Yet many of these people live in countries fronting on waters teeming with nourishment in a variety of delicious forms. Therefore, the cheapest and most efficient way to alleviate their suffering is through food from the sea. It is not that all these people do not get enough to eat, rather, a large percentage of them do not get enough protein for good health and well-being. According to the National Academy of Sciences (NAS) a 50 percent increase in the present catch could provide enough nourishment for these 500 million protein-starved people. But the report adds, "This is much more easily said than done."

Many of the protein-starved inhabit nations whose shores are washed by the Indian Ocean. Cooperative endeavors such as the International Indian Ocean Expedition are needed to fill gaps in our knowledge of sea animal stocks in such unexplored parts of the world. From 1960 to 1965 some 40 research ships from 28 nations, including the United States and Russia, crisscrossed the 28 million square miles of the Indian Ocean. What are believed to be rich untapped populations of sardines, shrimp, tuna, lobster and crab were discovered off the coasts of Africa and Asia. Concentrations of crab and bottom fish several hundred miles in extent exist off eastern Arabia. Large numbers of jumbo shrimp live 750 feet deep off Kenya, perhaps in commercial quantities.

---

* The remainder of the catch consisted of over two million tons of shellfish and lesser amounts of seaweed, seal meat, etc. Whales are not included in this tally.

But locating sea food and getting it to the dinner table involve different difficulties. There are problems of transportation or lack of it and effective ways of keeping the game from spoiling. The high cost of refrigerated fishing fleets, storage, and transportation facilities would boost the retail price of fish beyond the reach of the families that need it most.

One solution to the preservation problem may be nuclear irradiation. Small doses of radiation kill spoilage bacteria and increase the shelf life of food from days to months without making it radioactive. The U.S. Bureau of Commercial Fisheries operates a $600,000 pilot plant that zaps flounder, haddock, clams, oysters, crabs and shrimp. Hence such goodies as atomic oysters and other seasonal seafood should soon be available to inlanders and coastal dwellers alike on a year-around basis. A second pilot plant has been installed aboard ship in the hope that in the near future skippers will not have to race the spoilage specter back to port every time their holds are filled.

At present, irradiated seafood still requires refrigeration since the heavy doses required to kill all bacteria alter taste, smell or vitamin content. Therefore, a more direct and practical solution is to reduce fish to a colorless, odorless powder that keeps indefinitely without refrigeration. Called fish flour, it is made by grinding up the whole fish then removing water, fats and odorous fractions by heat or chemicals. Because the word "flour" frightens farmers and millers as only competition can, politicians prefer the name "fish protein concentrate," or to get a little more innocuous, "FPC." By whatever name, it has a protein content of 70 to 80 percent and can be blended into bread, used as a milk substitute or added to soups, cereals and curries. An Indian or Malaysian housewife could pick up a pound for about twenty cents, that is if United States bureaucrats would let her.

The Food and Drug Administration has not approved FPC for human consumption because the whole fish goes into its manufacture—guts, head, bones, tails, scales and all. Americans are too well fed to be concerned about the ban,

Some fisheries experts have suggested that dolphins—such as the mother, baby and aunt shown here—would make a new and nutritious addition to the world's menu. This suggestion was brought on by claims that they ruin nets and gobble up fish stocks in some parts of the world. But as one official says, many people would no more eat a porpoise than eat their pet cocker spaniel.

but starving millions are deprived of health and vitality because officials of their nations look to the FDA for guidance. They insist on its approval before importing any American food product. Also, bureaucrats feel that distributing a food product to other countries that is deemed unfit for Americans would invite a Communist propaganda attack.

Many knowledgeable people cannot understand why FDA regards fish flour as "filthy" but makes allowances for rat dung in wheat. As some nutritionists point out, it is inconsistent to brand flour made from whole fish unwholesome when millions of Americans daily eat sardines, oysters, clams, pig's feet, tripe and tongue. Hopefully, hunger and reason will eventually win out over bureaucracy.

There are indications that it is going to. FDA recently reclassified FPC from a "food" to a "food supplement." As the latter it would be added to baked goods, baby food and other products, and different legal standards would apply to its approval. Also, the Bureau of Commercial Fisheries has perfected a process to make cheap, pure, stable, easily handled flour from hake. This fish is abundant in domestic waters, not used for food or sport, available most of the year and free of fat. The BCF process has undergone thorough testing and been found to be highly nutritious and completely safe.

But even if all barriers fall, will the Asian or African housewife, hagridden by religious taboos and outmoded customs, feed her family curries thickened with fish flour, or two-month-old irradiated tuna fillets? Man's stomach often refuses to break the rules of his upbringing. Most of the people of India and other countries who prefer a vegetable diet would be better off with animal protein. But even in a famine, religious vegetarians will sometimes die rather than eat meat or fish.

The United States Falls Behind

The world's population is expected to double by the year 2000. As it swells to six billion people pressure to obtain more food from the sea becomes greater. The world catch has increased more than tenfold since the beginning of the century. It doubled between 1952 and 1964. Although this increase exceeds the rate of population growth by a comfortable margin, the sea still contributes less than 15 percent of the animal protein eaten by humans.

More than 200 countries have fishing fleets. But nine nations account for about 40 percent of the catch: Peru, Japan, Red China, Russia, the United States, Norway, Canada, South Africa and Spain, in order of tonnage caught. Japan, where Mr. Average eats five times as much seafood as most Americans, led the field until 1963. Then Peru took first place by forging a remarkable industry out of the multitudes of anchoveta (*Engraulis ringens*) that swarm off her shores. These little sardinelike fish account for 98 percent of Peru's catch.

The Soviet Union tripled its production between 1948 and 1963, and its expanding fleet continues to meet and exceed Government-set goals. To her own benefit and that of underfed millions, Russia provides massive assistance to the fisheries of such countries as Ghana, Nigeria, Congo, Sudan and Eygpt. She is building fishing facilities in Cuba and at both ends of the Suez Canal which could conceivably serve as naval bases. Fleets of radar-equipped vessels working off West Africa keep an electronic eye on the Atlantic Missile Range and make a good living fishing at the same time. The Soviets have offered to land large quantities of fish on a regular basis in India, Ceylon and Brazil. "It's food diplomacy," notes one United States oceanographer, "and it seems to be working better than dollar diplomacy."

Although Russia zealously maintains a 12-mile limit off her coasts, Soviet vessels are free to come within three miles of United States shores, and they are coming in increasing numbers. Modern 150-boat fleets fish off both coasts. Accompanied by spotter planes and large supply ships, they work within photo and radar distances of early warning defense units, missile launching sites and naval exercises. Congressional reports call the Soviet flotillas "a peril to the United States fishing industry and a threat to the available supply of fish."

While Russia continues to expand, modernize, automate and subsidize its fishing industry, the United States continues to let its fleets run downhill. The industry is plagued with antiquated vessels, high shipbuilding costs, stubborn reluctance to try new methods, lagging progress in processing and an unstable market. While the world has increased its harvest from the sea United States landings have suffered a decline.

Russian and Japanese fishermen go out in fleets of fast, modern trawlers that have freezing equipment. These flotillas are shepherded by large mother ships carrying supplies and, in some cases, processing machinery. They freeze their catch immediately, store it and stay at sea for months. They can and do roam far from home in search of good yields and new fishing grounds. Unlike Russia and Japan, the United States does not intensively apply available technology. American fishermen go to sea in individual boats, which are slow and decrepit, and must bring their catch back to port for processing.

America's share of the world catch dropped from 13 percent in 1948 to 5 percent in 1963, and her take of food fish decreased from 3.3 billion pounds to 2.5 billion during approximately the same interval. This does not mean that Americans ate less fish. Seafood consumption actually increased from 1949 on, reaching 5 billion pounds in 1963. But this higher number simply reflects an increase in population not an increase in appetite. For many years the average American has eaten less than a pound of fish and shellfish a month. The gap between an increasing population eating a steady amount and the decreasing catch has been filled by imports, which have tripled since 1949.

Although half the seafood on our tables comes from other countries and the United States has dropped from second to fifth place among fishing nations, the outlook is not all bleak. The American catch of industrial or nonfood fish has doubled since World War II, although this increase lags behind that of other big fishing countries. These inedible fish are processed into fish oil and meal. The oil goes into the manufacture of paint, and the meal is used in chicken and cattle feed. Thus, a good menhaden catch can help push down the supermarket price of chicken.

As another plus factor, a significant part of the imported fish meal is produced by American companies in foreign countries, as is a good share of imported shrimp, tuna and lobster. Development of these foreign-based operations has accelerated since 1954, and increasing their output is one way to meet what many consider the principal challenge of the United States fishing industry—recapturing the domestic market.

Taking advantage of underexploited and unexploited stocks is another way United States fishermen can regain a greater share of the domestic market and maintain a leading

BLUEFIN TUNA is unloaded at Woods Hole Oceanographic Institution after a research cruise to gather information about its spawning grounds and migratory habits. Such information will improve the catch of both commercial and sport fishermen.

position among fishing nations of the world. Soviet and Japanese fleets catch over a million tons of ocean perch and bottom fish in the Bering Sea and Gulf of Alaska every year. There is no reason why American fishermen should not exploit the same rich populations.

The waters off California teem with anchovies (*Engraulis mordax*) in such abundance they reportedly could support a catch of two billion pounds a year. These fish compete with Pacific sardines (*Sardinella sagax*) for food, and such a catch might help rebuild the sardine stock which has, for unknown causes, been on the decline since the 1940's. But canners cannot afford to pack these small fishes profitably because of high labor costs, and California conservation laws make it difficult to take anchovies for fish meal or FPC.

A large untapped stock of hake exists off the Pacific coast, but U.S. commercial and sport fishermen alike hold this codlike creature in low regard. (Not so with some of the foreign fishermen who process it into fish meal.) Research reveals that jack mackerel off the Pacific coast could stand greatly increased exploitation. During recent years a new open ocean fishery for bluefin and skipjack tuna began in the Atlantic, where the presence of commercial quantities of skipjack was long unknown. Future tuna fishing in the Atlantic is expected to grow to the point of rivaling present efforts in the eastern Pacific, where yellowfin and perhaps albacore have come to the verge of being overfished. But the Pacific tuna industry can still continue to grow on increased catches of bluefin and skipjack.

Rational development of such stocks could result in a doubling of United States production in 10 to 15 years, according to the NAS Committee on Oceanography.

Filling the World's Fishbasket

What is true for the United States is true for the world. Says the Committee on Natural Resources: "The resources of the sea are multitudinous and immense, yet most of them are not exploited at all. . . ." According to Dr. Milner B. Schaefer of the Institute of Marine Resources, abundant pilchard and mackerel stocks in the North Sea and North-east Atlantic have barely been touched. Among the un-used populations of the North Pacific he lists anchovy, jack mackerel, hake, saury and squid. The fertile areas off Africa's west coast are just beginning to be exploited by the new African nations with enthusiastic help from the Russians. Nets now dipping into the vast anchovy schools off South Africa indicate this fishery may become as extensive as the one off Peru.

Food yield from the sea can also be increased by develop-ing imaginative new uses for familiar creatures. Smoked shark fillets have made a debut on the British delicacy mar-ket. "Very nice to eat, but very sweet," was one comment. Fish sausages are now available in Icelandic fish shops. Made of haddock and lumpsucker and lightly smoked, they look exactly like meat frankfurters. In Russia whale meat is blended into pork and beef sausage. Japan reportedly plans to build fish sausage factories in West Africa and the Carib-bean area. Japanese tuna hot dogs taste like meat sausage but cost far less. Students in United States schools have chris-tened them "Friday franks." Some creatures need what Brit-ish writer-scientist Richie Calder calls "gastronomical ano-nymity." Few Americans would order something called "rat-tail" or "dogfish" but change the names to "grenadier" and "rock salmon" and they become tempting new dishes. For years New England fishermen flung the ugly, sharp-spined redfish back into the sea as trash. But then filleting machines were invented that reduced them to succulent-looking chunks of white meat. Their name was changed to ocean perch. Gaily-colored packaging completed the transfiguration, and the once neglected redfish zoomed from obscurity to the seventh biggest catch in the United States.

There are undoubtedly hundreds if not thousands of good-tasting creatures in the sea that dietary unimaginative-ness and biological ignorance keep from our dinner plates. Only about a dozen species account for 75 percent of the United States catch and, Japan excepted, other nations ac-cept comparatively few species for human use. Badly needed is a biological census of the World Ocean together with a testing and tasting program. Combined with a public sea-food education campaign this would bring many exotic new dishes to our tables and help liquidate the world's protein deficit.

Sharpening Primitive Tools

Despite its importance to many nations, fishing remains one of the world's most backward industries. Man lives off the sea much as his ancestors lived off the land a thousand years ago. He hunts the creatures of the sea largely by instinct and tradition, and captures them with nets and hooks which have hardly changed in hundreds of years. However, the availability of the principles of science and the products of technology, together with the pressure of burgeoning populations, is now sparking the development of revolutionary methods of fishing.

The Soviets lower electric lights into the Baltic and Caspian Seas to attract fish, then pump them aboard ship through a large suction hose. Such pumping techniques are used by American menhadenmen to get small fish out of purse seines. Some of these fishermen use a hose with a copper mouth through which electricity flows. For as yet unknown reasons, fish align themselves with an electric field —tails toward the negative, heads toward the positive. The proper low voltage stimulates them to move toward a positively charged plate, which in this case is the end of a hose leading into the ship's hold. When this technique is perfected, the next step is to do away with nets and catch fish by current alone.

Electricity has been used to stun big tuna so they can be boated easily. Harpoons carrying 200-volt alternating currents electrocute whales quickly and efficiently. United States fishermen shock shrimp out of their daytime burrows by means of electrode-equipped trawls. Formerly many shrimpers worked only at night when their quarry came out to feed, but these shocking tactics enable them to fish around the clock. Such electric trawls could immobilize fish in their path, then scoop them up. Since different size fish will, theoretically, respond to different frequencies fishermen of the future may "tune in" on the size catch they want.

Sunday supplements already have manned and robot subs with long antenna-like electrodes herding fish into nets and hoses, but ocean engineers have not caught up to them yet. Other imagined devices include nets equipped with waterproof TV eyes and maneuvered by propulsion devices controlled from surface. The Bureau of Commercial Fisheries tested an unusually large trawl (317 feet long) and discovered that fish able to evade smaller nets get lost and become trapped in the big net before they realize what has happened. Perhaps such huge bags could be towed by submarines or closed with their own motors, allowing fishing in rougher seas than is now possible. In the future, self-propelled nets might be used to gather creatures corralled by bubble curtains or rounded up by dolphin cowboys.

Maine fishermen have already used bubble curtains to confine sardines in shallow water. In the future they might lure the fish to nets or hoses by sound or chemicals. Fish are so sensitive to odors that a fisherman can disperse a school of salmon by washing his hands in the sea. They might be attracted in much the same way. A network of hydro-transmitters might round up fish by broadcasting noises the animals themselves make when they are mating or frightened.

Fish-finding sonar is now used routinely, even in small trawlers. The Norwegians employ an acoustical finder that reveals the size and number of creatures in an area. Future fishermen may peer several hundred feet down into the ocean with the aid of laser-beam searchlights. Boat skippers may carry fish forecasting charts along with their weather maps. Biologists have already enjoyed some success predicting the times and places where fish will appear. The Bureau of Commercial Fisheries makes such reliable forecasts of haddock and groundfish abundance off New England that fishermen and processors plan their operations a year in advance. The Japanese Government runs an elaborate fish prediction service. Daily maps drawn from data supplied by fishermen themselves indicate, among other things, where water movements bring large quantities of nutrients to the surface.

Before fish forecasting becomes a reliable day to day process, however, biologists must learn a lot more about the sea and its inhabitants. They need information about the entire life cycle not only of commercial species but of the creatures they eat and those that eat them. Mortality among baby mackerel before they learn to feed and fight, for instance, may be as high as 99.996 percent. Halibut may experience a large and successful spawning in a particular area but a nearby population of hungry salmon could devour most of the helpless infants. When such knowledge is obtained scientists will be able to tell fishermen where and when to concentrate their efforts for the best catch.

Basic knowledge also lubricates the complex machinery of fishery management which, like land management, has the goal of harvesting as much as possible without damaging the ability of a resource to reproduce itself. Fisheries people talk about "maximum sustained yield"—catching the maximum number of fish without causing a decline in the total population. With knowledge to guide them, managers can set closed seasons and areas, regulate the mesh sizes of nets, etc., so this ideal can be achieved.

Helping Nature

Knowledge sired by research enables man to increase his yield from the sea by integrating his efforts with nature. One way he has done this is by transplanting fish from one location to another. Although mixed with some colossal failures, several extremely successful movements have been carried out. In the late 1800's about a million and a half baby shad were taken from New York's Hudson River and released in the Sacramento River-San Francisco Bay area. In 60 years the shad catch increased from one hundred thousand to four million pounds, and today these fish inhabit waters from southern California to Alaska. Descendants of less than 500 striped bass, taken from New Jersey to California, have supplied commercial fishermen with millions of pounds of fish flesh and become one of California's most important game fishes.

In Europe, plaice were moved from unsuitable "slum neighborhoods" into waters with more ideal living conditions. Young fish, not developing well in overcrowded areas off Denmark and Holland, were moved to locations much richer in food and space. With more room and less competition for food the undersized youngsters grew three, four and even six times faster than those left behind in the old neighborhood. The latter also became healthier and fattened faster when the congestion was relieved. In one operation, carried out yearly in Danish waters, the value of the increased catch has exceeded the cost of transplantation by 500 percent. Since the 1930's biolgists have considered it economically sound to transfer plaice from the overpopulated Dutch and Danish coastal waters to the fertile Dogger Bank in the North Sea. But no one country or fishery association will finance an undertaking which will benefit all nations and associations equally.

In other cases enthusiasm outpaced knowledge, and fishes were transplanted to conditions unfavorable enough to cause wholesale mortality. In some moves transplantees competed for food with more valuable native species and brought about the disappearance of the latter.

Competition from less desirable or inedible creatures lessens the size and number of individuals that reach the dinner table. Therefore, another method of increasing our take from the sea is to get rid of as many "trash" species as possible. Oceanographer Columbus Iselin puts it this way: "At the moment, we are picking the flowers and leaving the weeds. We must find a cheap way to get the weeds out so the flowers will bloom." He and many others feel that we could afford to weed the animal gardens of the sea by using trash fish as raw material for fish flour and meal.

Not every biologist and seafood fancier will agree on what are flowers and what are weeds, but starfish are sure to be near the top of everybody's list of undesirables. According to Danish zoologist Dr. Gunnar Thorson, starfish, snails and other invertebrates eat about four times as much food as fish. He says that these beasts, feeding on the same bottom dwellers as piscians, leave them only one or two percent of the available victuals. If Thorson is right, here is a good place to try weeding with mechanical devices or chemicals that kill selectively. Says Prof. Alister Hardy: "If man could eliminate just a quarter of the pests and so allow the fish to have some twenty instead of two percent of the potential food supply, then he could make a given area support ten times the quantity of fish."

Hardy goes on to describe a futuristic scene wherein the latest starfish eradicators are pulled across the sea floor by pressure-proof, atomic-powered tractors driven by frog-men farmers. The starfish would be ground up into chicken feed. Besides combing out weeds, Hardy believes the tractors could "roundup fish in nets of novel design." Tractor drivers and bags of fish would be "drawn up at intervals through an opening at the bottom of the ship."

Submarine tractors working along the bottom would stir up the sediments, which are like a vast compost heap laden with stagnant fertilizer. Plowing this up so that mineral nutrients rise to lighted layers would provide nourishment for the grasses of the sea—the foundation of the food pyramid. But in the age of remote control and telemetry do we need manned tractors, or do we even need tractors?

Laid on the bottom, pipes with compressed air bubbling through holes might stir up enough minerals to fertilize shallow waters. The rising bubbles could also be used as a sea fence. In bays and sounds where tides and winds are not strong enough to mix the water from top to bottom, circulation can be stimulated by increasing the roughness of the sea floor. This might be done by dumping old autos and streetcars there. Such debris sunk off California provides a shelter and gathering place for a variety of fish and invertebrates, much to the delight of sport fishermen.

Dr. Columbus Iselin thinks large areas of the Atlantic off southeastern Florida could be fertilized by using the energy of the Gulf Stream as it flows between Florida and Cuba. If the bottom were roughened enough, swirling turbulence might bring up cool, nutrient-laden water, vast volumes of which would then flow into the Atlantic. As an added advantage, onshore summer winds blowing across this colder water would cool the Miami area.

In deep, seasonally stagnated water, plowing might be done with a nuclear reactor set on the bottom. A NAS Committee suggests that heat generated by radioactivity could warm the bottom waters enough to make them rise and carry minerals to the surface. Ocean waters might also be turned over by a unique device called a "salt water siphon." A pump starts water flowing upward through large, heat-conducting pipes extending down 500 to 1,000 feet. Subtle differences in temperature and salinity—and so weight—between water inside and outside the pipe causes the former to keep flowing after the pump stops.

Speeding up natural overturn could convert some of the ocean deserts into fertile pastures or it could cause undesirable, even disastrous, changes in local climate. NAS has recommended that money be appropriated to acquire the tool boxes full of knowledge scientists and engineers need before tinkering with the delicately balanced machinery of nature. If research shows that artificial upwelling is feasible and desirable, then engineering development and pilot scale trials will follow.

Farming the Sea

Once scientists learn to weed and fertilize the sea, which they will certainly do in time, it would still be wastefully inefficient to hunt for the results by blindly dragging bags below the surface. The ulitmate in exploiting the sea is to fence off part of it and raise fish and shellfish as we do cattle and crops.

This is no new idea. Asians and Pacific Islanders have raised aquatic animals in salt ponds, fresh water and rice paddies for at least 500 years. Mainland China gets over half its fish food from inland farms. In the United States commercial fresh water farms produce about six million pounds of trout annually and some farmers raise bass, buffalofish, catfish or sunfish as a money crop. But only since

Scientists may soon raise fish like these JACK CREVALLES *(Caranx hippos)* on salt water farms. In western Scotland a 5-acre bay has been closed by a dam and stocked with postage-stamp-size plaice. These were hatched and reared on the Isle of Man where a pilot plant for mass producing young plaice rears about half a million fish a year.

World War II have salt water farms received increasing mention in the technical literature of the West, and only now are commercial fishermen beginning to think in terms of seafood farms.

Floodgates close off thousands of acres along the coasts of Southeast Asia to form simple farms, which are merely large fish traps. Creatures enter with the flood tides but are prevented from leaving as it ebbs. Like cattle on a range, they feed on whatever is naturally available in the enclosures. In this method predators and competitors enter with food species and they grow and fatten, too, at the latter's expense. On better organized farms pests are fished out or poisoned with chemicals that do not harm the crops. Also, the water can be fertilized to encourage seaweed and plankton growth, or the fish fed directly as pigs are slopped on land.

As a further step the farm can be started like a hatchery operation. Specially prepared enclosures free of hostile species are stocked with eggs that have been cultured or caught in the sea. Instead of following the hatchery procedure of turning the fry loose to grow and be hunted, the farm animals are raised through their period of most rapid growth then sent to market.

In 1963 an experimental fish "factory" was established at Port Erin on the Isle of Man and stocked with plaice eggs from a British hatchery. Dr. J. E. Shelbourne has developed methods of hatching the eggs and raising the fish to postage stamp size, and these techniques were put into practice at Port Erin. In 1965 this pilot plant produced a half-million young plaice. Transported in plastic bags these youngsters were placed at various sites in Scotland, including a small bay in western Argyllshire. Here a 5-acre inlet has been enclosed by a dam and converted into Britain's first experimental marine fish farm. If the farm is successful it could lead to the establishment of commercial fish farms in the many lochs on the west coast of Scotland.

After World War II several of these lochs were manured with chemicals, and plant and animal plankton in them quickly underwent an immense increase in population. Plaice introduced into the lush bays added two years' growth in six months. In this experiment the precocious fish were free to leave, but now engineers are investigating bubble curtains, electric fences and mechanical barriers to block the loch mouths without preventing the flow of water.

Plaice spawn in winter, thus a fish factory could conceivably raise another species that lays in spring or summer, such as sole. Both species could be used to stock farms which would produce a year-round supply of consistently good tasting and uniform sized fish. The latter would be a tremendous bonus for canners and packers. Fish farmers might also be able to increase the growth rate of their crops by special diets or keeping the water uniformly warm.

Many square miles of brackish lagoons, tidal flats and swamps along the coast of the United States would be ideal sites for fish farms. At present most of this land is ignored, used for waste disposal or filled in to accommodate speculative, mosquito-ridden housing developments. Some tidal lands are already hopelessly polluted. Oysters and clams inhabit other sections but their numbers have been declining for many years. Applied to these areas, methods of shellfish culture developed in Asia might produce millions of pounds of additional food a year. There are, of course, problems to be solved first. After World War II a number of veterans tried clam farming on intertidal flats in Massachusetts, but invading armies of crabs and boring snails quickly wiped out their crops.

Some sections of brackish coastal land serve as nursery grounds for shrimp and fish. The young, hatched offshore, migrate to these protected waters to grow to maturity. These creatures undergo their most rapid growth in areas where they would be most accessible for farming. Closing off such areas with a tide gate and letting the fish and shrimp grow naturally would yield more seafood than the 100 to 250 pounds an acre averaged by fishermen. By careful selection of stock, feeding, fertilizing and predator control it is estimated that sea farms could produce 2,000 to 6,000 pounds of fish an acre each year.

But many pitfalls await those who hope to make a commercial success of sea farming or *mariculture,* and not all of them have to do with the vagaries of nature. One American who knows this from bitter experience is John Hart Knox, an enterprising industrial engineer who attempted to pioneer shrimp farming. Knox became aware of the experiments of Dr. G. Robert Lunz, who reared natural-born shrimp from infancy to maturity in tide pools at Bears Bluff Laboratories in South Carolina. Knox reasoned he could do the same on a commercial scale in many natural sites along the thousands of miles of coastline from the Carolinas to Texas.

His calculations showed that the greatest expense would be the cost of building earthwork ramparts and gates for controlling tidal flow. Screens on the opened gates would let young shrimp in but keep bigger predators out. They would also prevent large shrimp from leaving. Many more individuals would reach adulthood in the safety of these enclosures than in enemy infested open water. When their rapidly maturing bodies caused them to seek the offshore mating grounds the gates would be opened, and the crustaceans harvested as they rode the tide out. Knox figured a 40 acre pond, yielding 500 pounds per acre at $.50 a pound, would make $10,000 less operating costs. And the shrimp would do most of the work.

But as things turned out, the shrimp did nothing while Knox worked against politics, prejudice and greed for 18 expensive, fruitless, frustrating months. In South Carolina his way was blocked by outmoded conservation laws which forbid leasing intertidal land for any purpose but oyster cultivation. In Florida less than 100 miles of coastline appears promising enough for a one-try pilot farm and conservation laws make even that illegal. Greed raised the price of worthless swampland beyond any hope of profit. Stubborn resistance to "outsiders" and new ideas kept him out of potential locations. From November 1960 to March 1962 Knox devoted all his energy and personal funds to knocking down these barriers, but in the end he was beaten. In a modern, progressive country that prides itself on a tradition of free enterprise and the pioneering spirit, John Hart Knox was beaten.

In Japan Knox might have made it. He might have gotten as far as Motosaku Fujinaga, a former fisheries official who developed techniques for raising shrimp from eggs to cocktail size on a commercial scale. His "farms" are tile nursery tanks and concrete rearing ponds where the handsome dark brown and white *Penaeus japonicus* are spawned and reared to their full ten-inch size in six to ten months. Under scrupulously controlled conditions the newborn eat a baby food of diatoms cultivated on Fujinaga's own farms. Then before they start eating each other their diet is changed to oyster and clam eggs, copepods and brine shrimp. Of the 300,000 to 1,200,000 eggs laid by each mother as many as 10,000 may reach maturity, while in the open sea only two or three would survive.

Japan is unquestionably the world leader in sea farming. Some 44 million pounds of eels harvested annually from nearly 800 farms go to thousands of restaurants specializing in eel dishes. Every year 40 million pounds of oysters mature while suspended in clusters from rafts, which can be floated to other locations if unfavorable conditions develop. The Japanese cultivate many types of seaweed; grow octopus and squid on experimental farms; and breed halibut, mullet, bream, bass and blowfish. The intestines of the latter contain deadly poison and must be carefully removed before eating. By adding hundreds of millions of artificially bred animals, Japan's Fish Breeding Center plans to double the fish population of the 240-mile long Inland Sea before 1974.

In years to come sea farms may be stocked with improved varieties of fish and shellfish produced by selective breeding. For years man has made land animals more suitable to his needs by permitting only those offspring with desirable traits to reproduce. Both the meaty Rhode Island Reds and White Leghorns which lay as many as 200 eggs a year were bred from the same scrawny, poor-laying wild stock after generations of such artificial selection. When much more is learned about marine genetics it should be possible to produce meaty, disease-resistant fish that grow fast and give birth to large numbers of healthy young.

Experiments in this direction have already increased the length, egg production and disease resistance of hatchery-reared trout and salmon. These and other marine fishes that breed in fresh water lend themselves especially to selective breeding since it can be arranged so their home spawning grounds are in a hatchery. "I'm using the ocean like a pasture," says experimental breeder Lauren R. Donaldson whose salmon and trout return to his ponds like a herd of cows wandering back to the barn. Working out of the University of Washington, 62-year-old Dr. Donaldson has reduced the age of reproduction of chinook salmon from four to three and even to two years, in addition to increasing their average weight, length and egg production. Early maturation reduces exposure to predators at sea and 10 to 30 times as many university-reared salmon survive as their natural cousins. Dr. Donaldson sees his research as a possible key to halting the decline of the Pacific Northwest's once great salmon fishery.

He has also crossed rainbow and steelhead trout and produced a fish that is strong, mean and full of fight. Other breeders are attempting to cross chum salmon, which have a fine flavor and run every year, with pink salmon, which are quick to take a lure. Other experimenters think it may be possible to breed oysters that are resistant to the more than 30 diseases which take a tremendous toll of these mollusks every year.

If produced in large enough numbers, improved strains could be turned loose on marine farms or in the open sea to interbreed with and meliorate wild creatures. But so far man's achievements in selective reproduction are too meager to exert any influence on the prodigious stocks of the unfenced ocean. However, hormones such as *gonadatropin*—which causes previously infertile women to give birth to twins, quads and even sextuplets—kindle hope for artificial breeding of improved stocks in numbers that begin to compare with Mother Nature's offspring.

The Inexhaustible Sea?

Such progress in finding, catching, weeding, farming and breeding holds great promise as at least a partial solution to the problem of feeding Earth's rapidly growing population, millions of whom do not now get enough to eat for good health. Although no one knows how many stomachs seafood can fill, one thing is clear: no justification whatever exists for the popular and comfortable notion that ocean resources are inexhaustible. The World Ocean can be forever bountiful only if man does not harvest faster than nature or he himself replaces. Today, the sea's living wealth is being spent at a greater rate than ever before in history, yet without knowing how well nature can keep up. A few valuable species already hang on the verge of commercial extinction, and increased efforts in some areas are not yielding increased catches.

Many regulations, supposedly written to conserve sea creatures, do more harm than good. Some fisheries seem to be regulated not on conservation grounds but along lines to maintain the highest prices. Along with 20 other countries the United States is a member of 8 international commissions organized to regulate fishing on the high seas. But in no field of international relations is agreement and compliance so difficult to achieve. Increasing consideration is being given to the creation of a single international agency, a world fisheries group, to work on the scientific, legal, political and economic problems of exploiting the wealth of the sea, both living and nonliving.

One area needing immediate international attention is the extent of territorial waters and the zones of restricted fishing contiguous to a nation's shores. Three international conferences, including one called in 1960 specifically for this purpose, failed to settle the questions. Meanwhile more and more problems arise and nations have been on the verge of war over fish and lobsters. In 1964, twelve European nations agreed to restrict fishing as far as 12 miles from their shores. Very probably the long-accepted 3-mile territorial limit will soon be replaced by a 12-mile limit, at least as far as fishing is concerned.

Another area requiring international consideration is the disposal of radioactive and other wastes. Human and industrial refuse around parts of the United States and western Europe has reached such alarming proportions many knowledgeable persons express concern over the potential damage to open sea fisheries. Traces of DDT have been found in fishes living far from land, even in the Antarctic Ocean. Frightening uncertainties remain attached to the disposal of radioactive wastes. Almost any degree of radiation may harm developing eggs. Marine plants and animals can concentrate low-level material to what may be a harmful degree, and radiation is known to produce thyroid cancer or tumors in fish.

Besides acting to conserve and protect known stocks, an international agency could coordinate the search for and the exploitation of new resources. It could act as a clearing house for information on new developments in fishing gear and techniques, and on progress in such fields as transplantation, sea farming and selective breeding.

Whether under international agreement or not, progress in these areas will alter the evolution of creatures in the sea. Species decreed useless from the point of view of feeding humans may become extinct. Others may develop greater strength and speed to escape more efficient catching gear. Some may evolve surprising responses or resistance to new types and intensities of electricity, sound, light and chemicals. We may see new lines of disease and parasites. Any changes will affect not only food fishes but also their prey, predators and competitors.

Selective breeding will lead to entirely new varieties and perhaps even to man-made species. United States hatchery biologists are now attempting to control the sex of fish progeny. Perhaps seaweeds will be hybridized to become tasty fruits and vegetables.

The course of man's evolution is being affected, too. Like his cousins the whales, he is going deeper and staying longer to exploit this "new" environment. It is not competition from other species that forms the driving force but intellectual curiosity and competition from himself, sheer pressure of his own numbers. American and French divers remain in the sea as long as a month without surfacing. Scientists are experimenting with silicone rubber "gills" that enable hamsters, mice and rabbits to breathe oxygen directly from sea water. It is only a matter of time and technology until man equips himself with such gills.

Jacques-Yves Cousteau, pioneer French aquanaut, envisages fathoms-deep factories that will transform the raw materials of the World Ocean into useful products. "Anything our contemporaries can do on the surface, the mermen of tomorrow will do under the sea," he prophesies. Dr. Athelstan Spilhaus, ocean-minded dean of the University of Minnesota's Institute of Technology, proposes the establishment of sea grant colleges to do the great things for aquaculture and ocean engineering that land grant colleges did for agriculture. He says: "Man will use the oceans in the future as completely as he uses the land. . . . He will essentially occupy the sea as an extension of the land, creating space to live equivalent to 15 extra continents."

The sea gave birth to life and without its waters no living things could ever survive on Earth. Now man, rightly or wrongly, is looking to the ocean as his ultimate safety valve, the answer to his problems of food, waste and even space. But the sea has no mind and the sea is not inexhaustible. It cannot be man's salvation without man's help. The salvation will come only if he obtains the necessary knowledge and uses it wisely. By controlling his numbers and exploiting land and sea intelligently man can save himself from himself. And what is more, instead of plunder, pollution and pandemonium, he can leave a protein legacy for posterity.

A lobster in every pot—what a magnificent gift for his children's grandchildren and for the children of all mankind.

Bibliography

GENERAL

CARSON, RACHEL, *The Edge of the Sea.*
New York: The New American Library, 1959.
CIAMPI, E. and C. RAY, *The Underwater Guide to Marine Life.*
New York: A. S. Barnes & Co., 1956.
CROMIE, WILLIAM J., *Exploring the Secrets of the Sea.*
Englewood Cliffs, N.J.: Prentice-Hall, Inc., 1962.
HALSTEAD, BRUCE, *Dangerous Marine Animals.*
Cambridge, Md.: Cornell Maritime Press, 1959.
HARDY, ALISTER, *The Open Sea—Fish and Fisheries.*
Boston: Houghton Mifflin Co., 1959.
————, *The Open Sea—The World of Plankton.*
Ibid., 1956.
RICKETTS, E. F. and J. CALVIN, *Between Pacific Tides.*
Stanford University Press, Third Edition, 1952.

EXPEDITIONS

DARWIN, CHARLES, *The Voyage of the Beagle.*
New York: Bantam Books, 1958.
HYERDAHL, THOR, *Kon-Tiki.*
New York: Rand McNally & Co., 1950.
Members of the Expedition, *The Galathea Deep Sea Expedition.*
New York: Macmillan Co., 1956.

EVOLUTION

COLBERT, EDWIN H., *Evolution of the Vertebrates.*
  New York: Science Editions, Inc., 1961.
DARWIN, CHARLES, *The Origin of Species & The Descent of Man.*
  New York: Random House Inc., The Modern Library.
OPARIN, A. I., *The Origin of Life.*
  New York: Dover Publications, Inc., 1953.

THE SEA

CARSON, RACHEL, *The Sea Around Us.*
  New York: Oxford University Press, 1951.
ENGEL, LEONARD & the Editors of LIFE, *The Sea.*
  New York: Time Inc., 1961.
SVERDRUP, H. U., M. W. JOHNSON and R. H. FLEMING, *The Oceans.*
  Englewood Cliffs, N.J.: Prentice-Hall, Inc., 1942.

SEAWEED

CHAPMAN, J. J., *Seaweeds and Their Uses.*
  New York: Putnam, 1952.

PLANKTON

DAVIS, CHARLES, *The Marine and Fresh-Water Plankton.*
  Michigan State University Press, 1955.
NEWELL, G. E. and R. C., *Marine Plankton: A Practical Guide.*
  London: Hutchinson & Co., 1963.
RAYMONT, J. E. G., *Plankton and Productivity in the Oceans.*
  New York: Macmillan Co., 1963.

INVERTEBRATES

MACGINITIE, G. E. and N., *Natural Hitsory of Marine Animals.*
  New York: McGraw-Hill Book Co., 1949.
BUCHSBAUM, R. & L. J. MILNE, *The Lower Animals.*
  New York: Doubleday & Co., 1960.

SQUID AND OCTOPUSES

LANE, FRANK, *Kingdom of the Octopus.*
  New York: Pyramid Publications, 1962.

SHARKS

Sharks and Survival, ed. Perry W. Gilbert.
    Boston: D.C. Heath Co., 1963.

FISHES

CURTIS, B., *The Life Story of the Fish—His Manners & Morals.*
    New York: Dover Publications, Inc., 1961.
LAGORCE, J. O., ed., *The Book of Fishes.*
    Washington, D.C.: National Geographic Society, 1961.
LANHAM, UHL, *The Fishes.*
    New York: Columbia University Press, 1962.
NORMAN, J. R., *A History of Fishes.*
    London: Ernest Benn Ltd., 1960.
OMMANEY, F. D. & the Editors of LIFE, *The Fishes.*
    New York: Time Inc., 1963.

DEEP LIFE

BEEBE, WM., *Half Mile Down.*
    New York: Duell, Sloan & Pearce, 1931.
IDYLL, C. P., *Abyss.*
    New York: T. Y. Crowell Co., 1964.
MARSHALL, N. B., *Aspects of Deep Sea Biology.*
    London: Hutchinson & Co., 1954.

ANIMAL NAVIGATION

CARR, ARCHIE, *Guideposts of Animal Navigation.*
    American Institute of Biological Sciences, 1962.
————, *The Windward Road.*
    New York: Alfred A. Knopf, 1963.

WHALES AND WHALING

BULLEN, FRANK T., *The Cruise of the Cachalot.*
    London: Smith, Elder & Co., 1901.
MELVILLE, HERMAN, *Moby Dick.*
    New York: The New American Library, 1955.
SLIJPER, E. J., *Whales.*
    New York: Basic Books, 1962.

DOLPHINS AND PORPOISES

ALPERS, ANTHONY, *Dolphins, The Myth and the Mammal.*
    Boston: Houghton Mifflin Co., 1961.
KELLOGG, WINTHROP N., *Porpoises and Sonar.*
    University of Chicago Press, 1961.
LILLY, JOHN C., *Man and Dolphin.*
    New York: Doubleday & Co., 1961.

MARINE RESOURCES

TRESSLER, D. K. & M. McW. LEMON, *Marine Products of Commerce.* New York: Reinhold Publishing Co., 1951.
Marine Resources by National Academy of Sciences-National Research Council, Washington, D.C.: Publication 1000-E, 1962.
Economic Benefits from Oceanographic Research.
    Ibid., Pub. 1228, 1964.
Oceanography, The Ten Years Ahead by Interagency Committee on Oceanography of the Federal Council for Science and Technology, Washington, D.C., 1963.

The Bureau of Commercial Fisheries, U.S. Fish and Wildlife Services, issues excellent booklets on virtually every commercial marine species found in American waters. These cover biology, methods of catching or rearing, and methods of preparation.

Index